ROSES IN DECEMBER

"God gave us memories that we might have roses in December"
J.M. Barrie

Front cover:
Detail from a photograph, c. 1914, showing the author's
father & mother, second and fourth from left, with two
friends in front of "Overton", Ashgrove Park, Belfast,
their first home in married life

Text prepared by Willow Books
www.willowebooks.org.uk

ISBN 978-1-909473-02-7

First published 2012

ROSES IN DECEMBER

AN ULSTER CHILDHOOD IN THE NINETEEN-TWENTIES

by

Hilary Gibson

Published by Willow Books

Hilary Gibson was born in Belfast in 1922 where she lived for 60 years. She has one son and three daughters and now lives in England but her heart, remembering times long gone by, is still in Ulster.

ACKNOWLEDGEMENTS

I know my sincere thanks should go to many people, and if, here, I omit anyone's name, I apologise.

To my friend June Hamilton for her constant encouragement as I wrote this memoir, and to my cousin, Joan Currie, in Seattle, who had a bound copy made for me in the early days which immediately seemed to give the whole venture more substance.

To my children, Margaret, Moira, Marian and Hugh John for their unfailing love over the years, and for whom I particularly wish to preserve these memories.

To Michael Longley and the Northern Ireland Arts Council for their support, and to the Tyrone Guthrie Centre at Annaghmakerrig for allowing me to spend a month there, revising the script.

My thanks also to my niece, Lesley Wilson, and to my cousins William Davison, Marion Francis, Anne Campbell and Maxine McConnell, for the loan of many of the photographs which appear throughout the book.

Most of all my thanks go to my son-in-law, Roland Goslett, without whose kindness, patience, forbearance and constant advice, help and encouragement this book might never have become available to a wider audience.

The quotation of the opening lines of 'Carrickfergus' by Louis MacNeice (1907-1963) is from his 'Collected Poems', published by Faber & Faber, by kind permission of David Higham Associates, London, and of John Montague's 'Like dolmens round my childhood, the old people' from 'New Collected Poems' by kind permission of The Gallery Press, Co. Meath, Ireland

**This book is
dedicated with love
to the memory of
AGNES WALSH,
(died January 1942 aged 60)
'Aggie',
the angel of my
childhood**

Agnes Walsh holding Hilary, aged 1, in 1923

CONTENTS

Part I : The Town Child

Part II : The Country Child

INTRODUCTION

This is the story of my childhood in Ulster in the Nineteen-Twenties and early Nineteen-Thirties. I was half a town child, because I was born in Belfast and my home was there. The other half of me was a country child, seeing and absorbing the life in South County Derry at that time, with my mother's family. I was a shy, rather solitary child. Five years younger than my only sister, I was in my early years isolated from the normal sibling rough-and-tumble, spending most of my time with adults, and elderly adults at that. I felt safe and comfortable with them. They made no demands on me, emotional or otherwise. Conversations were held in my presence, arguments were conducted and secrets were told, just as though I were not there at all. Of those years, and of the people of my childhood world, who seemed imperishable as rocks and sometimes as unyielding, I have almost total recall.

Life has changed so much since then, both in town and country, that my children, who grew up hearing me tell stories of that time, now more than eighty years ago, have encouraged me to write down my recollections. I hope that a wider circle of readers may enjoy these too, and that perhaps they may help to re-awaken their own memories of childhood .

Hilary aged 8 about to present a bouquet to the Lady Mayoress of Belfast at the opening of a church sale of work, 1930

Part I : The Town Child

"I was born in Belfast between the mountains and the gantries
To the hooting of lost sirens and the clang of trams."

From 'Carrickfergus' by Louis MacNeice (1907-1963)

Anna Todd, Hilary's mother, c. 1918

Chapter 1

Early Days

Everyone loved Mama. She was plump and jolly, and when she laughed she shook, her face turned pink and her eyes disappeared into the folds of her face. We laughed too, and told her she could not see the joke if she laughed too much. This never failed to convulse her into further mirth. She wore wool suits and favoured shades of warm raspberry or soft pink, and each afternoon around two o'clock, when the household chores were finished, for Mama ran a tight ship and the house was kept, as an old friend of hers used to say, "scrup'lous", Mama changed into just such a wool suit and always wore a pretty blouse. Blouses were her passion and she became known for them. She would go to town, spend too much money on a new blouse and show it to us, saying, "Well, you know I can't wear a cheap thing," to excuse the small extravagance.

Her surprisingly well-shaped legs, always clad in beige silk stockings with "clocks" embroidered up each side from ankle to mid-calf, ended in tiny feet shod in high-heeled court shoes. She had a high instep, she claimed, and could not wear sensible lace-ups or low-heeled shoes of any kind. The clip-clip of her little feet could be heard moving briskly over the kitchen floor with its red and black quarry tiles as she chatted to whoever was there with her. If on a rare occasion she happened to be alone, for she loved company, her cracky singing voice was raised in some of the songs she had known when she was young. "Good-bye, Dolly Gray" was a special favourite of hers and of mine, and I felt sad to hear about the young man going off to the far wars and marching with the soldier boys at the call of the bugle.

Mama, who had been a nurse, was in London at the time of the Boer War doing what she called her "fever-training". I have the Certificate she obtained then and when I look at it, all the memories of her come flooding back. She used to tell me, over and over again, that she remembered Charlie McKee, who came from her home district in the country, being in London then and calling to take her out. Charlie had joined the army and was ready to ship out to South Africa to fight the Boers. Mama remembered how he wore his uniform with its red coat with such pride, and how handsome he looked as he squired her along Piccadilly. "Poor Charlie," she would say, "Poor Charlie. He was killed at Spion Kop. And he had thought it all such a big adventure. His mother died of grief when she heard the news, for Charlie was her favourite." I thought of Charlie too, and wondered if Mama, so young then, had loved him. Maybe so, but she never said, though her eyes had a faraway soft look when she spoke of him. He had been part of her young life, far in the past when I remember Mama, but she had the ability to bring to life in conversation all the people she had known in her youth, and I felt that I, too, knew them. They became as familiar to me as my own childhood friends, though most of them were either dead long since or had emigrated to America or even Australia, and had never come back.

Neither of my parents was young when I was born, Mama being forty-three and my father forty-five. They had met when his mother was dying and Mama, as a nurse, came to care for her in her last illness. By that time Mama was not in the first bloom of youth and she had already been disappointed in love. As a young probationer nurse in hospital, she had fallen in love with a handsome young doctor. He had loved her, too, but after a two-year courtship he had, he said, fallen in love with someone else, the only child of rich parents who were able to help him establish himself in his profession. Mama could not even begin to compete with this glittering prize and she was devastated.

Father, who was a kind man but rather weak, saw her and recognised her inner strength and essentially jolly nature. He decided that as his mother was dying – and he loved her very much – here was his chance to find someone to look after him. Mama had, he felt, somehow been supplied by Providence, and at exactly the right moment. To her he probably seemed quite sophisticated, with a fairly smooth line of talk, and somehow or other they decided to make a match of it.

He was engaged to someone else when he first met Mama

Henry and Anna Todd, Hilary's parents, c. 1915

Hilary's mother in nurse's uniform when training at the Royal Victoria Hospital, Belfast, c. 1898

Henry and Anna Todd on their wedding day, 8 July, 1914, Castledawson, Co. Derry

and when she entered my grandmother's room for the first time, neat and trim in her uniform, he was there and my grandmother said jocularly, "This is my son – and he is engaged to be married, so you mustn't fall in love with him!" Could there have been anything better guaranteed to make any woman do exactly that? Father must have had doubts about the reigning fiancée, who lived in Dublin, for she was jettisoned somewhere along the line and in July, 1914, my parents were married.

They had a large and splendid wedding in my mother's home village of Castledawson. She wore a wreath and veil and a white satin dress with a hobble skirt which was quite the latest style. My Aunt May, ten years her senior, made a rather elderly bridesmaid in blue silk and lace with a large picture hat to match. Father in the wedding photograph looks truly elegant in a morning coat and wearing a black silk hat, his cravat held by a pearl tie pin. His hair was, as ever, polished to the shine of patent leather, smoothed down by an unguent called Anzora Viola, which he used all his life and which became a permanent feature of his shelf in our bathroom.

After the wedding they went on honeymoon to Paris and Brussels, returning home hurriedly when the Belgian army began to mobilise for war. They were settling down happily in a pleasant little house in Ashgrove Park when suddenly my father realised that he had very little money, a wife to support, and that most likely on account of the Great War his business endeavours would collapse. He was agent for confectionery and exotic imported comestibles, none of which contributed to the war effort. Mama remembered with irritation that he had "lain down on the bed and cried" when he thought of this sad state of affairs. However, he gathered himself together and went back to work and as it happened things turned out very well.

Mama had a miscarriage about a year later and was dangerously ill with peritonitis, was operated on and recovered. When this happened Father wept again at the thought of being left alone to face the world. However Mama was made of stronger stuff than the doctors had thought and emerged from her ordeal in reasonably good order. Three years later my sister was born, to their great delight, and five years after that I was born. My arrival must have caused them some surprise and perhaps consternation, but they never made me feel it and I grew through my first few years feeling cosy, wanted and loved.

That those years were so happy was in great measure due to Aggie. Aggie was in name a maid, but she was in reality my great fount of love and comfort, my bulwark against the world, the fire at which I could always warm myself, the one to whom, no matter how naughty I had been, I could always turn and be sure of shelter. Her white-aproned bosom contained a heart which seemed to beat, I felt, only for me. In the security of her love I grew through early childhood comparatively unscathed by the changing circumstances of my parents' financial situation. Aggie was only five feet tall, with dark hair, rosy cheeks and bright, brown, kind eyes. She must have been in her late forties. She was deaf, which was a great tragedy for her, but it was never a barrier to communication between us. She was dearer at that time to me than Mama. I was her darling and in her eyes I could do no wrong.

When I was born the war had been over for more than four years. Father's business had flourished in spite of everything and he had made a few successful deals in stocks and shares. Money had come fairly easily and for that reason had been spent easily, too. A large house was bought on the Cliftonville Road, Belfast, where I was born, which was then a pleasant residential area. It had been carefully and expensively furnished, carpeted and curtained. Outwardly all appeared to be well. The trouble was that neither of my parents had any money behind them, and no clear idea of how to manage what they had. Mama and Father enjoyed life to the full while they could. My sister remembered the really good times, when money was more than plentiful, and I remember life being happy and comfortable with, if not all the things small girls long for, at least some of them.

The first familiar and best loved sound that I can remember from early childhood is the rattle of the trams as they passed the house. At night I lay snugly in bed, with the covers pulled up and around my neck, looking at the outlines of the familiar furniture by the light of the street-lamp outside as it shone wanly between the dark green wooden slats of the venetian blinds. The picture of St. Agnes wearing a pearl head-dress on the wall smiling benignly down upon me, I listened for the high whine of the trams as they laboured up the incline from the Antrim Road. They went "aaaaaaaahhhhh, rattlety-bang-bang-bang-bang" on the tram-lines and then "ping!" as the conductor pulled the bell for the driver to stop when someone wished to alight or board at the stop, which was situated outside our house.

On cold winter nights I lay cosily still, thinking of the tram driver standing in his draughty compartment in front of the tram with nothing to shield him from the weather. Wearing his heavy dark overcoat piped in red and peaked cap to match, he forged his way on and upwards towards the terminus at the top of the road, like a sleigh-driver in one of Hans Andersen's fairy tales. I imagined myself standing beside him, the two of us like Kay and Gerda in The Snow Queen, driving through a blizzard.

In summer the road lay quietly in the evening sunlight, for there was little traffic, and I, a reluctant prisoner in my bed, would rise and peep out through the slatted blinds to watch the trams swaying past. The driver and conductor were then minus their overcoats and wore white covers on their caps. They donned these on May 1st each year and took them off again at the beginning of October.

This love affair with the trams only flourished when I was allowed to sleep in the spare room, which was at the front of our house on the first floor, across a broad landing from my parents' bedroom. My own bedroom was behind the spare room and I hated it, furnished as it was with a Victorian mahogany dressing table and wardrobe and a large brass double bed, the knobs of which rattled maddeningly each time I moved so much as a toe joint. The floor was covered with green and white patterned linoleum and had a braided rug by the fireplace and another by the side of the bed. When I had to put my bare feet on the cold linoleum I thought it vastly unfair, for it was the only uncarpeted room in the house apart from two of the attic rooms on the top floor which Mama used as store rooms. These held such treasures as a spinning wheel and a German officer's spiked helmet which an uncle had brought back as a trophy from the war. My sister Joyce, whose room was behind my parents' room, had carpet on her floor and a window which looked out on Manor Street, not exactly the hub of the world, but it was better than my view of the yard.

My complaints about this discrimination were loud and long, and finally an arrangement was arrived at. I was to be allowed to sleep in the spare room more and more often, only being moved back if visitors came to stay or if there was a party, when the lady guests were conducted upstairs to take off their wraps and coats and lay them on the bed.

The bell at the Poor Clare Convent on Cliftonville Road tolled out its melancholy sound at odd hours of the day and night. I now realise that it was used to denote the times of prayer for the nuns, but those neighbours who were not Catholics believed that the nuns were so selfless and their vow of poverty so inflexible that they were not allowed to buy food. Therefore, when the nuns grew hungry and could bear the pangs no longer, they tolled the bell for their co-religionists to bring food at once. No one doubted the truth of this and it was accepted quite literally along with the story that the nuns had no beds, but slept in their coffins. This bizarre and uncomfortable state of affairs settled my mind once and for all that I could never be a nun and especially not a Poor Clare. I was all for enjoying the pleasant things of life when they chanced to come my way.

The author's father & mother, second and fourth from left, with two friends in front of "Overton", Ashgrove Park, Belfast, their first home in married life, c. 1914

Chapter 2

Home and Family

In front of our house there was a neat garden with two small squares of grass, one on each side of the front path, sprinkled with white daisies. Flowers – London Pride, Canterbury Bells, money-musk – were in the beds which edged it. Here I learnt to make my first daisy-chains, necklaces and bracelets, and stood gazing through the wrought-iron gate to watch the passers-by.

The front door of the house was mahogany, with a handsome engraved glass panel inset. This led into a wide hall, carpeted in dark blue patterned with green and red. To the left of the hall was the drawing room, with the morning room behind it, separated by folding doors. After a time the morning room was abolished and it all became one large room. The paint-work was white, the walls were papered in a soft blue, grey and fawn leafy design, the carpet was pale blue with fawn medallions woven into it and the furniture was upholstered in blue damask.

It was an elegant room with a pale grey marble fireplace surmounted by a mahogany top which could be lifted off. When this was in place it made a platform which held a selection of Mama's treasures, small pieces of silver and of porcelain. No clock, for she held that the drawing room was not a place to be conscious of time, but a room for relaxation. The delicate spindly-legged mahogany-framed china cabinet contained other precious possessions, small pieces of ivory, our silver christening mugs and other memorabilia, but it was dominated by Mama's best china, a Royal Crown Derby Imari pattern tea set, brilliant and splendid with its red and blue design heavily overlaid with gold. This was used only on special occasions, like Christmas, because each piece was dated 1918 and therefore could not be replaced if by some ghastly mischance it got broken.

The curtains reached to the floor and were of heavy creamy material edged with silk braid and at either side of the bay window were long blue brocade curtains. In the bay was a blue beaded seat measuring about four feet by three, supported on carved mahogany legs, on which I loved to sit when visitors came, for two reasons. The first was because I was fascinated by the pattern of the multi-coloured beads imprinted on my bare legs, and the second because I liked, surreptitiously, to pick off the tiny blue beads. If I was caught doing this I was severely upbraided, for if one bead was picked off a thread came loose and several dozen beads came away immediately, ruining the pattern. In the centre of the seat was a design worked in clear, grey and black beads, and the whole thing was very handsome indeed.

The piano stood near the back of the room and was used when Mama and Father gave parties. Their friends, like Father, sang songs to entertain the other guests. Each performer required very little coaxing to sing, and there was always someone who could play the accompaniment. The only fraught moments occurred when perhaps a new guest stood up to sing a song which was considered and acknowledged to be the property of someone else. Everyone had his or her favourite song and no one else was allowed to sing it. My father's favourite songs were "The Bold, Bad Baron" and "I Can But Trust You and Believe You Still", a sentimental ballad which he sang with great feeling. Other popular songs were "Passing By", "Oft in the Stilly Night", "When Other Lips and Other Hearts Their Tales of Love Shall Tell", and "The Gentle Maiden", which I liked best. At the end of the recital, and after everyone who was willing had had their turn, all the guests would join in singing "The Bells of Saint Mary's", accompanied on the piano by a man who at other times liked to entertain the company with a piano concerto or two which was far above their heads. Nothing annoyed this man more than the sound of talking as he played, and as one or two of the ladies grew restive and whispered remarks to each other he darted fiery glances over his shoulder and banged angrily on the keys, causing them to move uneasily in their chairs and pretend they were searching for handkerchiefs in their handbags.

Although neither Joyce nor I could play the piano nor showed any aptitude for music, we enjoyed having a piano because it contained a pianola. A door opened in the bottom half of the piano and two large pedals were folded out, then the centre panel of the upper part of the piano was slid back, a paper roll pierced all over with tiny holes was inserted, hooked on at each end and, hey presto! as we pedalled frantically, the roll began to turn and the most delightful music came out. Instant music! There were several music rolls, but my favourites were "Coppelia" and Chopin waltzes, run a close third by the rousing "Marche Militaire" and "John Peel".

The dining room on the right hand side of the hall was also divided in two by folding doors, but it had not the bright airiness of the drawing room and was decorated in shades of brown. A large oak dining table which at its smallest dimension seated eight people in comfort, chairs to match and a dumb waiter were in the back part of the room.

The front part of the room was where we sat during the week, for the drawing room was only used on Sundays. It had comfortable leather chairs and a sofa with velvet cushions, a large sideboard which matched the dining table but would not fit in the back part of the dining room, and various smaller tables and chairs. The sideboard had two large drawers and two cupboards in which were kept innumerable interesting objects, including a Mah-Jongg set which had been brought home from Hong Kong by Mama's cousin who lived there. This was really my favourite plaything. It was not used as a game, for no one knew the rules, and as long as I was careful not to lose any of the pieces, Mama allowed me to play with it. I spent hours making patterns with the ivory and bamboo bricks with their red, green and blue characters. I laid them out in rows, first of all selecting each row of the same colour; then I varied them, taking them out of their little baize trays in the leather case and rearranging them to my heart's content.

Packs of cards were kept in the bottom drawer of the sideboard and could be used to build card houses or to play patience, which, with other card games, I learnt early. A large jigsaw puzzle cut from three-ply wood was kept in a black japanned box with an inlaid design of mother-of-pearl on the lid, which had once held chocolates. It made a picture of an ocean liner, and I liked to work on this when I tired of the Mah-Jongg set, as I sat in the space underneath the sideboard, which had high legs. No one objected to this arrangement provided the jigsaw was kept within bounds and no pieces were left where they might catch in the Hoover.

The Hoover terrified me when I was small and I perched on the highest chair I could find, my legs tucked safely beneath me, as Mama drove it into every corner. Its ballooning grey bag was very alarming and I feared it would swallow me up. Mama felt that by owning a genuine Hoover she was a cut above all other vacuum cleaner owners. Aunt Emma, who lived next door, had an Electrolux which had a brown corrugated metal cylinder to catch the dust from a long snake-like tube with a suction nozzle attached to it. This was said to be easier on carpets than a Hoover, but Mama said she would rather take the risk of having to get a new carpet many years hence than give herself a bad back by stooping to haul the Electrolux around. Aunt Emma, however, had the edge on her by owning that miracle – a washing machine. It was a huge, tank-like monster called a Thor, which, like everything else in that house, was the best and most expensive of its kind. Each spring Aunt Emma accorded Mama the privilege of washing the blankets in it, which meant a great saving of labour.

Mama's family, who lived thirty-five miles away in County Derry, were often with us. Our house was the focal point of all their visits to Belfast, and they had the irritating habit of not letting us know when we might expect a visit. They considered Mama as being there to accommodate them and to cater to their needs when they thought fit to make the journey to see her. To be fair, if we had arrived with them without notice they would all have welcomed us. Mama did make them welcome, but found it disconcerting when, perhaps, we were sitting at lunch and the front door burst open and a group of people appeared in the dining room, all smiles and bunches of flowers, baskets of eggs and butter and usually a chicken killed that morning, in every hand. Mama had to stretch her resources very cleverly so that they might all be fed instantly, for they had come a long journey and were usually ravenous. It was as though a swarm of locusts had descended on us. In the twinkling of an eye, or so it seemed, their hats and coats and scarves lay in disarray around the sitting room and they seemed to penetrate every corner of the house, talking, laughing and gossiping to Mama about all that had happened to them and their neighbours since they had last visited.

Joyce and I learned to look quickly to see if a suitcase or

two had been placed by the grandfather clock in the hall at the foot of the stairs, indicating that one or two of the visitors had plans to stay for a few days or, according to the size of the suitcase, even a few weeks. No matter how inconvenient this might be we had to smile and say how pleased we were to see them and how welcome they were, and as often as not double up to make sure there were enough beds to accommodate them. They appeared to have a firmly-held belief that during the times they were absent from us we had no life at all, but revived, like the Sleeping Beauty, when they reappeared on the scene. These invasions were a sore trial to Father, who never really liked his in-laws, a feeling which was heartily returned.

Aunt Ruth, too, visited us regularly, though as she only lived on the other side of Belfast, her visits were fleeting in comparison with those of Mama's relatives. She was my father's half-sister, the matriarch of the family and the only one who had any real control over Father. If he stepped out of line in any way she had only to fix him with her cold, grey eye and say, warningly, "Henry!" and he cringed, transported back to the time when he was a small boy, living in a divided household with his parents, siblings and half-siblings. He never challenged Aunt Ruth.

She lived with her two daughters, both of whom were teachers. Their mother was a dragon, frightening off any men who might have shown an interest in either of them and dooming them to spinsterhood. Her son, who was her pride and joy, had escaped from her clutches and lived in England, coming home each year for Christmas, when she held a family gathering in his honour. All only sons of Irish mothers were treated as though they were the Messiah.

Aunt Ruth was tall and stout, with high-piled white hair and long dangly jet earrings. She always occupied the best armchair by the fire and wore black georgette dresses which reached to her ankles, with much pin-tucking on the bodices and topped, like the froth on a glass of Guinness, by cream lace collars. She owned a car and a wireless with a loudspeaker, and we envied her both.

Joyce and I felt very grown-up when we visited her house. We were always made to feel welcome and we knew that they were really glad to see us, that we were not just appendages to Father and Mama. Our cousins – half-cousins really – drew off our coats and admired our dresses and said how pretty we looked, then settled us in comfortable chairs before offering drinks to my parents. Mama usually had a glass of sherry and Father a whiskey and soda. Aunt Ruth had a mellow port wine and as this was being poured out by Cousin Nellie, Cousin Dorothy took two tiny liqueur glasses from a cupboard in the sideboard and Cousin Nellie half-filled each of them with delicious dark red port wine for us. "It'll strengthen them," observed Aunt Ruth benignly, sitting nodding at us, like a large Buddha in the corner. We had about a thimbleful each, but we were delighted. We were at one with the company and we, too, were important. We too were honoured guests in spite of being children, for children in those days really were expected to be seen and not heard. Occasionally, in celebration of a birthday or anniversary or an achievement on the part of a family member, Aunt Ruth produced a bottle of champagne, always Veuve Clicquot. We were given a little, this time in the bottom of a saucer-shaped champagne glass, and felt that we were living the high life indeed.

The Christmas family gathering – for it was not a party – was something of an ordeal for everyone. It was a command performance. Any members of the family who lived in Belfast were there, and some of them brought their close friends. Aunt Minnie and her daughter Dolly always came to these gatherings. Dolly, who was profoundly deaf, enjoyed the company, smiled at us and was greeted warmly by everyone.

Mama always warned us beforehand, on pain of death, that we were not to stare at either Aunt Minnie or Dolly, especially when they communicated in sign language, but it was hard not to look at and be fascinated by the quick movements of their hands. "Tell Dolly!" Aunt Ruth commanded, after some story had been told and laughed at, whereupon Aunt Minnie, tiny and bright-eyed and dressed in black, turned to Dolly and, her hands flickering like flames, recounted the episode. Dolly and she would nod and smile at each other, then Dolly would look at all of us and clap her hands with pleasure and her eyes would crease into slits as she laughed. Dolly liked to play board games with Joyce and me, and draughts was her favourite. Joyce was good at this and could always see the moves she should make, but I was hopeless, and Dolly always had to tap a finger and make the strange little sounds she used to attract attention, to alert me to the danger of losing a draught.

Once another distant relative called George brought with him the man with whom he lived. At that time homosexuality was never even thought of, and in our circles no-one remembered or spoke of Oscar Wilde, for none of them were literary in taste. I think that George's friend Mervyn was more than a friend, however, although such a thought would not have entered anyone's head then. Mervyn was a pretty young man, always beautifully dressed with matching tie and silk handkerchief arranged tastefully in his breast pocket and socks of the same colour. He wore a gold ring on his little finger which he was constantly twisting around.

Mervyn was always fussing about, helping Cousin Nellie to arrange the tea table, folding the napkins into fantastic shapes and then standing back, hands clasped under his chin, to admire his handiwork; asking Cousin Dorothy for a new cake recipe and telling her about a new way he had found to make biscuits crisp and light. "Such a nice boy" sighed Mama innocently, later on, and I could see that she wished she had a son like Mervyn. "George is so lucky to have a friend like that! Imagine, Ruth says he does all the cooking and washing and ironing for George. I just don't know what George will do when Mervyn gets married!"

"H'm" snorted Father, who realised deep down inside that perhaps George and Mervyn's ménage was not quite what it seemed, but did not wish to discuss it with Mama. He thought it seemed odd for men to be as fond of each other as were these two, but even he could not have conceived that they would "do" anything, or indeed what, in that case, they would, or indeed could "do". Father was always an enthusiastic heterosexual in outlook.

On this never-to-be-forgotten December evening, in the midst of preparations for tea, Mervyn, who was in the dining room with Cousin Nellie adjusting the table decorations, came back into the drawing room to find George laughing and talking to a strange young man who had just arrived with my Cousin Bill. George, who was forty and grey-haired and not at all attractive, had his hand on the newcomer's arm. When Mervyn saw this he blinked his long dark curly eyelashes over his dark blue eyes, looked reproachfully at George, put his hand on his cheek and burst into tears. Everyone was thunderstruck. In Ulster men do not cry except when their mothers die, when it is permissible but not advisable, so this outburst surprised everyone.

"What's wrong, Mervyn?" asked Aunt Ruth, wondering if Cousin Nellie had scalded herself to death in the kitchen. "Nothing, nothing" came the muffled reply as Mervyn turned and rushed out of the room to the bathroom where we could all hear him slamming the door. "Goddammit," swore George, which drew a hiss of disapproval from Aunt Ruth who did not allow anyone in her house to take the name of the Almighty in vain. George left the room, leaving the company open-mouthed. Everyone began to talk at once about the weather, the season of the year, what they were doing at Christmas, in fact everything but the happenings of the last few minutes. Dolly and Joyce and I continued with our game of "Old Maid"; Joyce and I had heard and observed the whole episode, but Dolly who had her back to the company knew nothing of the drama.

After fifteen or twenty minutes George and Mervyn came back into the room, George looking white, angry and embarrassed, and Mervyn with hurt eyes and pouting like a sulky schoolgirl. They sat down together, Mervyn laid his hand in a proprietary fashion on George's knee, and began to make party conversation. Aunt Ruth, not understanding the situation at all, said kindly, "Are you all right, Mervyn? Were you hurt?" for she now thought perhaps he had cut himself with the cake knife, or even twisted his ankle.

"It's all right, Ruth" said George evenly, removing Mervyn's hand from his knee in the manner of a gardener removing a caterpillar from a rose-bush. Father, rushing in to cover the moment of embarrassment, began a long rambling tale of how he and Mama, on one of their annual visits to London to the Confectioners' Exhibition at Olympia, had gone to a night club. There they had met Haydn Wood the composer who had invited them back to his flat in Park Lane and had played the piano for them including in his recital, especially for Mama, "Roses of Picardy".

Everyone present had heard this story before many times, so that no one needed to listen but just had to say "Mmmmmm" appreciatively at the high points. Inside they were all busy with their thoughts about Mervyn's outburst. The ladies were much puzzled and of course Joyce and I had no idea what the implications were. I could hear Bill say to his friend, "He's a pansy!" jerking his head towards Mervyn. Bill, who had lived in London for some years, knew about these things, but to me this remark was incomprehensible. Mervyn was certainly pretty, with pansy blue eyes, and I thought this was probably what Bill meant.

Soon after Christmas Aunt Ruth came over to see us one Sunday evening and said to Mama that George and Mervyn were not living in the same house now. In fact Mervyn had moved away to England, she said, where he said he thought his opportunities would be better.

"Opportunities for what?" sniffed Father, and rattled his newspaper loudly.

"It's such a pity," resumed Aunt Ruth without glancing at him, "I just hope George finds some nice girl to look after him now. Any girl would have found it hard to move into that house while Mervyn was there – he was such a good housekeeper. He did beautiful embroidery, too, and knitted pullovers for George. Not many men can do that," she mused. Father snorted.

On a visit to the Mourne Mountains, c. 1930:
left to right, back row – Cousin Dorothy Hampton,
Aunt Ruth Hampton, Hilary's mother, Hilary, Hilary's father;
in front – Cousin Nellie (Helen) Hampton

Back row (l to r) – Auntie Daisy Cleland (Hilary's father's sister), Hilary's mother Anna Todd, Aunt May Garvin (Hilary's mother's sister) – Front row (l to r); Hilary's father Henry Todd, Hilary's sister Joyce, Auntie Daisy's daughter (Hilary's first cousin) Margaret – c. 1919

Henry Todd and Hilary, aged 9 months, summer 1923

Chapter 3

Father's Story

Father had had a difficult childhood. His father, Grandpa Henry, had been left a widower with six children, the youngest less than a year old, and then married my Grandmother Margaret, for reasons which I have never been able to fathom, for temperamentally they were totally unsuited to each other.

Grandma Margaret's life had been a sad one. She came from a good family, one which was well thought of and firmly established in the community. According to the information in the family Bible she had three sisters and one brother, the latter only surviving for one day. The sad little entry reads 'James Gunning, born 11th and died 12th September, 1844'. Her sister Anne died young and was laid to rest beside the infant boy in the family grave at the Old Priory, Holywood, County Down.

Grandma Margaret was a pretty, ladylike creature by all accounts, who had been gently brought up. The oldest of her family, she remained at home, caring for her parents who lived at the Kinnegar, near Holywood, whilst her two remaining sisters, Emily and Elizabeth, set off for Australia to search for Great-Aunt Emily's husband who had departed hurriedly from Ireland under a cloud. This was not only traumatic for Great-Aunt Emily, but cast a gloom, socially and financially, over the rest of the family.

The story was that my great-grandfather, Grandma Margaret's father, had large financial interests in the Carrickfergus Salt Mines and was engaged in shipping salt. Great-Aunt Emily's husband, John Smith, who he had taken into his business – for he had no son to succeed him – failed to insure the ships and cargoes as instructed by Great-Grandpa, thinking there was no risk, and pocketed the money instead. A storm blew up, the ships went down, and Great-Aunt Emily's husband thereupon lit out for Australia, abandoning his young wife. When she recovered from the shock she gathered herself together, wiped her tears, and taking her younger sister, Lizzie, with her – because a lady could not travel alone – set out for Melbourne, where she met her husband walking down the street! Great-Aunt Emily had a hard life after that because John Smith was a ne'er-do-well, and poor Great-Aunt Lizzie came to a sad and sudden end after eating contaminated oysters whilst on holiday somewhere near Sydney.

Meanwhile, Grandma Margaret, left in Ireland with her parents, was briefly engaged to be married to a learned divine, but this fell through, probably because of her diminished financial status after the shipping insurance episode. In her mid twenties she married my grandfather, a large, rich, virile and rumbustious character, who was totally unsuited to her quiet and religious nature and gentle upbringing.

Grandpa Henry was not an unkind man, but he was selfish. His older children viewed their step-mother without enthusiasm. In fact they openly resented her and encouraged the younger ones to do the same. The baby – whose birth had been the cause of her mother's death – was tended and looked after lovingly by Grandma Margaret, but when she was old enough to understand, her older sisters encouraged her to defy her gentle stepmother, who by that time had three children of her own, my father and his two sisters, Daisy and Harriette. Harriette was to die in her early twenties.

There were then, to all intents and purposes, two families under the same roof but living and eating in separate rooms. Father's half-sisters – one of whom was Aunt Ruth – proceeded to make my grandmother's life very unhappy, influencing their father against her as long as they were able. Fortunately for Grandma, he loved her even though he did not understand her.

Grandpa Henry dealt in property and made money easily. He attended race meetings throughout Ireland with great enthusiasm as well as going each March to the Grand National at Aintree. He drank heavily twice a year and in the intervening months was a total abstainer.

When he embarked upon one of his drinking bouts he drank for some days and was then brought home in a cab by friends and put to bed by the family. One of the men whom he employed in his business was then sent for, and when he saw Bob Morgan poor Grandpa began to groan, for he knew what was in store for him.

Bob went into Grandpa's bedroom, and a case of whiskey was placed on the landing just outside the door. The bedroom door was then firmly closed, and Grandpa and Bob began the long days of agony which had to pass, it was recognised, before Grandpa was himself again. Bob fed him whiskey and only whiskey until Grandpa thought that if he ever had to taste it again he would die. He did not die, and after five or six months he had forgotten all about the treatment, as women, giving birth to each child after their first, cannot remember the pain until it begins once more, and then it is nine months too late.

Bob was an evangelical Christian and a strict teetotaller, and he preached regularly at the Customs House steps on Sunday evenings – a favourite gathering-place for citizens out for a stroll – dwelling on the evils of drink. He described the agonies of "a poor sinner" he knew well, but not, luckily, mentioning Grandpa by name. "He feels the flames of Hell licking him, and his whole body burns," Bob would thunder, and his audience would stir uncomfortably, thinking of the sizzling flesh.

Into this strange background my father was born and brought up. His mother cherished a great wish for him to become a clergyman, for she was a gentle and good woman, and when he was a tiny child, just beginning to talk, she taught him to say, "The Reverend Henry Todd, D.D.," when strangers asked his name. Poor Grandma Margaret, living in her own little fantasy-land. Grandpa Henry owned streets of houses in the area of Peter's Hill and York Street in the City and he also owned three pawnshops which had come to him through his first wife, and all this was extremely lucrative. He expected his son to join him in business.

Father had no taste for either the Church or following in his father's footsteps. His ambition was to join the Royal Navy. This idea was firmly squashed by both parents, though one of Grandma's forebears had been a surgeon in H.M.S. Temeraire - a ship of the line at Trafalgar - in the distant past. She could not bear the thought of parting with her only son and Grandpa was angry when Father would not conform to his demands. He was therefore apprenticed to a firm of linen merchants, Richardson Brothers, in Donegall Place, Belfast. After he had served his apprenticeship he drifted into the leather trade, and then into insurance. Any of these would have been a safe and secure place for him to work, and the references he received on leaving each of them were impeccable, testifying to his industry, cheerfulness and good manners and regretting his departure.

The reference provided by Richardson Brothers, Linen Merchants, to Henry Todd, on completion of his apprenticeship in 1902

Father was born out of his time. If he had been born later, and perhaps in London, he would have a made a marvellous impresario, a theatrical agent, or even a manager of a pop group. He adored the stage and everything to do with it. He was good-looking and had a good singing voice. In his youth he had singing lessons from Dr. Koeller, who was foremost in musical circles in Belfast at the time. He pleaded with Grandpa to send Father to the Conservatoire at Leipzig, for he felt he had real talent. Grandpa flatly refused – such high-falutin' notions cut no ice with him, so poor Father missed his chance. He had to be content with becoming a member of a "concert party", a group of young men like himself who sang, played the ukulele and entertained with élan at charity performances and even sometimes at hospitals, in their spare time in the evenings.

This was his only taste of the bright lights, but it gave him a thirst for the stage, even at one remove. He made friends with the manager of the Grand Opera House in Belfast, a man called Harry Downs, and became quite a stage-door Johnny, meeting the pretty performing ladies after the performance, squiring them to supper and possibly to further delights afterwards. He did not reminisce to us about the pretty ladies, but he never tired of telling us about the great performers and actors whom he had met when they visited Belfast. His hero was Houdini, and no matter whose name was mentioned in connection with escape performances Father always closed the conversation by saying with great finality, "I'm sure he was very good, but there was never anyone like Harry Houdini."

I am sorry that I did not know Father when he was young. I was not born until he had reached his mid-forties and was realising that life had passed him by, that all his golden dreams had faded and could never now become reality. Father really ought to have married an heiress who could have kept him in comfort. He, a true butterfly, would have liked that.

Grandpa Henry died at the age of eighty-two, a rich man. He cut my father off with one hundred pounds, the rest of the forty thousand – in 1908 a large sum – going to two of the daughters of his first family, one of these, Aunt Maggie, having been the baby whom my grandmother had brought up and looked after. Grandma Margaret herself was left almost destitute and was allowed two pounds a week from the estate.

This story was related to us with great regularity by Father at Sunday lunch, which seemed to spark off the thought of the incident in his mind. He told always, and bitterly, of how the will had been read to the family after Grandpa Henry's funeral and of how he was joined afterwards in another room by the officiating clergyman, Dr. McIlveen of the Crescent Church, who said to him in extreme anger, "Judas Iscariot will never be dead as long as Maggie Todd is alive!" This was because Aunt Maggie and her sister Aunt Anna had taken Grandpa, two months before his death, when he had become slightly ga-ga, to a solicitor, one Valentine Wilson, who was a cousin of theirs, related through their mother, and had had him make a new will for Grandpa Henry, leaving everything he possessed to them, apart from a few tiny bequests, to the great fury of all their siblings of the half and the whole blood. Father ended the tale, as he helped himself liberally to the underdone roast beef and red dish gravy, by saying, ". . . and I hope he is roasting in Hell now." With this pious thought, and having attended church that morning, he attacked his lunch with good appetite.

Aunt Maggie came to a sad end, well deserved according to Father. All her money spent or given to strangers, she died in much pain in Woking, where she went to live after coming into her inheritance. Aunt Ruth, strong-minded woman as she was, and the oldest of the whole family, kept telling us that, "Maggie spent all her money buying fur coats for soldiers." She never explained this bizarre statement, which conjured up all sorts of images in our minds, and I still do not know what she meant, but it was certainly derogatory. Maggie did not enjoy her inheritance – her ill-gotten gains, said Father – and neither did her sister Anna, who was the other conspirator in the plot to do Grandma Margaret down. As soon as they laid hands on Grandpa's money, Anna and Maggie went for a sea voyage to South Africa. Anna became so ill that she was unable to go ashore when they reached Cape Town. She died on the way home and was buried at sea. Father and Aunt Ruth insisted that Aunt Maggie had poisoned her, but they felt no grief at her demise.

Chapter 4

Sundays

On Sundays we went to church. Mama rarely came with us, claiming that my father was never ready in time and that she would not walk into church during the second hymn for anyone. She scolded him and told him that he would be late for his own funeral and doubtless would also be late rising on the Resurrection Morn. With a sniff, he rattled his newspaper and continued to read the latest scandal. He meant to be early, he felt, and that was what really mattered.

On Sunday mornings Aggie rose early to go to Mass, and before leaving she brought everyone's breakfast to bed. This we felt was no great luxury but merely our due, and I remember the milky tea in its white and gold cup with a pink flower on the side. The toast was slightly burned because it was difficult to get it evenly golden when it was made by holding it in front of the fire in the range on a long metal toasting fork. Porridge was the usual fare – we had eggs also on weekdays – and this was served in my very own porridge plate which had a fluted edge and a picture of the Babes in the Wood on the bottom, with a verse which read;

"The birds were trying hard to sing,
The babies cried like anything.
The robbers fought – the savage thieves!
The robins winked, and gathered leaves."

I adored this plate which Aggie had bought for me while I was still in a high chair, and I refused to eat breakfast out of any other. Hot milk, both for pouring and for drinking, came in a small jug shaped like a cow, its tail forming the handle. Aggie insisted on pouring the milk for me before she left, lest I be scalded in a milky avalanche among the sheets, where the toast crumbs formed a scratchy base to sit on.

Father, Mama and Joyce also had their trays and then Aggie, after lighting the drawing room fire, went off to Mass. We did not think it strange that her church was different from ours, and every Christmas we went with her to see the crib. It was so pretty, so holy, the inside of the church so dim, hushed and still, so different from ours with its utilitarian interior, that we were moved and impressed. When we knelt with Aggie before the crib we were borne away in thought to far Bethlehem and the Christmas Story came alive for us. At first I cherished the vain hope that someone, somehow, would give me the baby doll in the manger to take home, but Aggie explained to me that He had to stay with His Mother, and I was content.

After eating breakfast, Joyce and I got out of bed and went down to the kitchen to see if there were any biscuits or cut pieces of cake which we could eat, and usually there were. Bought biscuits were absolutely unheard of in our family where everything had to be home-made. Mama, like all her sisters, thought it a mortal sin to buy biscuits, cake, jam or marmalade, except for biscuits like cream crackers or puff cracknels, which could not be made at home, or the occasional packet of ginger snaps. Quickly we took what we could carry in our hands and what we thought would not be missed, and made our way back to our rooms in bare feet so that we should not be heard. Joyce got back into bed with the Schoolgirl's Own, and I got into mine with a picture book, or perhaps the latest issue of Tiny Tots.

After what seemed hours, Aggie came back, having completed her devotions, and came up to dress me in the clean clothes already laid out on the bedroom chair. Father was up by this time and was shaving in the bathroom. He shaved with a cut-throat razor which he wiped after every few strokes on a piece of thin paper torn from a sheaf inside a red leather cover marked "Razor" in gold. This hung from a hook by the window beside the hook for his razor strop. The sharpening of his razor on this strop was conducted in silence except for the slap-slap-slap-slap of the razor as it moved up and down. One memorable day Father's hand slipped and he sliced the strop through. Everyone in the house knew of this happening in record time as his shouts of fury echoed through the house.

I was dressed and waiting in the hall below with Joyce for

ages before Father descended. He was dressed in his Sunday clothes, black coat and striped trousers, black waistcoat, white shirt, stiff white collar and black knitted tie, held by a pearl tie pin. The pearl in this pin, which Father wore every day, was the size of a dried pea and milky-white in colour. It had been found in the River Mourne near Strabane years before by a former admirer of Mama's and given to her, and she had had it set as a tie pin for Father and had given it to him for a wedding present. He did not seem to mind about its origin, but wore it, peacock-like, to set off his ties.

He was most fastidious about his clothes, and when he took them off they were always brushed from top to bottom, the pockets turned inside out to remove any fluff and then turned back in again. The turn-ups of his trousers had the same treatment before they were hung in his wardrobe. He wore a bowler hat, and would have been uncomfortable in any other, except at weddings and funerals, when he wore a silk hat and morning coat. This silk hat was kept in a leather case with red satin lining. It had to be handled with care, and a small red velvet cushion was kept in the case also. This was used to achieve the regulation high shine. The top of the hat was the most difficult part to shine. It was necessary to stroke it in small circles from the centre to the outside with the little velvet pad which was embossed with the name of the hatter "Gideon Baird, Cornmarket, Belfast".

Now Father began to make his final preparations for the walk to church. His boots stood by the fire, polished to a high shine by Aggie, and topped off with a soft cloth so that he himself might give them a final dusting. Later on, when he wore shoes, these stood polished and ready, and his spats, dark fawn in winter and pearl grey in summer, were placed beside them together with a buttonhook to help with fastening.

Finally Aggie carried in his hat and coat. Mama held his coat, warming it before the fire first, and then he took his hat and warmed it also before placing it on his head. Now he was ready. Father was a true sybarite. He expected others to cosset him, but if they were not there he did not skimp on his bodily comfort.

Joyce and I were issued with pennies for the collection and hymn books before starting off on our long walk to church, which was on York Road. In winter we wore warm tweed or reefer coats and usually velour hats with elastic under our chins, long wool socks and Sunday shoes buttoned across our insteps. One winter we had matching coats of rose pink tweed trimmed with grey squirrel and real silver buttons with a pierced design. We had pink berets made of the same tweed, these outfits having been thought up by Mama in a moment of inspiration and made by Jinny the dressmaker on her autumn visit. The fur had once trimmed a coat of Mama's and had been saved when the coat was worn out.

In summer we wore white silk socks which came up to our knees and were held there by white elastic garters, the socks folded over the garters by exactly half an inch, black patent shoes, summer Sunday dresses and panama hats.

Mama bought our hats down town in a wholesale drapery warehouse to which she had access because she knew the owner, and sometimes she even bought them when we were not with her to try them on. She like to do this because if we were with her we begged her to let us have straw hats trimmed lavishly with multi-coloured ribbon rosettes, artificial flowers and streamers which hung down at the sides, and which we envied on other children. She steadfastly refused to allow this and informed us tartly that, "Nice little girls always wear panamas," to which we had no reply. The only concession she ever made was to allow us to have a narrow, coloured ribbon round the crown of our hats, tied in a neat bow at the side, to match our Sunday summer dresses. These hats also were held on by elastic under our chins.

Off we would set for church, by now late already, Father walking briskly in the middle, a daughter on each hand. My legs grew tired before we got half way to church, but the pace could not be slackened and I was borne along regardless. If I really flagged too much I was transferred from my isolated position on Father's left hand and given the middle track between Joyce and him, one hand held by each of them to hurry me on, which meant that I had to yield up custody of my hymn book and collection penny to Father.

On we rushed, like the Erlkönig in the poem, and finally arrived at church, late of course. We panted up the steps and stood in the vestibule for a few minutes while the minister, whom we called Uncle Abbie, for he and his family were close and dear friends of ours and lived a short distance from our house, finished a prayer. This gave our hot pink faces a chance to cool down before we marched up the aisle to our pew, immediately behind the manse pew, where Uncle Abbie's wife, Auntie Jessie, and her four boys were already installed, usually flanked by their Grandmother Smyth, who came from Dublin to stay on long visits. She was a pretty plump little lady, dressed in black, with nodding ornaments of jet on her small bonnet which nestled above her snowy hair like a black polka dot on top of an ice cream cone.

Uncle Abbie ceased to speak for a few seconds and regarded us with pained affection, for he knew Father's inability to be on time for anything and I suppose he was glad to see that we had finally arrived. We settled into our pew and Uncle Abbie resumed the service. I liked lively and bright hymns and it was better still when I knew the words. "There is a Happy Land, Far Far Away" was a favourite. The words were easy to remember and the tune cheerful and I loved to sing. Father lifted me up to stand on the seat as I was not tall enough to see over the front of the pew. Granny Smyth's bonnet was scintillating as she moved her head while singing and I longed to touch it.

When the hymn was over we sat down and did not listen to the Scripture reading, for this was the time to prepare for the sermon when the children, the four manse boys and Joyce and I, were given sweets to eat. On most Sundays Father provided these and four faces swivelled round from the pew in front to see what he had to offer. Without removing his glance from the pulpit he removed a bag of sweets from his pocket and handed them to Duncan, the eldest boy. The bag was firmly grasped, a quick perusal of its contents made and a sweet removed. Then the bag was handed to the next boy, when the same ritual was performed, and so until each brother had in his mouth a large sweet to suck throughout his father's sermon. The bag was handed back over the pew to Joyce, who took one and then Father took the bag and selected a sweet for me, as I was considered too small to trust with the bag in case I let it fall and spilled its contents over the dusty floor.

Sometimes Granny Smyth provided the sweets and when she did there was no variety – she always made the conservative choice of Fox's Glacier Mints, which could not be crunched, a prerequisite for all church sweets, which had to be quiet. When the sweets had been passed round and everyone had had one, Auntie Jessie, who had snow white hair and a young face, looked round her own flock and then turned round to check that Joyce and I were comfortable. Then Uncle Abbie began the sermon.

Sermons then were long and tedious and after a few minutes I began to have an uncomfortable feeling that I needed to go to the lavatory. This was impossible, I knew, as it was unheard of for anyone to get up and go out of church for such a reason. Bodily functions were unmentionable, even for children, and many a bladder must have been ruined because of long sermons. Sometimes, after my long walk to church, I fell asleep, my hat falling over my eyes as my head bent forward and I leant against Father's arm. Sleep relieved the agony of my (mostly mental) need. Then the elastic of my hat began to cut into my chin and I woke up again. The sermon droned on and on for what seemed eternity to me and the only thing I could see which brightened my view was the jewel in the shawl of the kilt worn by one of the boys in front. This kilt was passed from boy to boy as it was outgrown by each in turn, though I only remember it being worn by the two youngest, for they were all older than me. It was a magnificent outfit, mostly red in colour; indeed it was the most fascinating set of garments I could imagine. The shawl pin was silver, with a lustrous red jewel in the centre, rather like a large round winegum, and as winegums were almost my favourite sweets (and were often brought to church, being silent when they were picked over), I longed to suck this jewel as it twinkled at me from the shoulder of the boy who wore the kilt. Desperately I wanted to have it in my hand, to finger it and then to put it in my mouth. It tantalised me for several seasons, but I never even got to touch it.

The collection was taken by stern-faced men in Sunday suits and creaky boots who looked as though they had come to collect the rates. The first time I was taken to church I thought they had come to hand out money to everyone and I was delighted to think that I, too, was included in this largesse. Eagerly I put my hand into the plate and grasped as many coins as I could, like a sort of lucky dip. Outrage spread over the face of the man who was handing the plate, horror spread over the faces of my parents – for Mama was there that day to keep an eye on me – and surprise registered on the faces of everyone who could see what was happening. Father grasped my hand and tried to prise my fingers open, but without success. I would not let go what I thought was mine. Then he shook my hand, and in shock at this I let the coins shoot all over the floor of the pew. Everyone in the manse pew turned round and twelve eyes regarded me with interest. I squirmed with embarrassment at my gaffe and sat in misery for the rest of the service with a scarlet face and tried to hold back the tears which burnt behind my eyeballs. I would not be comforted, even by the offer of a lemon squash gum. I could not join any more in the singing, for I had a lump in my throat and only longed to be home again with Aggie.

Harvest Thanksgiving services were a focal point of the church's year and special collections were taken at that time. Each congregation vied with other churches in its effort to have the best decorations and the women members spent a whole day before Harvest Thanksgiving Sunday making their church beautiful.

Many congregations had members who had come to the city to work, but their hearts were still in the country, and few were more than one generation from the land, so that it was easy to get masses of flowers and huge quantities of fruit and vegetables for decoration from farming relatives. Sheaves of corn were brought in and small bunches of corn were made and tied to the end of each pew with red ribbons. The pillars of the church were wound like barley sugar canes with evergreens and flowers were twined among the leaves, mostly dahlias with blazing yellow, red and purple blooms and orange and bronze chrysanthemums.

A bowl of late roses, their colours soft and pale, rested on the communion table, flanked by pyramids of shiny green and red apples and russet pears. The window sills were lined with symmetrical patterns of green laurel leaves from which trailed fronds of red Virginia creeper and a row of apples glowed on top of each bed of laurel leaves.

Great bunches of autumn leaves and flowers formed two huge splashes of colour on each side of the choir and from the pulpit hung, always, three bunches of grapes. The one in the centre was lustrously purple and bloomy and those on the sides an appetising yellowish green. All were perfectly triangular in shape – upturned isosceles – and at the service on Harvest Sundays I wondered if a grape might fall plop on top of the hat of one of the choir ladies, or even better, into the mouth of one of the singers should he happen to look upwards while hitting a high note. Would he choke if this happened, I wondered? These grapes looked so delicious that I longed to taste them and hoped that somehow I might be offered a few at the end of the service.

Usually there was a visiting preacher for this service, and if he smote his fist to emphasis a point the bunches of grapes quivered excitingly and everyone secretly hoped they would be dislodged, but it never happened and we were all disappointed. The Black boys and Joyce and I sucked our sweets contentedly and the sermon was listened to without much interest by the occupants of both our pews, though Father and Auntie Jessie and Granny Smyth had, for politeness sake, to look as though they were receiving the Message from the Source. Joyce felt she should be allowed to bring a book with her to church to while away the sermon time, and so did I, when I learned to read, but neither of us dared mention this to Father.

The church porch at harvest time was the best part of all. On the table where the visitors' hymn books normally rested was a pile of fruit and vegetables, all washed and clean. Great green cabbages, orange carrots and creamy parsnips, with a few purple globular turnips, made a colourful display, and on the floor, flanked by sheaves of corn and wheat, rested an enormous yellow vegetable marrow with a text engraved on it. When the marrow had been the size of a small courgette, early in the season, its owner had taken a pin and scratched carefully and evenly "GOD IS LOVE" or some equally short and telling text, along its side. As the marrow grew so grew the text, becoming a raised scar on the smooth skin. Finally, when it was harvested in time for this special Sunday, the text was there for all to see, in large clear letters.

In pride of place, on the porch table, centred carefully among all the produce, was a huge harvest loaf. Sometimes this was made in the shape of a large wheat sheaf, with perhaps a tiny harvest mouse at its base, and sometimes it was shaped like a platter, bearing the five small loaves and two fishes mentioned in the Gospel. Whatever its shape, it was golden and glossy and always in the centre of the display, setting the seal on the whole proceedings.

Harvest hymns were sung, for these were always popular and everyone knew the tunes. It was considered to be not quite cricket on the part of the organist or choirmaster to choose an unfamiliar tune, and if he did this he could count upon being soundly berated by the Ruling Elder who remembered the days of tuning forks and thought that system far superior to the strains of the organ, over which the congregation had no control and which bore them along, willy-nilly, in its wake.

When the service was over everyone would cluck-cluck with delight at the beauty of the decorations, and Auntie Jessie's sister Mignon, who was known as Minnie, leant over to kiss us from where she sat in the pew behind, with her husband. Her husband was handsome and dashing and he smiled at us. Minnie was pretty and soft and billowy and floated in a cloud of Arpège. She had an enchanting slight Dublin brogue and after she kissed me, bending low to do so, she always said, rather wistfully I think, 'Isn't she a dote?' for she had no children of her own.

Once again in the fresh air we walked home as fast as we could, or as fast as I could "to give us an appetite" said Father, though he never needed a walk to stimulate his. It was enormous, to Mama's irritation, for he was as thin as a rail, while she ate little and was plump.

Sunday lunch was nearly always roast beef or lamb, though veal was sometimes bought from the veal shop on the Shankill Road, if Aggie had time to make the bus journey to fetch it. The beef had to be underdone for Father who liked "to see the blood running out of it" and Mama ladled this red "dish gravy" over our roast potatoes, to strengthen us. Pudding was usually rice with raisins, or perhaps stewed apples and custard. Father had a liking for prunes, which came to the table in a shallow oval glass dish. Simple food was served but it was always good and well cooked. I loathed carrots and parsnips, which were often mashed together, making an orange and cream speckled mixture, and I gagged at having to swallow them. Inevitably I was told by both parents to "eat them up and it will make your hair curly" or "Lots of little girls who have no dinner today would be glad of carrots and parsnips". I wished fervently that they would parcel up my share and send it off to these children so that their hair might curl, perhaps, as mine never did. It was some time before I caught on to the fact that this was a blatant lie on Father's and Mama's part, and I used to go to bed on Sunday nights looking with dissatisfaction at my straight fair hair and thinking jubilantly that the very next day I would wake up with a mop of golden curls.

After lunch Father had a short nap and then, if the weather was good, he took us for a walk. He did not want to go for a walk and neither did we, but it was obligatory, so, dressed in our Sunday hats and coats again, we walked to the top of Cliftonville Road where there were still green fields, and back again. Father did not hold our hands this time, but swung his Malacca cane with its silver handle as he strolled along. The road was busy with walkers, families taking their Sunday exercise just as we were, and groups of boys and girls walking quietly along. Everyone was dressed formally and many of the girls wore high-heeled shoes on which they teetered along uncomfortably. No one thought of comfort – appearance was paramount. There was not much noise, only the occasional burst of quiet laughter rising above the gentle babble of the walkers. The Ulster Sabbath still held full sway.

When we came back from our walk Father and Mama read the Sunday papers, which they did with a slight feeling of guilt, for in many Presbyterian houses it was considered sinful to buy a paper on the Lord's Day. We always had a plentiful supply, Father apparently feeling that he might as well be hung for a sheep as a lamb, and to this end he bought no less than six, the Sunday Express, the Sunday Chronicle, the Sunday Dispatch, the Sunday Graphic, the People and the News of the World, from which it can be adduced that Father did not wish to have his mind improved on Sundays. He read them all avidly, saving the News of the World until last, like an after-dinner liqueur. Joyce and I read or played Snakes and Ladders or Ludo on the hearth rug before tea. Before going to bed, and before I could read very well myself, Father read me a story from Grimm or Hans Andersen. Mama had to forbid him to read "The Little Mermaid" or "The Little Match Girl" because they made me cry so much.

Sundays hardly ever varied, except when friends who had cars invited us to go "out for a run" which meant in effect a drive to Bangor. They felt they were doing us an enormous favour, but we would just as soon have remained at home.

On Sunday evenings my parents often went to visit friends who now occupied the house in Ashgrove Park where Mama and Father had begun their married life, a short tram-ride from where we now lived. They always caught the tram at the same time each Sunday, and if they were not at the stop near our gate when it arrived, the tram-driver would wait for a few moments, ping-pinging on his bell for them to hear. They would rush out of the house, waving to us as they left and to the tram-driver as they passed him to board his tram at the back, and would be borne off on their journey. The drivers nearly always worked the same routes and got to know their passengers very well.

Chapter 5

Callers and Sadnesses

Our telephone was in the cloakroom behind the morning room which later became part of the drawing room. Between the morning room and the cloakroom was a window of frosted and engraved glass and as the cloakroom window on the opposite wall would have looked out on the yard the window on that wall was made of coloured glass. The cloakroom had a glass roof for lightness and the walls were of tongued and grooved varnished wood. A lavatory led off it and a white wash-hand basin was close by the telephone. A large cupboard held our Wellington boots, shoes which my sister had outgrown and which had been brushed and put away until I grew into them, and Father's boots and shoes which were kept on wooden shoe trees made to the shape of his feet. There were two boxes of shoe-cleaning materials, one for brown shoes and one for black. No one wore any other colour.

When I first became aware of the telephone I thought that a lady lived somewhere at the other end with whom my mother was extremely friendly. I also thought that she lived with a friend called Norah Ply. Mama frequently returned to the morning room from whence she had gone to make a call, to tell us, in great irritation, that it was "Norah Ply". I felt sorry for poor Norah, for Mama never wanted to speak to her.

Then it dawned gradually on me that other people, apart from Norah Ply and her companion, could actually be contacted by means of the telephone if one knew a magic number. Sometimes, when Mama was out, I stood on the chair by the telephone, unhooked the receiver from its rest, turned the little handle of the wooden box below it as I had seen the grown-ups do, pressed down the bar of the receiver, which for me was quite a hard thing to do as my hands were small and not very strong. When the voice saying "Number please?" was heard, I made up a number – any number – and asked for it. "Belfast?" queried the disembodied voice in the telephone and I said "Yes", not knowing that there were other exchanges in the city such as Malone, Fortwilliam and Knock. Occasionally the information would come back that there was "Norah Ply" but frequently an irritated voice would answer me as I kept saying, "Hello – hello!" As I had nothing more to say to this unknown person I hug up and tried again, fascinated by this outlet to the world so much that my stutter did not bother me. Aggie, being deaf and in the kitchen, could not hear or see me, and my game went unnoticed until I tired of it.

My stutter was a great trial to me and did not clear up until I was eight or nine, when it disappeared almost miraculously. I used to pray that people would not speak to me, or ask me questions which I would have to try to answer, for if I did not know the questioner well a great fear came over me that I would not be able to speak at all, or that I would stick at a given word, which of course meant that I always did. Strangely, people who came to do any kind of work in the house were easy for me to chat to, and I hung around them, watching and talking to them until Mama called me away, saying that I was wasting their time which she was paying for.

Aggie's nephew Jack often came to do carpentry work, as he was very clever with his hands and could put up shelves and make cupboards at a very reasonable cost. Mama loved cupboards and our house had many, all of them full.

Another visitor was the man who "stitched" china. If by some mischance a good dish was cracked or even broken in two, this man, who called at the house about once in six months on his rounds, was brought in and set to work in the kitchen. He would quickly set the broken pieces together and then put in tiny metal rivets to hold them, rather like surgical stitches after an abdominal operation. Once the sink in the cloakroom was badly cracked – someone had dropped a flower vase accidentally into it while filling it with water – and the stitching man came and put in a neat little row of stitches which remained for years. Anything which needed his attention was put away carefully in the china pantry on the top shelf, to await his next call.

The china pantry was a tiny room opposite the cloakroom, with shelves all around where Mama kept her "good" dinner service, various tea sets and vases and bowls for flowers, together with cut glass tumblers and wine glasses. Aggie was never allowed to wash these things and indeed was glad not to have to do it, for she had one fault. She was what was known as a "breaker". Things did seem to come apart in her hands and that was not the time of planned obsolescence. Things were brought to last a lifetime and it was a major tragedy if something should prevent this.

I liked to watch the knife-sharpening man, who pushed his sharpening wheel about on a little cart, calling at doors and asking if there were any knives which needed his attention. Mama loved sharp knives and always had some work for him. In summer he sharpened hedge-clippers and lawn-mowers too. All these callers were brought in and given tea in the kitchen after they had done their work. A special mug and plate were kept for their use on a shelf in the scullery just by the large iron mangle. Mama, who was still and always a countrywoman at heart, could never bear to send anyone away from the house without giving them something to eat, so tea, bread, butter and jam were always provided.

Dust bins had not been heard of, and when they did come were an amazing innovation. In early days we had a small dark house called the "ashpit" in the yard, with an aperture leading to the back entry. All household refuse was put in this and it was collected each week by men from the Corporation with a horse and cart, who shovelled it all away. The dust men were regular recipients of tea, but Mama did not encourage them to come into the house, for she had strict ideas about hygiene. They ate and drank in the yard, while their horse and cart bearing the noxious, smelly cargo of refuse, waited in the entry. Sometimes they asked Aggie for a bucket of water so that the horse might have a drink, especially in warm weather, and Aggie willingly provided it, her brown eyes softening at the sight of the sweaty animal.

Once, to Mama's irritation and consternation, Father came back from a business trip to England and announced that he had arranged to have six fantail pigeons shipped over. These had been given to him by one of the directors of the firm he represented, and he, unable and unwilling to refuse, had foolishly accepted this unsuitable gift. Mama and Aggie realised, with sinking hearts, that the care of these birds would fall to them, as Father was not one for soiling his hands, but all their protests fell on deaf ears. Father had a taste for the bizarre and the unknown. He knew absolutely nothing about birds, save for the five hens next door in Aunt Emma's yard which clucked around fluffing out their white feathers and producing eggs for the family's breakfast.

Aggie's nephew Jack was called in, wood and netting wire were bought and an enclosure was made in the yard with perches for the pigeons. Father supervised the work grandly, without any idea of what was needed, but luckily Jack had a neighbour who was a pigeon fancier and he supplied free advice. After a few weeks the pigeons arrived in baskets. Father looked slightly nonplussed. Jack was sent for and brought his neighbour, who released the pretty birds into their new quarters. They spread their tails in a most delightful way and strutted upon their perches. Even I, who was afraid of birds, thought them beautiful.

The worst fears of Mama and Aggie were soon realised. They had to feed and care for the birds and as the weeks went past they grew more and more irritated with Father, who by now had lost all interest in his new pets. He had shown them off to all his friends and now did not know what to do with them. Spread their tails and preen their beautiful white feathers how they might, all their charms were wasted. One day Mama, who could bear it no longer, sent for Jack and his neighbour. The pigeons were placed once more in their baskets, the enclosure was dismantled and the whole issue removed. Jack's neighbour was delighted with his new stock, but it was a long time before pigeons could be mentioned again in our house.

Father kept saying that he would like to own a monkey or even a marmoset. He often came home announcing to Mama that he had seen a lady in the tram that very day with a dear little marmoset. No one else ever saw these and I think he had really seen an occasional monkey or marmoset in a pet shop in Gresham Street which was near his office. He would ask Mama what she thought of the idea and, when she told him in no uncertain terms exactly what she did think, he retired to fume silently behind his paper. He did eventually succeed in introducing a parrot into the household. It lived with us for several years and was the one bird I was not frightened of, I think because it had a curved beak and its legs were not spindly. I was terribly upset when it developed a cyst under its wing. A friend, who was a bird fancier, offered to take the parrot and have it treated and looked after, and offered five love-birds in exchange. Mama agreed and the love-birds duly arrived, but one day she left the cage hanging outside in the sunshine thinking that it would do the pretty little birds good. The cage was empty when she went to it in an hour's time. The bars had been just a fraction of an inch too wide apart to prevent the occupants from flying off. After that she bought a canary, a bright yellow one called Paul, named after Paul Robeson whose voice she admired, and she got great pleasure from its singing.

The first dog I remember was Sue. Sue was a fawn Pekingese who was already nine years old when I was born. I recall Mama and Aggie crying as she lay in her basket in the kitchen, giving little moans. Then one day Aggie wrapped her in a shawl and carried her tenderly to the vet's on the Antrim Road. Aggie came back with the shawl neatly folded over her arm and her eyes full of tears and Sue's basket was put away for some time.

Then came Jimmy, a small smooth-haired black and white fox terrier. Jimmy was a tremendous fighter and kept on coming home with his silky ears torn and bleeding. He was then kept indoors for a time and Mama would dress the wounds gently, but as soon as he recovered he was off again to do battle for the favours of a spaniel bitch who lived up the road. In the end his ears were almost like tassels when he shook his head, but he was a dog of great personality and his injuries did nothing to mar his charms in our eyes. He had one disconcerting characteristic; he was subject to fits. He did not tremble, but just suddenly went unconscious, and always behind the gas stove. Aggie would drag him out, supine, like a small, smooth bolster, and lay him in his basket until he recovered when he was given a teaspoonful of brandy to restore his strength. This made him fall asleep again quite quickly, and when he woke up he was as good as new. One day he was knocked down by a passing car as he was out on another amorous foray and was carried into the house barely breathing. He died almost immediately and we all cried, even Father, for days.

After that we were given Tiger, a stripey pregnant cat. She produced three kittens and Joyce and I wanted to keep them, but

Mama found them homes and off they went. Tiger was a gentle and intelligent cat who came to a sad end. One day as she sat quietly at the garden gate a man came past with three greyhounds on leads. When they saw Tiger they pounced on her and killed her almost instantly. Mama and Father were away from home at the time, and Aggie was beside herself with grief and horror. I have detested greyhounds ever since.

Some time later Father bought another Pekingese and excused this lapse to Mama by saying that it was for me. He had a friend who bred these little dogs and it had an impressive pedigree. We called it Fah Wong after a gardener employed by my cousin Eva who lived in Hong Kong and we all felt most cosmopolitan with our choice of name. Wong was a very handsome dog, though too large for a Peke, and I loved him dearly. He became almost like a person to me and seemed to have many human foibles and virtues. He grew cross in his mid-years and one day he bit Aggie very badly. Amid all my shrieks and wails he was taken away, I was told to another home in the country, but I am afraid that poor Wong went to his last long home.

My cousin then gave us a bulldog called Punch, of whom he had grown tired. Punch was white and very gentle to everything but horses. If he saw or heard a horse he went berserk and it was always an anxious time when the coal man came to deliver coal. When the baker called, three times a week, or the milkman twice daily, or the lemonade salesman on Fridays, all of them had vehicles drawn by horses. Punch had to be shut into the kitchen and there he would bark and hurl his considerable weight against the door, almost cracking the wooden panel, until the caller departed hurriedly, thinking that he had come on the residence of the Hound of the Baskervilles. Punch was wonderful with young children and sat quietly allowing any small child to take countless liberties with his dignity, gazing sadly at them with his soft, brown eyes. Finally it was decided that no one in our family could or would devote enough time to exercising him properly and he was given away to someone who could give him the care he needed. I was inconsolable for days and missed him dreadfully, but I had no say in the matter.

Our most regular caller was the paper boy, who came six

nights a week, Monday to Saturday. Paper boys were not employed by newsagents, but collected the bundles of Belfast Telegraphs from the newspaper presses in Royal Avenue. Some of them ran around the centre of the city calling out, "Telly – Telly!" selling their papers to passersby, and others worked up their own rounds for delivery. They were usually small boys aged around nine or ten years and were always cold and pinched looking, and mostly barefoot.

The boy who delivered our papers was called Frank. He was small and delicate, with the face of an angel and golden curly hair and he always arrived as the grandfather clock in the hall boomed six. Frank wore a small grey jacket and trousers and a clean but worn shirt and had no shoes or socks. A couple of weeks went past after he took over our delivery from an older boy, and the weather turned chilly. Frank's small feet were pink, and then blue with cold. Mama, the kindest of women, noticed this and asked him gently if he had any shoes. Shyly he admitted that he had not, his father was unemployed, like so many others at this time, and there was no money for clothes.

The next night when he arrived Mama had set by a chair in the hall a pair of Joyce's outgrown school shoes and two pairs of long grey socks, neatly mended. Frank arrived at the door with his bundle of papers under his arm and she brought him in and fitted the shoes and socks on his feet. His little face beamed with pleasure as he looked at them, walked, a few steps in them and gathered up his papers to continue his round. The next week a jersey was added by Mama to his clothing and he looked much better.

The following week he came to the door without the socks or shoes or jersey and seemed embarrassed. When asked, he said the clothes had had to be pawned for a few pence as the family had had very little food.

After that it became a ritual to leave a glass of milk and a thick slice of bread, butter and jam on the table by the hall door each evening for Frank. He would hand in the paper, drink the milk quickly and run on his way with the bread in one hand and his bundle of papers in the other. This went on for about eighteen months, and then one night a strange boy appeared. He was asked where Frank was and said that he had been taken into hospital.

Frank was ill, he said. Now the new boy was given the milk and bread and jam each night, but he brought us little news of Frank. He did not even know where Frank lived, as he was just one of the other paper boys who collected their bundles outside the Telegraph office. We did not know Frank's other name or where he lived, and had no way of finding out.

One night Sammy, the new paper boy, came, and as he drank the milk he told us that he had heard Frank was dead. Tuberculosis, he said. This was my first experience of death and that a child could die seemed inconceivable to me. I went to bed that night and wept. I wept for Frank, for Mama and Father who would probably die one day and leave me alone in the world. I wept lest Aggie, dear Aggie, should die, for I knew I could not live without her. I was drenched in grief and would not be comforted, even though I went downstairs to ask Mama, Father and Aggie to promise that they would not die, or at least would not die before me. Frank was gone and would not come back. Never again would I be able to hand him his milk and bread and jam. I could not understand it and therefore could not bear it.

Shortly after that my Uncle Willie who lived in Coagh died. He was my Aunt Sara's husband and I loved him because he was kind and gentle and quiet and held me on his knee when he visited us.

He came to stay overnight with us about once a month, for he was receiving treatment at the Royal Victoria Hospital. Of course I did not know what the treatment was for, but in fact it was cancer of the throat. He seemed to grow thinner and greyer as the months went on and I remember one evening when he was with us and my parents were out. I had a bad dream and Aggie brought me downstairs in my blue dressing-gown, crying in fright. Uncle Willie drew me on to his knee and we sat, my sobs growing quieter, companionably by the fire in the morning room, not talking at all, I because I was drowsy, he because talking was now so painful to him. After a while, warmed by the fire and his kindness, I was put back to bed again by Aggie.

I never saw Uncle Willie again. Some months later I awoke to find the house in a great flurry and Mama and Father dressed in black, getting ready to go off to the station in a taxi. Where were they going? I asked. No one had time to think of breaking the news gently and I was told that Uncle Willie had died. I rushed back to bed and covered my head with the blankets thinking that if I did not listen to this dreadful news I would find out eventually that it was not true. But it was true and I began to realise that Uncle Willie, like Frank, had been taken from me and that in some dreadful way I too had been diminished. Death became frighteningly close and real.

When I was seven my Auntie Daisy died. She was Father's widowed sister, a pretty woman with light brown hair and grey-blue eyes, only fifty years old. She had a great sparkle and verve for life and was very musical. She was first violin in the Belfast Philharmonic Orchestra and, we were always told, bowed with her left hand. She was also an accomplished pianist and I remember her sweeping into our drawing room and sitting down at the piano to play all the latest melodies. "Charmaine" was her favourite and she would sing, "I wonder why you keep me waiting, Charmaine, my Charmaine," with great feeling. "Ramona", "Three O'clock in the Morning", "Always" and "What'll I do?" were part of her repertoire too, and I never hear these old waltzes without seeing her once more sitting on our piano-stool and flashing her graceful hands with their jewelled rings up and down the keys while I sat silently on the blue beaded stool, listening and enjoying it all.

For birthdays and Christmas, which for me were only four days apart, she always gave me shell pink socks for parties and Celanese knickers in white and pink, also for parties. These replaced the starched lawn knickers with their Valenciennes lace frills which were so scratchy, and I welcomed the change. They came wrapped up in a bag from the Bank Buildings, and if she had bought the wrong size Mama and I made a special journey downtown to change them.

I was called after Auntie Daisy, whose name was not Daisy at all, but Jeannie. Mama thought fit to call me Jeannie, and added May to placate her oldest sister, but she did not want me to be known by either of these names as she knew there would be trouble from whichever aunt she did not favour. She could not think of a name she really liked for me, so just a few days after I was born her young friend Hester decided to take a hand in the choosing. She came on New Year's Day, while Mama was still in bed recovering – for at that time no woman who had given birth even dreamt of putting her foot to the floor for at least two weeks – bearing a book of Christian names.

Over and over the list of names they pored, discarding this one and that one for very frivolous reasons. Perhaps they had known a dog called this, or an actress they disliked had been called that, or a woman whom they both detested had called her daughter by yet another name. Finally the choice was narrowed to two, Cynthia and Hilary. After much deliberation they decided on Hilary, largely because no one they knew was called by that name.

Auntie Daisy brought life into the house when she came. She wore pretty clothes and had a warm, scented presence. When she came to parties at our house she wore a dark blue velvet coat with a white fox collar over her dress. The fur framed her face becomingly as she went upstairs to leave her coat on the spare room bed and came into my room to kiss me good-night.

Then one day the news came that she was ill, had developed pneumonia – and shortly later we heard that she was dying, then that she was dead! That glamorous, lively woman did not fit the word 'dead'. How could she be dead? But it was true.

It was decided that Joyce and I must go to see the dear, dead aunt for the last time. Mama and Father were already at Auntie Daisy's house, so Aggie was instructed to get us ready in our Sunday dresses and coats, which emphasised to us the solemnity of the occasion. She was grave-faced as she scrubbed our faces and hands and knees, which always seemed to be covered in cuts in various stages of healing. She told us that Auntie Daisy had gone to Heaven. She said this to comfort us, as Aggie, being Catholic, did not really believe that anyone could go to Heaven without stopping off for a time in Purgatory first, but she was too kind to tell us this.

I felt a chill wind blow round my heart all the same. Auntie Daisy was gone. There would be no more graceful hands playing our piano, no waltzes, no more Charmaine.... The world seemed suddenly bleak and unsafe.

Aggie dressed herself in the clothes she wore to go to Mass on Sundays, and we were collected by a taxi. We had a silent journey across the city and as we swept into the driveway of the house we could see lights in every room shining dully through the drawn blinds as befitted a house of mourning. It was dusk and it was cold, for it was March, but inside the house there was the usual warmth and the scent which Auntie Daisy had always used still floated in the air.

Joyce and I made the rounds of the gathered relatives and friends and were kissed by everyone. Soon Father took our hands and led us upstairs to see his sister as she lay peacefully on her bed, dressed in a pink nightgown and pink bed-jacket trimmed with swansdown. There were flowers everywhere and the overpowering scent of hyacinths filled the room.

We stood by the side of the bed where our aunt lay looking as though she had just lain down for a short rest, her brown hair combed in its usual way and the pink of the nightgown casting a glow on her pretty features. We did not know what to do or say. This was the first time either of us had seen a dead person, but the experience did not frighten us. Auntie Daisy looked pretty, just as she had done in life. I knew that she was dead, that she had gone from us and would not come back, but the memories I have of her as she lay, quietly and contentedly among the flowers, remain, and death lost its bitter sting for me that March evening.

Auntie Daisy Cleland (née Todd) c. 1903 when 23

Chapter 6

Christmas

Christmas began halfway through December. Not until then did Santa Claus appear in Robb's shop in Castle Place and live there in Fairyland, approached by a magic aeroplane which took children to visit him, until on Christmas Eve he took his departure to prepare for his great journey that night. Visiting Santa in Robbs was a great thrill and when a full complement of passengers had been loaded up in the "plane" a loud rumbling took place and things flashed past the windows in wonderfully realistic fashion. All the children present were quite convinced that they had actually flown far away and out of the shop. When they arrived in Fairyland Santa was waiting, avuncular in scarlet and with a long white beard, with a large pile of presents already wrapped, pink for the girls, blue for the boys. The return flight was no less exciting, the passengers emerging dazed and flushed with excitement, to be greeted by their parents as though they had been away for weeks.

Robbs was the first, and for a long time, the only shop in Belfast to stage this attraction, and it became obligatory for any self-respecting parents to take their children there. John Robbs was an old-fashioned shop, not quite so soignée as the Bank Buildings or Anderson & McAuley's, and certainly without the panache and style of Robinson & Cleaver's or Lindsay's, but it was solid and homely. Apart from the Santa visits I loved it because of the way payments were made. Little overhead railway tracks ran from each counter to the cash department. When purchases had been completed, the money was put into hollow wooden balls, which were screwed in half to receive it, and the balls were then placed on the railway tracks and sent on their way. Change was returned to the department for the customer in the same way, the balls running very, very slowly – and sometimes I held my breath lest they stop altogether, but they always completed their little journeys successfully.

I loved to go to town with Mama before Christmas, to walk through the brightly-lit shops, feeling the cold, sharp air on my bare knees, jostling in the crowds and sensing the air of hurry and excitement. If it was raining the wet, shiny pavements gleamed in the lights from the shop windows and the sea of umbrellas drifting up and down Donegall Place and Royal Avenue heightened the glamour.

Soon the excitement of Christmas entered the house. Cooking preparations began in real earnest and Aggie and Mama had great cooking sessions in the kitchen. The Christmas cake and three Christmas puddings had been made months before so that they could mature. Mama called them plum-cake and plum-puddings. One pudding was scheduled to be eaten at Christmas, the next at New Year and the third at Easter. Excitement mounted during the week before Christmas as friends of Mama's came and went, often bringing small gifts for Joyce and me. These were placed out of reach by Mama, and when Christmas Day came and we rushed downstairs to open our presents under the tree at the back of the drawing room, there they all were. The Christmas tree was never decorated until late on Christmas Eve when we were in bed, so that we might come down and find it, bright with its glass balls and tinsel and candles – no fairy lights then – on Christmas morning, that heavenly smell of pine needles filling the air.

I played with my presents until lunch, which was usually a light meal, perhaps vegetable broth and a pudding, and then had a short nap as I was to be allowed to stay up until late that night. I got up about four in the afternoon and was dressed by Aggie in my silk party dress, she insisting on my wearing an extra woolly vest underneath to keep out the cold. Then I floated downstairs, feeling special, and went into the warm drawing room which held that strange expectant air which all rooms have when they are made ready for a party. It was a still, breathless, lamp-lit atmosphere, the only noise being the flicker of the flames in the fireplace where the coal was piled high because of the cold winter evening.

Christmas Day was always a party day. Mama never thought of having less than eighteen to dinner at seven, and always included friends who she thought might be alone or lonely or sad.

Friends of Father's in England sent an enormous turkey every year all the way from Norfolk. Mama was sometimes a little anxious that it might not arrive in time, but it always did, coming by carrier to our door packed in straw and in a woven straw basket with handles. It weighed twenty pounds and Mama and Aggie together hauled it in and out of the oven, stuffed at one end with bread-crumbs, onion and parsley, and at the other end with chestnuts. So delicious was this chestnut stuffing, a specialty of Mama's, that no matter how much she made and put into the breast of the turkey, there was never quite enough to satisfy everyone. There was also a large baked ham, and two of the gentlemen guests did the carving. Father was not a good carver, so he looked after the vegetables and sauces. Wine was not served, other drinks such as whiskey, gin and sherry being offered before and after the meal. The only wine which was ever used, and this on only the most special occasions, was champagne.

The dinner table at Christmas was always pretty. Mama used her best cut glass tumblers for the home-made lemonade which was served with the dinner, the silver cutlery shone, polished to a high shine by Aggie, the white linen damask cloth was stiffly starched and gleaming and the linen napkins were folded into the shape of water-lilies or bishops' mitres before being set at each place. All this paled into insignificance against the magnificence of the crackers. Father had an agency for these and his best sample boxes were brought home for us, for by Christmas they were no longer needed for display purposes. This meant that the most expensive kinds of crackers decorated our table in the most wonderful colours. Sometimes ornaments like crinolined ladies, tiny dolls with frilly skirts, were attached to the sides, sometimes silk artificial flowers which looked better than the real thing, and once they had small ivory fans with feathers in pale shades of pink and blue and mauve.

Down the centre of the table there was an enormous cracker, perhaps four feet long, exclaimed over by all the guests. At the end of Christmas dinner, when all the turkey, ham and plum pudding and Mama's trifle drenched with sherry and decorated with glace cherries and crystallised violets, had been enjoyed, the cracker was lifted bodily from its place and pulled by the children, supported at each end by one or two grown-ups. All the crackers, including the monster one, contained hats and toys in great variety, celluloid dolls, games and puzzles, and these provided entertainment for us for the rest of the evening, while the grown-ups repaired to the drawing room to talk or perhaps play cards. The men smoked Havana cigars and for me the smell of cigar smoke is still the most evocative scent in the world, taking me back over the years to those long-ago Christmases.

Sometimes there was not room at the table for the children, and then Joyce and I, together with the two young sons of friends who joined us at Christmas, were seated at a small table just beside the large one. Ours was a perfect replica of the large table where the grown-ups sat. We had decorations and crackers exactly like theirs and joined in all the fun and laughter. We felt important and rather special, and although the other three were older, they let me pull crackers with them and saw that my paper hat was on straight.

After dinner, when everything had been cleared away, Joyce and I, with our two companions of the dinner-table, who were older than either of us and had the added glamour of being at boarding school, stayed in the dining room playing board games, card games, listening to records on the cabinet-style wind-up gramophone with the picture of the small dog inside listening to His Master's Voice. Our records were not new, but we liked them, and listened to "My Blue Heaven", "Bye, Bye, Blackbird", "All Alone", "It Ain't Goin' to Rain No More", "Show Me the Way to Go Home" with impartiality. "What'll I do?" was then and still is, my favourite.

We ate tangerines, which were only available at Christmas, pinching the soft peel for its wonderful scent, and spitting the pips as far as we could into the fire to hear them pop as they hit the hot coals, and then, our appetites not one whit abated by the large dinner we had just eaten, we started on the confections which in our house were available in great profusion at this time of year, these too being part of Father's business. There were hand-made chocolates in black japanned boxes with lids inlaid with designs of mother-of-pearl and tiny keys to lock them, like the one we later kept the jig-saw puzzle in. Crystallised fruits imported from France, sticky and rich in their plain wooden boxes, were no novelty to us, and we checked them over pickily, eating first the apricots and peaches which were the most luscious, then passing on to the white pears and pink pears with their tiny stalks still in place. After that we ate the pineapple rings and greengages, leaving the plums, cherries and figs until later, and the kumquats till the last.

This order of eating was in direct contrast to my past usual habit which meant that if I were given a plate of fruit salad I left the cherry until the last, it being for me the pièce de résistance. Once I was visiting Auntie Daisy for lunch and was sitting listening to the grown-ups talk and admiring my cherry which, glistening and ready on my spoon, was to be such a luscious last mouthful. Suddenly Alice, the maid, came along, and quietly, thinking I did not like cherries, removed my plate, the cherry quivering gently as it was carried off. My disappointment knew no bounds, but I could not protest. A similar calamity took place, again at Auntie Daisy's, when the pudding was baked rice with raisins. I waded laboriously though the rice, sorting out the raisins as I ate and saving them for the last few juicy mouthfuls. Again Alice whipped my plate away with its precious cargo and presumably dumped all the raisins in the bin. After these experiences I decided it was best to enjoy the good things in life as I went along.

As we played the records and games, Aggie and her sister, who lived not far away, sat in the kitchen, prostrate with exhaustion in chairs before the kitchen range, pleased that everything had gone well. Aggie's sister always came to lend a hand at parties, and was sometimes supplemented by a maid belonging to one of the guests. The maid, dressed in her crisp afternoon cap and apron, was brought along by her employers and helped in the kitchen and in serving the meal. Aggie often helped out in the houses of my parents' friends in this way, too.

After dinner the gentlemen guests usually subscribed a small sum of money which, when it was collected, was taken into the kitchen by one of their number and given to Aggie as a sort of present, not exactly a tip, and she and her helpers were thanked for all their hard work. Maids were known to their employers' friends by the names of the families for whom they worked, Mary Allen, Aggie Todd and so on. It was a great shock to me when I found out that dear Aggie's surname was not really the same as mine.

After a time, when we had feasted upon the crystallised fruits and Heller's chocolate dragees in brown cardboard boxes, imported from Vienna and the best in the world, we repaired to the drawing room to join the adults. Some of them were sitting by the fire talking, others were playing cards. One regular guest at Christmas was a dear old clergyman, the Reverend Parker Major, who to Mama's huge amusement was a Minor Canon of Downpatrick Cathedral. "Minor Canon Major!" she would chortle, "It sounds like a peal of bells!" He came with his wife and his dog, a small, plump, smooth-haired fox terrier, white with brown and black patches, called Palmolive. Palmolive had perfect manners and accompanied him everywhere. She lay on the hearth rug, quivering with joy if her master spoke to her in his gentle pulpit voice. His wife was unattractive and not only in appearance. For some reason, though, he doted upon her as well as upon Palmolive, and if anyone asked him a question he always answered, placing his hands delicately together in the praying position, "Well, now, what does my darling wife say?" I think that if she had suggested taking a trip to Outer Mongolia in a hot air balloon he would have accompanied her readily, always supposing that Palmolive could go too.

We mingled happily with the grown-ups, someone always moving up to make room for us to sit down. I as the youngest was often accommodated on someone's knee, an uncomfortable position as my bare arm was pressed against hard waistcoat buttons. At about ten o'clock Aggie would wheel in the trolley bearing supper. Already stuffed to the gills, all the guests would declare themselves unable to swallow a mouthful and would then go on to do full justice to the mince pies and Christmas cake hospitably pressed on them by Mama. The tea was served in Mama's Crown Derby cups, and it was all very festive.

I was allowed to stay up right until the last guest had gone, and then I was shepherded up to bed by Aggie, both of us tired and half asleep. Christmas was over . . . over . . .

Christmas time was children's party time, and the round of gaiety was quite intense for a few weeks during the school holidays. Sometimes we were invited to a Rotary Club party at the Grand Central Hotel, where the entertainment was lavish and finished with a Punch and Judy show. We also attended the parties of our friends and those of our parents' friends' children, some of whom we did not know very well. Someone usually called for us in a car, as often these parties were at other ends of town, Knock or Malone, and we enjoyed driving there and arriving in style, going into warm, bright houses to join with the other children in all the old games. The agony of wondering whether one would be chosen to enter the magic circle of "The Farmer Wants a Wife" or "Down on the Carpet" was exquisite and the relief when one was chosen was like the lancing of a boil. I felt I would die of shame if no one liked me enough to take me by the hand and draw me into the centre of the ring to be perhaps the Farmer's Child. "Hunt the Thimble", "Musical Chairs" and "Musical Bumps" were all played with great enthusiasm. The game of "Postman's Knock" was greeted with shrieks of delight and excitement from the little girls and reluctance on the part of the little boys, who were much embarrassed by it.

After the games tea was served, with innumerable sandwiches, biscuits, cakes and jellies and sometimes, if the household was very avant-garde and had a refrigerator, ice cream. Mama's last words to us before we left home rang in our ears: "Two sandwiches first. No cakes until you have eaten two sandwiches." We obeyed this edict unquestioningly.

The thing which terrified me about parties was that after tea, when all the games had been played and the hostess could not think of what to do, it was the custom to hold a "concert". This whiled away the time until the children were collected to go home and meant that each child was called upon to perform in some way, perhaps saying a short poem, playing the piano, doing a conjuring trick (attempted only by the bravest and mostly unsuccessful), singing a song or dancing. This was a test indeed. I prayed that it would be time to go home before my turn came and I tried to make myself small and unnoticed. I would have to "dance" for the audience, I knew, though my knowledge of dancing was nil, but it was impossible for me to recite because of my stutter. Everyone had to contribute something to the occasion, and I can still see, in my mind's eye, one small five-year-old boy, shy and pink-faced, his straight fair hair brushed to one side, dressed from head to toe in white apart from his black and yellow school tie. He tucked his thumbs into the pockets of his short white trousers and his fingers beat agitated time to his recitation of "I had a little dog and his name was Spot". I thought how lucky he was to be able to do this and envied him greatly, even though I knew he, too, hated this part of the proceedings.

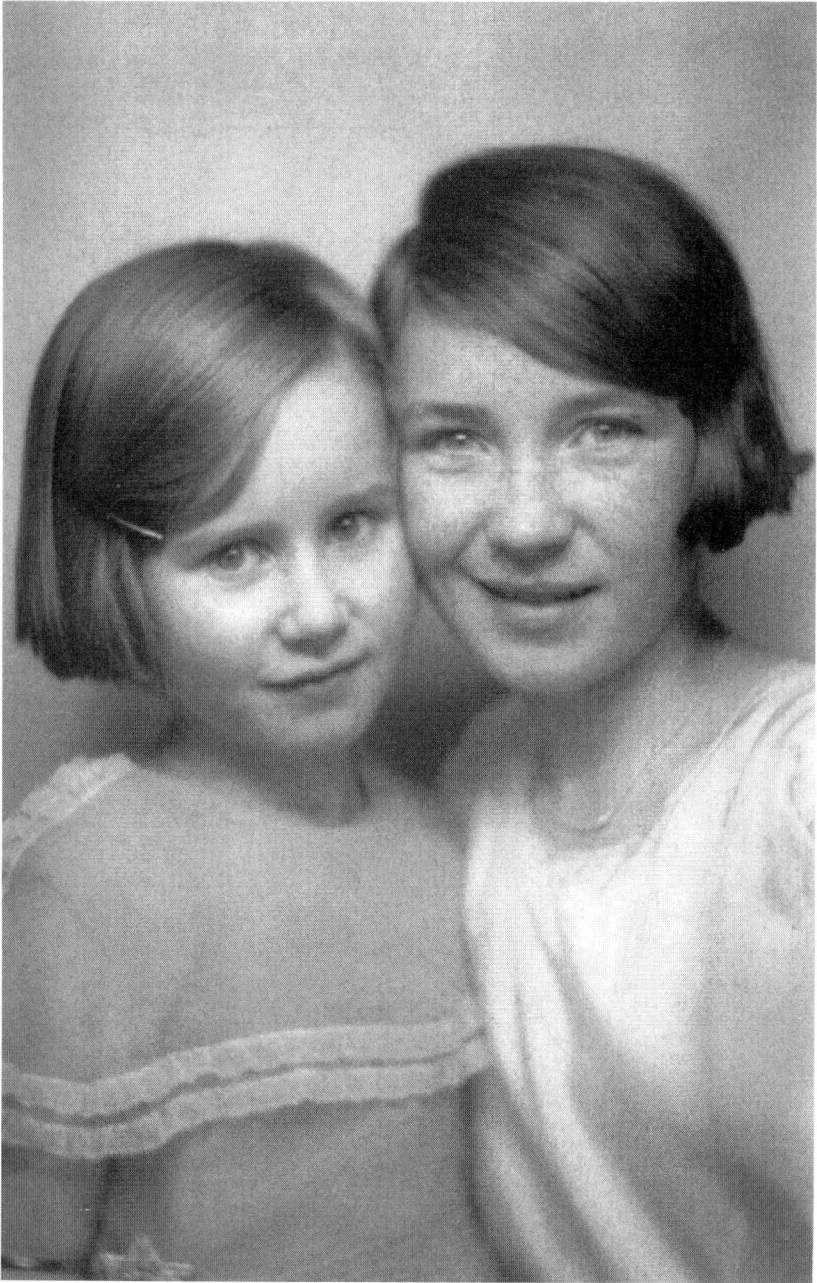

Hilary (6) and her sister Joyce (11) in party dresses, 1928

Chapter 7

Next Door

Next door to us lived Aunt Emma, Aunt Annie, Uncle Tempy and Uncle Joss, together with Carrie the maid, a Pekingese dog called Chin and five hens so that the family might have fresh eggs for breakfast every morning.

The aunts and uncles, who were brothers and sisters, were related to Mama through marriage, her uncle Robert having married their eldest sister Sarah Little. All were in their sixties except Uncle Joss.

Uncle Joss, the youngest of the family, was in his mid-fifties, a debonair man who exuded an air of glamour and wickedness and wealth. He owned a large yellow motor car, at a time when most cars were black. He was tall and slim and elegant. He wore beautifully cut pale suits in summer, dark in winter and tweed at weekends. These were made for him in Savile Row in London and his handmade shoes came from Lobbs. Uncle Joss smelt of bay rum and sported a moustache, luxuriant iron-grey hair and a marvellous tan which he kept up by constant visits abroad. He had a mistress whom he shared amicably with a friend who was also a man of the world, but liked to cut costs. I do not know whether they each had visiting rights on certain days of the week, or whether they ever met at her door, one coming and the other going, like the weather man and woman. I always knew of this association, though I had no idea what a mistress was, except that Mama kept stores of food in the mistress's pantry at home. We were family and therefore entitled to know about and comment on Uncle Joss's life, though not of course to him.

Uncle Joss had once been married and the story was told by Mama in hushed, excited tones. He had been, Mama said "very fond" of a woman called Isobel. One day Isobel, a tall, thin woman in her early thirties, with dark hair and grey eyes with a green tint, whom he had not introduced to his family, arrived at the house in floods of tears and asked to see Aunt Emma. Aunt Emma, rather taken aback, asked her in and gave her tea.

Mopping her tears with a large white linen handkerchief belonging to Uncle Joss, Isobel told her story. She was in an interesting condition, she said, and the father of her child was Uncle Joss. With remarkable aplomb for a maiden lady who was not suppose to be au fait with the facts of human reproduction, Aunt Emma questioned her closely, calmed her down and sent her home in a taxi, assuring her that all would be well.

When Uncle Joss arrived home from his office that evening Aunt Emma confronted him with a fait accompli. He found to his horror that arrangements were already being made to have the banns called. Rant and rage as he might, his gentle older sister would have none of it. Reasoning had no effect either. Uncle Joss was issued with an ultimatum. Isobel's honour must be vindicated, said Aunt Emma, who had now called Uncle Tempy in on her side. The child must be given a name and home. Faced with his two siblings and finding them unyielding in the matter, he, having no alternative, furiously agreed to do as they said. Isobel came often to the house to visit Aunt Emma in the following days, but after he had cross-examined her Uncle Joss refused to speak to, or even to be in the same room with, his paramour.

The day of the wedding came swiftly and Uncle Joss, Uncle Tempy and Aunt Emma, who wore her best hat with osprey feathers to honour the occasion, bowled off to the church in a taxi, Uncle Joss looked angry and madly handsome in a dark suit with, appropriately enough, a black tie, and the other two had set jaws like warders escorting a condemned man to the scaffold. They were implacable. They did not want this dreadful Isobel, who they considered slightly common, to become a member of their family, but their principles would not allow them to search for another solution. Uncle Joss, they felt, should never have put them in this upsetting position. Isobel was really a Fallen Woman and now she was to be their sister-in--law. It was really too bad of Uncle Joss and most inconsiderate.

When they arrived at the church Isobel was already there, waiting for them at the door. She looked remarkably composed in pale grey with a large grey picture hat wreathed in white daisies.

Her greenish eyes had a triumphant gleam and she carried a grey suede prayer book.

Out of the taxi stumped Aunt Emma and the uncles. Uncle Joss looked straight ahead and did not greet his bride, but marched into the church, the other three almost running to keep up. The ceremony was short and to the point, and when he observed Uncle Joss's scowl the minister omitted the homily he had planned to deliver. Uncle Joss, he could see, was in no mood for homilies. Aunt Emma did not even have time to take her lace handkerchief out of her handbag to dry the tears she had planned to weep. Uncle Tempy sat beside her, majestic as ever, in the front pew, looking as though he wished he were anywhere else in the world, his white leonine hair brushed to the consistency of whipped egg white and his long, lean legs hooked under the seat in front. These two were to act as witnesses to the marriage.

The minute Uncle Joss and Isobel were pronounced man and wife and the register was signed, Uncle Joss turned and marched back up the aisle with the new Mrs. Joss, who now looked slightly pink with apprehension, the look of triumph fading rapidly. When they reached the church steps Uncle Joss turned to her and said in clipped tones, "Now you are married. I hope you are satisfied. I never wish to see you again as long as I live." Whereupon he leapt into the taxi which was waiting and drove to his club, leaving his bride open-mouthed on the pavement.

Isobel began to weep loudly and Aunt Emma turned even paler than usual when she realised what had happened. Uncle Joss always meant what he said. Uncle Tempy got another taxi and Isobel was conveyed back to her own house and deposited there, the daisies in her hat by now slightly wilted.

Back to Cliftonville Road and home drove the other two and Aunt Emma went to bed at once, not emerging from the safety of her room for three weeks. The doctor was sent for and he ordered immediate bed-rest and a sedative. Uncle Tempy, fortified by a double brandy, was left to face the music when Uncle Joss came home. The words the brothers had were short and sharp, but the upshot of the matter was that Uncle Joss flatly refused to have anything more to do with Isobel, and no amount of pleading could alter his decision. He stated this fact unequivocally and then locked himself in the smoke-room, where he paced the floor and smoked Havana cigars until three in the morning. This was his private sanctum, for Aunt Emma would not allow him to smoke elsewhere in the house, and no one else was permitted to use it.

Their sister Annie was staying with relatives in Bangor when all this happened. She always disliked those relatives afterwards and said, most unfairly, that they had made her miss all the excitement.

Time went by and Aunt Emma recovered from her ordeal and began to take up the threads of her quiet life again. She reluctantly contacted the bride, who had remained strangely silent since the wedding, and found to her astonishment that Isobel was not pregnant at all. It had been a ruse to achieve a safe and wealthy marriage. Aunt Emma almost returned to her bed permanently when she heard this. What, oh what, would Uncle Joss say now? Timorously she informed him of her fact-finding mission, only to be told with quiet fury that he had suspected this all along and that, while he would make financial provision for Isobel for the rest of her life, it would be best if she left the country and her name was never again to be mentioned in the house.

Aunt Emma had to agree. Never again was Uncle Joss challenged upon any subject. She felt that she had jumped the gun and ruined any chance he might have had of making a good and happy marriage. Here he was, married and yet not married, all because of her impetuosity and good faith. Now she upbraided Uncle Tempy for aiding her in this, though of course she had given him no alternative.

All her life she would remember that she had pushed Uncle Joss into an impossible position, and she suffered dreadfully from guilt. Isobel was shipped off, barren, to England, and though Aunt Emma kept in touch with her occasionally by letter, she never saw her again.

Uncle Joss, who was handsome, dashing, urbane and completely irresistible to women, continued to play the field, bowl around in his yellow motor car, go on holiday to Italy and the South of France and sometimes Spain, with an occasional Mediterranean cruise thrown in, to deepen his sun tan, and visit his mistress twice weekly. His maleness pervaded the house as soon as he entered it, and though I was slightly shy of him, he was always kind. He was my first experience of a really glamorous man of the world. He was to me the epitome of the word "panache".

Uncle Tempy was completely different. He had been a very successful business man in Dublin and when he retired he sold all his assets and re-invested them in stocks and shares which were safe and secure. He was tall, immaculately tailored and good-looking, but not in the sexy way that Uncle Joss was handsome. Uncle Tempy's face was pink and his hair white and he had a bushy white moustache to match. He wore glasses with gold rims and was kind and gentle. Every morning he sat by the drawing room fire reading the Belfast Newsletter, his brightly polished tan boots twinkling like newly shelled horse chestnuts in the firelight and saying, "A-hmmmmmmmm," at intervals when an especially interesting item of news caught his eye. He and Aunt Emma were kindred spirits, quiet and serene in their ways.

I visited this house daily. I sensed the rarefied smell of wealth there. I cannot describe it, but it seemed to be a mixture of furniture polish, good food, expensive cigars (Uncle Joss's) and money. I sniffed it and wondered why, although our house smelt good too, the essential ingredient was missing. What was missing was money, of course, though I did not realise it at the time.

Carrie, the maid, dressed in red with a white morning cap and apron, opened the door when I rang the bell. I walked across the thick turkey-red carpet in the hall to the drawing room to kiss Uncle Tempy good morning. His white moustache swept my face as I sat down on a small hassock by the warm fire. "Draw up a boss," he would boom. Only the Aunts and Uncles, in my experience, called a hassock a boss. We chatted a little, he putting down his newspaper to regard me kindly. My stutter, so distressing to me in the company of strangers, never troubled me in this house, for it was a gentle place without rush or strain. I told him what I had been doing since I had seen him the previous day, which did not take long. He looked at me over his glasses, nodding and smiling, and then returned to his newspaper while I warmed my hands and knees at the fire as I crouched on the boss.

Sometimes Aunt Emma joined us in the drawing room and we sat there quietly until Carrie came in bearing a tray with beef tea or chicken tea in a large cup, accompanied by two cream crackers on a matching Rockingham plate for Aunt Emma, China tea with a Bath Oliver also on Rockingham china for Uncle Tempy and a glass of milk and a piece of seed cake for me. My cake came on a pink plate with "A present from Portrush" written on it in gold. This little collation was to sustain us until lunch time. If Aunt Emma was in bed, as she frequently was, Uncle Tempy and I would have our "elevenses" together, while she had hers upstairs.

Uncle Tempy – whose real name was Templeton – went out most afternoons for a walk or to visit his stockbroker, and each Friday he went into town about midday. There he lunched at the Bonne Bouche Café upon grilled fillet of plaice, followed by apple pie or crème caramel, and afterwards visited a cinema, arriving in time for the first performance of the afternoon. He settled himself in the back row of the balcony so that he could rest his head on the little wall behind. Then he slept. Soundly and well he slept until the programme had completed one round. He woke up greatly refreshed and watched the second round with enjoyment. This allowed him to be home in time for tea. He never varied this routine and Fridays were a highlight in his quiet life. He owned a wireless, a crystal set with a cat's whisker and earphones, and sometimes he would place the earphones on my head, holding them over my ears so that I, too, could hear the music he enjoyed so much.

Aunt Emma herself was the frailest of the four, but was nevertheless an indomitable woman. She ran the household beautifully and without fuss. She never did any housework or cooking – Carrie did that – but meals arrived on the table on time and were well chosen and nourishing. Each morning just after breakfast Carrie appeared at her bedside to receive instructions for the day. Uncle Joss dined at his club each evening with his friends, but lunched at home, so that the family met once daily and discussed any necessary business and family news.

Aunt Emma was subject to bronchitis and it was not unusual for her to spend the winter months in bed. Then her room became the centre of the house. The other three visited her daily, as did the doctor. A fire burned cheerfully in the grate and Carrie staggered upstairs several times during the day with buckets of coal to refill the mahogany and brass coal-scuttle and to build up the fire.

She was the heart of the house. She never raised her voice but her wishes were carried out to the letter, even when she was bedridden. When she was sick I made my way to her room each morning after visiting with Uncle Tempy downstairs. There she lay, her grey hair neatly brushed into a soft knot at the back of her neck, upon a cloud of pillows and wearing a scarlet bed jacket. On Sundays she wore a rose-pink jacket, which was more flattering. She smelled of lavender water except when she had a cold, when she smelled of eucalyptus oil, which she sniffed from a liberally-sprinkled handkerchief.

She had a pile of books by her bed and read constantly. Mama rarely read books (Father did – and always until three o'clock in the morning, for he loved thrillers and could not put them down, once started), so Aunt Emma seemed different to me even in that way. She never failed to say that she was pleased to see me, as I sat on a small chair by her bed. Sometimes she asked me to sing, and while I was no diva, I would obligingly pipe up. The songs I knew best were those that my sister learnt at school and which I picked up from her, but the words were sometimes missing here and there and I had to make them up as I sang. One of these was "The Minstrel from Sorrento" and I sang this to her almost every day, going on to the waltzes from the gramophone records we had at home, in which I was word perfect. I usually ended with "Horsey, Keep Your Tail Up" and "Jesus Loves Me", after which she gave me a sweet, a buttered ginger, and with a bulging cheek I kissed her good-bye until tomorrow and went home to lunch.

Once a remarkable thing happened. Aunt Emma decided to spend a winter in Italy. Italy! I was desolate. I did not know where Italy was, but I knew it was a long way from Belfast and that the winter would be long and dreary without Aunt Emma's calm presence next door. She had been inveigled into this arrangement by two friends, the Misses Munce, who wished to visit Alassio and knew that if they could persuade Aunt Emma to join them their living expenses would be much less. I did not like these women, who shooshed me away from Aunt Emma's room, where I felt I had more right to be than they had, because I was "family". They asked me questions and when I answered them seriously and to the best of my ability, laughed at me and repeated my foolish answers to each other in raucous tones of mirth and then told me it was time to go home. Aunt Emma seemed powerless to come to my rescue when they were there and I could not understand this. Uncle Tempy would stroke my hair comfortingly and put his arm around me as though to shelter me as I stood by his chair, and when they had tormented me in their loud English voices for as long as I could bear, I slipped out of the room and went home to Aggie, who always had a biscuit or a currant bun to soothe my ruffled feelings.

The three ladies set off for Italy and arrived at Alassio safely, where they passed the winter. Aunt Emma came back in the spring looking tired and slightly weary. She never repeated the experiment. Perhaps the loud voices and bossy ways of the Misses Munce had upset her, too. She did not say.

Aunt Annie was the fourth member of the family. She was short, stout, white-haired, wore glasses and always dressed in black. She was a widow and had two sons, one married and living in Canada and the other, a bachelor called Laddie, though he was thirty-five and his real name was Eric. In her youth, when the family lived in Stewartstown, she had fallen in love with a young man who worked for her father in his business. Her parents, dismayed at their daughter's intention of marrying "beneath her" threatened and cajoled, but Annie would not back down, declaring that she intended to marry her penniless suitor no matter what they thought. Marry him she did and was cut off from her family immediately. She lived with her husband and later her two children in a small house in a poor district where they eked out a meagre existence.

By a stroke of fortune, or misfortune, depending upon how and by whom it was viewed, within a few years Aunt Annie's husband was killed in a quarry accident; whereupon her parents descended upon her and swept her and her two sons back into the bosom of the family. As she had no money to speak of she had no option but to agree to this arrangement and soon she settled back into the old ways. Her two small sons were sucked into the family too, but somehow they were never quite accepted and were left no money by their uncles and aunts, nor by their grandparents when they died.

Aunt Annie was a fussy little lady and in my earliest memories she did not live with her brothers and sisters, but just paid them long, long visits. When her sons were eventually settled, she returned to the fold permanently and disturbed the even tenor of life in the house by her irritating habit of just being there. She did not read, as did Uncle Tempy and Aunt Emma, and she and Uncle Joss were poles apart in temperament and outlook. Indeed, he barely acknowledged her presence save at lunch times when he was forced to face her over the table.

She spent much time making batches of biscuits in the kitchen and would sometimes give me one, but even this did not make me like her. She doted upon the Pekingese dog, Chin, and when he grew to be almost senile at the great doggy age of sixteen she was to be found each morning holding him in her arms, he dressed in a bib, like a baby, and feeding him beaten-up egg-white on a silver spoon.

Aunt Annie had a horror of being buried alive and had a clause written into her will directing that when she died a vein in each of her arms was to be opened so that everyone would be sure that she was dead before burial took place.

One night there was a great commotion at our front door and I got up from sleep to go to the top of the stairs to see what was happening. I saw Uncle Joss and Uncle Tempy, together with Aunt Annie's son Laddie, all in a great state because Aunt Annie had had a heart attack. They had come to fetch Mama, as almost everyone who knew her did when there was illness, and had sent for the doctor, but Aunt Annie died that night. Her veins were opened as she had requested and when she was pronounced dead the funeral arrangements were permitted to go forward.

This family had the strange custom of burying their dead very early in the morning, eight o'clock being the time set, and as a journey of forty-five miles or so had to be completed before the funeral service could take place in the church beside their family vault in Stewartstown, they started off at six in the morning. This was a great trial to Father, who was the hardest person in the world to get out of bed in the mornings. Mama would have needed to have installed an ejector seat beneath him to achieve this. To hear him complain about these funeral arrangements one would have thought that a member of the Little family died each week. However, Mama never failed to get him to the starting post on time, looking spruce and immaculate as always in morning coat and silk hat, the recognised wear for funerals.

Aunt Annie was laid to her final rest with all her relatives who had gone before in the vault which was just like a little house in the churchyard. It had a wrought iron gate and shelves on either side where the coffins were placed. Every three years these coffins were removed, re-varnished and presumably caulked where necessary. After Aunt Annie died there were only three spaces left on the shelves, one each for her brothers and sister.

I was grown-up, married and a mother when Uncle Joss died. He and Aunt Emma were the only two left, for Uncle Tempy had died peacefully in his sleep some years before. They lived in a large house in another area, surrounded by a beautiful garden. My parents were dead and life had changed for everyone, but the atmosphere in that house was still redolent of the good life. When I heard Uncle Joss had died I went at once to see Aunt Emma, who was sitting, straight-backed as ever, in a chair in the drawing room, although she was then ninety-one. She was pale but calm. She kissed me and we talked a little. Then she asked me if I would like to see Uncle Joss for the last time. I said I would and she brought me into the smoke-room where he had spent most of the time in his last years, reading and viewing the huge television projector screen which he had bought because he would not, he said, strain his eyes to look at an ordinary television set.

We entered the room quietly and speaking in hushed voices as people do in any room where someone lies dead. There, in the coffin lay Uncle Joss, looking like a million dollars, elegantly attired in a dinner jacket and black tie. I fully expected him to open his eyes and ask me for one of his Corona cigars which lay on his desk. I said how well he looked and mouthed platitudes in the way people do in such situations.

Aunt Emma looked pleased and said she had not been able to make up her mind for a time as to whether he should be dressed in a dinner jacket or morning coat, but upon reflection she had felt that if he wore a morning coat he would look too much as though he were dressed for a wedding. She had finally decided on the dinner jacket, presumably feeling that it was better for him to look as though he was on his way to a dinner party.

Even in his coffin he looked glamorous and handsome and gave out that irresistible aura of sex and wealth, surely the best combination of all and the one which most men would give their eye teeth to possess in life.

Aunt Emma died at the age of ninety-five, slipping away as gently as she had lived. All the shelves in the vault were filled.

Chapter 8

Necessities

Mama was no mean cook and Aggie was a splendid ally, having been in her early days trained in the house of a titled family in London where she had been taught to cook by the chef. Her ideas, however, were usually wildly extravagant, calling for pints of cream and glasses of brandy, and Mama was torn between the longing to make an impression on her friends and the knowledge that she could not really afford larks' tongues in aspic, plovers' eggs or ortolans on toast. Chickens, ducks and geese, or even turkeys were obtainable in season from her family in the country and were despatched to her on request. Usually these arrived un-plucked, to Aggie's irritation, for it is more difficult to pluck a fowl when it has cooled and an easy matter if done as soon as the bird is killed, and still warm.

When the poultry arrived, Aggie sat in the kitchen with a large clean old sheet spread round her on the floor, plucking methodically, surrounded by a mound of tawny feathers if she was working on a chicken, or white ones if the victim was a duck or a goose. Ducks came in pairs for there was little meat on them and geese and turkeys arrived at Michaelmas and Christmas. Turkeys were hard to rear and were coaxed to maturity with difficulty by farmers' wives whose only income, apart from the egg and butter money, they represented.

The mistress's pantry, where Mama made her preparations for parties, was a small room between the kitchen and the dining room. On the floor were two crocks of eggs. These earthenware crocks, terra cotta outside and black-glazed inside, had wooden lids and contained eggs bought at Easter when they were cheap and plentiful, costing six pence a dozen, and preserved in water-glass. These were for use in cooking and baking over the winter when eggs were scarce and dear Mama always crocked sixty dozen eggs each year. The pantry was lined with cupboards and shelves filled with homemade jams, jellies, pickles and sauces.

There were always jars of stuffed and un-stuffed olives. For years I thought that stuffed olives grew that way, with salty red centres, and I wondered why on earth people bothered to grow the variety with the stones in, which were not half so tasty. There were jars of preserved tomatoes, peaches in brandy and cherries in maraschino, but the pièces de résistance were two large jars, one containing truffles and the other cockscombs. These last I could never relate to the proud, high-stepping, crowing roosters with their magnificent glossy red-brown feathers, nodding plumey tails and fiery red combs which I saw in my uncle's farmyard. The cockscombs in the jar were soft and cream-white, layered I suppose in brine in their glass prison, and looked altogether revolting. The thought of actually eating one filled me with revulsion, but Father only kept them as a doctor might retain an interesting specimen and never intended them to be eaten.

Once the pantry was used as the home of two leeches. Mama, who bruised easily, fell from the step-ladder whilst mending a fuse in the fuse-box which was perched crazily in the hall above the back dining room door. Mama was the one who mended fuses and did small running repairs like this, for Father was hopeless and confined his activities to sitting by the fire and looking over his newspaper at Mama as she teetered on the high rickety step-ladder, saying ineffectually, "Watch yourself, now!" She bruised her face and her eye was black and swollen next day. She despatched Father to the chemist's on the Antrim Road, telling him to bring back two leeches. When he returned with these creatures in a small black pill-box, Mama ascended to the bathroom and proceeded to apply them to her blackened face where they fastened on eagerly, feasting on the bruise, propped on Mama's cheek on a pillow of cotton wool. When they were thoroughly gorged and sated they released their hold and fell back on their cotton-wool bed, whereupon Mama arose from her necessarily semi-recumbent posture and tipped them neatly into a large wine-glass, sprinkled them with salt and water and covered the glass with a coffee-saucer. After a time they were ready to start their blood-sucking again. and so it went on until Mama's bruises had disappeared. Until then the leeches lived, when not working, on the pantry window-sill in their wine-glass and were visited daily by Joyce and me, when we looked at them in horror and disgust. Although we found them revolting we named them Minnie and Winnie, even though they did not sleep in a shell as in the poem. One day just after Mama's face was better, I went in to have a look at these black slug-like creatures, only to find they had gone. Mama said they had been sent back to the chemist, but I think Aggie had put them down the drain.

Mama made her pastry in this pantry and had a table there with a marble top specially for the purpose. Her puff pastry was delicate, high and flaky and was made with great ceremony, rolling out, dabbing with bits of butter, rolling again, resting. Seven times this ritual had to be carried out for the results to be good, and Mama never skimped.

When she made bread she used a baking-board about thirty inches square and with sides about three inches high along three of its sides. The fourth side, which was towards the edge of the table on which the bakeboard rested, had a groove to catch the unused flour or wheaten meal. She never used a rolling pin, claiming that it was too heavy and that a light touch was imperative, so she used a brandy bottle which was absolutely the right choice for it was clear, light, easy to clean and had a cleft in the bottom which made it easy to hold. To sweep the loose flour evenly around the board she used a goose's wing. Only someone who has used a goose's wing for this purpose can possibly know how well suited it is for the job, and there is no substitute for it. No grain of flour or meal escapes it and because it is flexible it gets into all corners and clears them instantly of any lurking waste. She had two new ones each year, which were removed from the Michaelmas goose before it was cooked, and these white feathery wings with their strong quills were thoroughly washed, well shaken and placed in the warming oven of the range in the kitchen to dry out gently, from whence they emerged white and new to serve their turn for the next twelve months.

Bread was made regularly twice a week. Mama had been taught this art by her mother, who, like all Ulster countrywomen, had made it a part of her life, a task which she performed every day and most likely, apart from childbearing, was the only creative thing she could do without feeling guilty about taking time off from caring for her family. Soda bread and wheaten bread were made with flour, or a mixture of flour and wheaten meal, salt, sugar, baking soda – cream of tartar being added in the case of soda bread to keep the bread white – and buttermilk. The bread could be cooked in the oven, from whence it came out soft and spongy inside and with a pleasant brown crust. On the other hand, and for variety, it could be cooked in the traditional way on a black iron griddle. The dough was mixed, kneaded on the bake-board, rolled out quickly and lightly into a circle about an inch thick, cut into four pieces which then – and this was the tricky part – had to be whisked on to the griddle which stood heated and ready on the stove. The farls had to be soft so that the resulting bread would not be tough, but still firm enough to keep their shape until they reached the griddle. Juggling the bread from board to griddle was a real test of skill. The shape had to be kept perfect, straight on two sides of the farl and curved on the outer edge, without a crack to mar its symmetry. The worst thing that could be said of a bread-maker was that her farls had bad edges.

Home-baked bread was supplemented by bought yeast bread called "plain bread" from the baker's cart. The baker – in country districts he was more realistically called the bread-server – called three times a week, on Mondays, Wednesdays and Fridays, with his horse-drawn cart. He dismounted from his high perch on top of the cart, hooked the horse's reins over the back of his seat, opened the back door of his cart and drew out a large wicker basket filled with different varieties of bread which he then carried to the customer's door. He had plain loaves, pan loaves, crusty loaves, basket pans, turnovers, cottage loaves, fruit loaves with raisins, cherries and peel, Veda bread and Hovis and usually Paris buns which were yellow and sugar-topped and so dry that they had to be eaten with a great deal of butter. The baker was a pleasant man – if he had not been he would not have had many customers – and always had a kind word for the children of the house. Sometimes he would even give a child a biscuit, a thick, round one, pierced with holes, not quite shortbread, but almost.

Our baker drove a brown cart with "Ormeau Bakery" in cream lettering on the sides. This bakery was considered to be the crème de la crème of bakeries and people of discernment liked to have its carts stopping outside their houses. There were several other large bakeries in Belfast, all of which I am sure were excellent, but somehow the Ormeau Bakery had the edge on all of them for style and dignity, and it was one of their carts which came to our house.

The milkman called twice a day. He kept his own cows in a field and milking shed at the top of the Cliftonville Road, and they were milked morning and afternoon. Pasteurisation had not then come into vogue. Mr. Wilson, our milkman, lived just around the corner from us in Cliftonpark Avenue and had a milk float drawn by a horse called Sadie. Sadie, like the baker's horse, knew the rounds of the customers as well as did her master and stopped at each one obediently, waiting patiently for him to reappear, when, at his word of command, she would move gently on.

The milk float was varnished and highly polished and the large metal containers for the milk shone brightly. Inside the lid of each of these hung a metal dipper by which the milk was transferred to smaller cans before being carried to a customer's door. Mama or Aggie brought a jug to the door and the milk was poured into it from the can. Refrigerators were in their infancy and the twice-daily delivery was necessary as milk soured so quickly, especially in summer. From about June until September the jug which held the newly delivered milk was plunged into a large basin filled with cold water which had been liberally salted to keep it cool. The whole thing was covered with a muslin square bordered with small square wooden beads of blue, yellow and red to weigh its edges down, and kept in the coolest part of the kitchen premises. In our house this was behind the scullery door, next to the mangle, where no ray of sun ever penetrated.

Many people, friends of Mama's, had "sewing ladies". These were ladies who came to the house for a day every so often to do mending, turning sheets sides to middle when they were worn, darning linen tablecloths, letting down and taking up hems of garments and other small tasks.

Some of my dresses were passed on from Joyce and an older cousin, but the one I remember and loved best had been bought especially for me when I was very young, not more than two years old. It was made of white organdie and had a border of appliquéd yellow chickens and a scalloped hem round the skirt which was gathered into a high yoke and the chicken motif was continued on a smaller scale around the yoke and the small puffed sleeves. Most of my other dresses at this stage were white, and under them I wore a fine lawn petticoat, fastened at neck and waist by tapes, with a narrow lace flounce at the hem. My knickers were also of lawn and had lace frills, only one frill for everyday wear, but for parties they had five or six layers of lacy frills and were starched so that the frills would stand out, and they were stiff and scratchy against my skin. On my feet I wore white kid shoes in summer and brown kid boots in winter.

As I grew older I wore woollen dresses in winter and bright cotton in summer, made by Jinny McAuley, a visiting dressmaker who lived in the country near Mama's old home. She came to stay for a week in spring and another week in autumn. In that time she fitted out not only me, but Mama and Joyce, with dresses for the coming summer or winter. We usually had two new dresses each if Mama had found suitable material at a reasonable price. She often bought remnants at sale-time, and Jinny was able to do wonders with them. Joyce's dresses which she had outgrown were made to fit me and my cousin's hand-me-downs were adjusted for Joyce. Mama had perhaps a new skirt or a dress and when all this was done, amid much poring over paper pattern books, Jinny did the mending. The sewing machine never ceased to whir until the week had sped past and it was time for Jinny to go home.

She was paid one pound for all this work, together with her bus fare, and seemed pleased and satisfied with it. It was a break in her rather dull life and during her week with us she usually had a jaunt into town on the tram. She did not buy anything, but just looked in shop windows and stored up ideas about the latest styles which she would use when she returned home.

Jinny had bright blue eyes like glass marbles, a mop of naturally curly blonde hair, a large pale shiny mole by the side of her nose, a cacophonous voice and breath like a flame-thrower. This last was very distressing when one was having what Jinny called a "fit-on". To have a "fit-on" was a great trial, especially for me as I was small and she had to kneel down beside me to arrange and rearrange the garment she was making. She was not too careful about where she rammed in pins and if I made a squeak of protest when she stuck one into my arm or chest, she smartly rebuked me and glared into my face, hissing, "Stay still," and emitting an anaesthesia-producing breath which filled my nostrils and brought tears to my eyes. She thought I was crying because of the pin-pricks and scolded me for being such a baby and I could never tell her the real reason for my misery.

She must have been about twenty-three when I first remember her, and while she was no Coco Chanel she was available and was imported regularly to keep us well and warmly clothed in winter and pretty in summer. Mama arranged the date for her arrival and on the appointed day Jinny appeared, dressed in her best coat and hat, her fair curls bobbing, and carrying a change of clothing in a small cardboard suitcase. She usually had a paper parcel full of patterns and carried a bunch of country flowers for Mama. Aggie disliked her intensely, as did Father, who only liked pretty ladies and could not bear this uncouth young woman with the raucous voice and the loud, vulgar laugh.

After a few preliminaries and tea in the kitchen she was wafted upstairs to the room which was my bedroom where a fire had been lit in the grate. This was, Mama felt, the best place for her to work, as all the loose threads and dropped pins and small scraps of material which she discarded as she worked could be easily swept up from the linoleum. The bed was pushed into a corner, the sewing machine was wheeled into the room, material was produced and the sewing marathon began.

When she came at first she liked to visit the Lyceum cinema on the Antrim Road occasionally in the evenings, and came back from these outings with her blue eyes shining in excitement at what she had seen. The film she had seen the previous evening was talked about all the next day and when Mama said, "Wouldn't it be nice to pipe that dress round the waist?" or, "What about a Peter Pan collar on that blue dress of Joyce's?" Jinny would pretend she had not heard and would say, "That woman in the picture last night – she was a kyo-boy! She had more dresses than you could shake a stick at – cupboards full of them – and some of them had necks nearly down to her waist. I was nearly dead in case one of her chests would fall out when she bent over. Such a cut! Do you think yon women really go about like that?" She prattled on, not expecting an answer, and Mama would go out of the room for a while.

After a few years Jinny got religion and was "saved". She said she now belonged to "the Dippers" and this put an end to the cinema visits, but it was her great pleasure on two occasions to go to the Crumlin Road and stand outside the gaol at eight o'clock in the morning when a murderer was to be hanged. When she returned from these grisly outings she demanded hot Bovril and sat at the kitchen table relating in excited tones all that she had seen, telling us of the reaction of the crowd when eight o'clock, the execution time, struck on the prison clock. She said that everyone had fallen silent for a moment or two and how later they all surged forward to read the notice which was posted on the door of the gaol saying that the execution had taken place.

Aggie could not hear these details but she could see the excited and unhealthy glow in Jinny's face and regarded her with distaste. She rattled the poker through the bars of the fire in the range and pulled the dampers in and out, making a great noise and filling the kitchen with sooty smoke, whereupon Jinny asked sourly if she was trying to suffocate her and when she received no answer, drank up the Bovril and went upstairs to lie on her bed for a time to mull over her experiences before starting into the sewing once more. At this Aggie opened the kitchen door which led into the yard and let in fresh air in a great gust. Later, Jinny's visits stopped. She would not leave her religious meetings long enough to come to us. Her fervour grew and she became completely carried away and, as often happens, her religious extravagances developed into a sexual abandon. She fell in love with a local lay preacher, a married man who behaved like a human dipstick, visiting his younger women converts with regularity and telling them to think of him as the Lord's messenger. Mama heard that she became pregnant no less than three times and had three self-induced abortions. After the last one poor Jinny bled to death, all alone in her small house amid the piles of material, the half-sewn garments and hundreds of paper patterns.

Chapter 9

Parties

Mama and Father were gregarious and enjoyed both giving parties and attending them. They adored dressing up for these evening gatherings and if the party was somewhere else, always came into kiss me goodnight before leaving, both of them smelling delicious, Father of Hungary Water and Mama of her favourite scent, Phul-Nana.

The Twenties wore on and money, because of the general economic situation, became scarcer, but my parents seemed to pay no attention to their changing fortunes. Their friends must have managed their finances more prudently, I think, for their lives continued comfortably. As far as we children were concerned, however, all was merry as a marriage bell and the parties and entertainments went on as usual.

On party nights the gas fire in the spare room was lit to warm the room and a small purple lustre bowl was filled with water and set before it to absorb the poisonous fumes. The fire burned brightly and pop-popped gently all evening and the beam from the pink shaded lamp by the bed was reflected in the looking-glass in the centre panel of the wardrobe which in turn made the silver brushes on the dressing-table glint in the soft glow. The bed was decked out beforehand with a blue silk counterpane and eiderdown to match and there was a small silver vase of flowers on the mantelpiece.

Joyce and I were put to bed by Aggie, bathed and in fresh nightgowns, before the guest arrived. It was a ritual for visitors to view the children of the house in bed and to kiss them goodnight. We sat in our beds waiting for the voices of the ladies to float past in the landing on their way to remove their wraps, comb their hair and re-powder their noses. Then they would swan into our bedrooms smelling deliciously of Otto of Roses or Chanel No. 5, and stand around the bed saying how sweet we were, how we had grown, telling us of their own children at home. It is strange how, when adults are friends, their children are expected to be friends also, and yet this hardly ever happens.

I felt that the children of my parents' friends were all rare creatures who inhabited a sort of fairyland, living in luxury, with scented, warm, pink, thickly carpeted bedrooms. Most of them were already at, or were destined for boarding-schools in England, for this was a true mark of their parents' financial success.

Slightly dispirited by all this, I watched the ladies twirl around the room in their smart Twenties dresses, some with fringes eighteen inches long at the hem, and shiny patent-leather pointy-toed strapped shoes which buttoned over their insteps. Their hair was cut short in the fashionable bob or shingle, or a bingle, which was halfway between the two. One or two wore lipstick – very daring and avant-garde, as many people still believed that only whores painted their faces. The others were content with leaves of papier poudre which they carried in their handbags and applied to their shiny noses and flushed cheeks during the evening. After they had gone downstairs, perhaps to enjoy a musical evening, and the light had been put out, I twisted and turned in bed, rattling the brass knobs and wishing that I, too, lived in a rarefied atmosphere, with a pink carpet in my bedroom and the prospect of an easy life.

Sometimes when the guests had laughed, danced and finished supper, they would troop upstairs again to see if we were still awake, which we usually were, the noise and excitement downstairs having banished sleep. They came into our bedrooms, the men this time as well, bearing plates of trifle or pineapple cream which Mama always made for parties. We sat up in bed, blinking our eyes at the light, and ate the puddings offered as they drifted across the landing between our bedrooms, as they chatted to us, but more excitingly to each other. I think the ladies must have felt deliciously wicked to be in a bedroom, even a child's bedroom with the child in bed, with other people's husbands standing around and chatting to them. Life could be dull for them.

I remember seeing one man standing behind a lady who was not his wife, as she leant on the end of my bed, and slipping his arm round her waist. She swayed backwards slightly and pinned his hand to her side with her bent elbow and they both laughed softly in a strangely guilty way as she turned her head and put her cheek against his. Years later Mama told me that these two had

had a long-standing love affair which was tacitly accepted by their spouses and all their friends as long as they were discreet and did not upset the apple cart socially.

One pretty little friend of Mama's called Hester, who was much younger than Mama, was married to William, a decent, kindly but dull man, who obviously could not fulfil her sexual needs, so she flitted around like a butterfly, to the fury of the other wives in the coterie, flirting with everyone's husband but her own, as William watched indulgently. She had provided him with two sturdy sons of whom he was inordinately proud and now he did not mind her flirtations, knowing that none of the wives whose husbands she charmed so beautifully would allow things to progress too far. The crunch came when she had an opportunity to spread her net further. Somewhere, at some party, she met an Englishman who did not know the rules, and she pouted when Mama refused to invite her new lover to supper. My parents felt that Hester was, in this instance, going much too far. There was an unhappy break in their friendship for a time until she got herself on to an even keel again, when her bright presence and delectable looks reappeared in our house. From that time onwards she confined her attentions to an older man called Alex, whose wife was rich but difficult.

Alex's wife Frances was years older than he was, and their marriage was childless. Frances dressed well but had a hard face and had missed out on any sexual attributes. I think she felt that as she had been born a virgin there was no need to change that state. Poor Alex was a frustrated man and had for years been attracted to the sweet-faced Hester with her milk-white skin, dark blue eyes and auburn hair and her melting voice. He had never been able to make any impact on her until she was forced to jettison her English lover, but suddenly, and for no apparent reason, one evening Alex made the great breakthrough. Frances appeared not to notice the languishing glances which passed between her husband and Hester, but according to Mama everyone else did.

When they were in the same room Hester's eyes would sparkle like electric torches sending out messages in semaphore. Alex gazed at her adoringly, all the time keeping a wary eye on Frances, who was fortunately so self-centred that she could never have imagined her husband admiring another woman, much less conducting a love affair. She droned on and on endlessly about her stocks and shares and her pains and aches. Hester and Alex always contrived to sit together at table where they could hold hands and press knees under the folds of the damask cloth. William regarded all this with benevolence and probably thought that the affair would soon fade and could, in any event, never be consummated as the opportunity would not arise.

According to Mama he was wrong. Alex visited Hester on the maid's afternoons off. Hester's sons were at boarding school and William was busy at his office, so on Thursdays the coast was clear and Hester and Alex had regular assignations. Mama said that she saw Hester once or twice on Thursday evenings about this time and she knew to look at her that she had been making love. Her eyes were huge and lustrous and she seemed to float around in a sort of dream, Mama said, looking absolutely marvellous and sated with love.

Masters and Johnston and their theories on sexual techniques had never been heard of, so most women on account of the lack of expertise on the part of their husbands – a condition not uncommon in Ulstermen – thought sex a vastly overrated pastime. They probably lay back patiently every couple of months or so and thought, not of England, but of their new spring wardrobes and how they would make their husbands pay up for taking liberties with them. Some, like Hester, were warm and passionate. They took lovers and enjoyed making love, looking younger and prettier than they had for years. Sometimes, suddenly, the whole scene would change like a kaleidoscope and new alliances would be formed, perhaps at a party when the accidental touching of a bare arm would spark off another affair which would burn brightly for perhaps six months, perhaps five years. No one knew why, but the reason must have been the great boredom of the women and the fairly usual frustration of the men whose wives denied them because they did not want any more children. Contraception was in its infancy and was never discussed. It was apparently considered "fast" to know about these things, and unless the men "took precautions" things were left to chance.

In the rare event of a woman becoming pregnant by her lover she would either hurriedly begin to sleep with her husband so that she might pass the child off as his, or have an illegal abortion. This, I heard years later from Mama, had happened to the couple whose love I had noticed when they stood by my bed. She had discovered that she was pregnant and had rushed off in a panic to a back street abortionist. Her husband found out what she had done and never forgave her, for he thought the child was his. As they had only daughters he longed for a son and felt she had denied him that. I do not know why she felt she must get rid of the child, but perhaps it was because her lover was a rather unusual looking man, tall and handsome, and she may have felt the child would resemble him too closely for her peace of mind.

Champagne has always seemed the essence of dash and excitement to me. Father had a friend, a rich elderly man who married a young and pretty woman less than a year after the death of his first wife. He was very proud of his second choice, who was thirty-five years his junior, and he loved to show her off. He liked to impress his friends and make them envious of him as they looked at their out-dated models. Before they left home to attend a party he always opened a snipe of champagne which he and his new wife drank, so that she would sparkle and do him credit and so that he would feel mellow and relaxed. She had charge accounts in all the best shops and he took her off to London and Paris on long holidays, but like all old men with young wives, he was madly jealous and difficult to live with. She died giving birth to a son, who died a few hours after her. "She was so pretty – and she loved me!" he said to Father after the funeral, adding peevishly, "I don't know how she could have done this to me!" Father told Mama that he seemed to feel that his wife had been most inconsiderate to die and that he regretted not being able to reprimand her for this behaviour. Soon he was on the lookout again for a third wife, once more marrying a young woman. She turned out to be neurotic and difficult and soon after the wedding she demanded separate rooms and locked doors, spending his money with abandon and having quite open affairs with every young man she fancied. Her husband died, but not before altering his will and leaving all his money to charity. She was left virtually penniless and all her young men who had been so attentive vanished like spring blossoms in a tempest.

"... and it served her jolly well right!" said Mama, who had never liked her.

Before I was old enough to go to school, Mama and I occasionally went for an outing with one or other of her friends who had cars. This meant that they were free during the day, with the use of the car, to jaunt around visiting their friends who sometimes lived out of town. We went to have lunch with the distant friends and set off in the car, Mama and her friend suitably dressed in tight-fitting cloche hats so that their hair would not be blown about on the journey.

The car I particularly remember belonged to Hester and was an open dark brown Morris tourer with a hood which was, when it rained, unfolded by hand from the back and fixed by some means to the frame of the windscreen. This I thought was an unsteady contraption and my feeling of insecurity was increased by the flapping of the canvas-edged mica windows which made all the world sepia as I peered out.

Mama and Hester, in the front seat, chatted merrily on about their friends and their problems, with particular reference to the friend they were about to visit. They discussed the state of her marriage which was known to be shaky, for her husband was a womaniser, or as they more delicately put it "fond of the ladies". In fact he was one of the greatest lechers in the North of Ireland and no woman was safe with him unless she was equipped with a chair and a whip to fend him off. Hester had had a narrow escape from him some months back when she went to leave a parcel for his wife in his office.

She told Mama that he had pinned her against the corner of his desk but she had managed to slip from his grasp, making him lurch against the sharp edge which was just at the right height to do him the greatest possible injury. "His face went all red and he sat down on his chair in a hurry," said Hester, and Mama laughed with delight as she visualised the scene, saying, "It served him right – he won't try that again." "He will, he will," said Hester, "but next time I'll have a hat pin handy." They tittered about this as Hester drove on, pomp-pomping the rubber bulb of the brass horn importantly as she rounded corners or if we met someone on a bicycle or even a stray hen, the lively chatter all the while growing more animated. I, in the back seat, worried in case the back part of the car, rattling like mad, dropped off, and Mama and

Hester might drive on to Bangor without noticing what had happened, leaving me, as in a rickshaw, somewhere along the way. My companion was Mick, Hester's brown spaniel, and clinging to him, my arms tightly round his neck, I slid and slithered about on the shiny leather seat. Mick and I shared many a hair-raising experience as we shot round corners, catapulting us to one side against the door with the brass handle.

Once we reached our destination, and sherry for the ladies and lemonade for me had been dispensed, I was sent off to the kitchen to talk to Lily the maid, or to eat raspberries in the sunny kitchen garden while the ladies gossiped until lunch was ready.

When it was time to go home in the late afternoon, laden with produce from the hostess's garden, I was tired. Mama and Hester discussed in detail the latest chapter of the domestic drama they were following with such avidity, and I fell asleep hearing one of them say, ". . . and did you hear poor Bertha say that she found him in the summerhouse with the next door maid? She should have taken the carving knife to him!"

"Or a hatchet!" Screams of laughter accompanied these remarks, but I heard nothing more. I lay against Mick's comforting side, breathing in unison with him as we both slept.

Women were bored beyond endurance with their narrow lives, and then came the great vogue for playing cards, which gave them something to interest them. Ulster was puritan in outlook and for many years cards had been regarded as the devil's pasteboards, used only by men in their club rooms. Now women began to play whist and soon took up bridge. Men, and some very emancipated women, played poker.

My parents were card-players, Mama more so than Father. They taught me to play poker when I was about four, using matches instead of money. Perched on two cushions on a fairly high chair, I learned to deal the cards and place my bets and tried to hide my delight when I filled to an inside straight or a full house. Joyce was an avid reader and was usually in the middle of an exciting school story, and besides, she was not fond of card games. Father and Mama could not play poker as a twosome, so I became a natural third. I loved poker. It was quick and each game was soon over. I learnt to play other card games like sevens, rummy, pontoon (which I found difficult as I couldn't count very well) and nines, all of which I have now forgotten. I had a natural card sense, but I never learnt to play bridge, which then and since has filled me with ennui, mainly because Mama was such a keen player and I developed an aversion to it because it took up so much of her time.

She and her women friends met about once a week at each other's houses. These ladies arrived about half past two in the afternoon, when they had got rid of their husbands who had the tiresome habit of coming home to lunch each day. When they arrived the hostess had the bridge table set up and ready for play with cards and markers and pencils. There was usually only one table of bridge as any larger number constituted a party. When the guests had removed their outdoor coats they put on their bridge coats and, after a few pleasantries, sat down to serious play.

Bridge coats were de rigueur for these gatherings, rather as prayer shawls are in a synagogue, and were made of velvet, or perhaps cut velvet. In the case of very dressy ladies the bridge coats might be made of brocade. These coats were hip-length jackets, shapeless, collarless garments with long sleeves. The really fashionable thing was to have one with a fringe round the hem which dangled and swung as its owner flounced into her seat. They were usually fairly dark in colour, black and maroon being favoured most of all, as these colours "went with" almost any colour of dress underneath.

The bridge game was never serious at these afternoon gatherings. Conversation rose and fell as the cards were dealt and played, and the game was constantly halted as some juicy item of gossip was divulged. Euphemisms were rife. Pregnancy was described as "being in an interesting condition" and was considered to be rather daring, even in married ladies. Cancer was referred to darkly as being "malignant". Hysterectomy was talked of as "having everything removed". These fascinating subjects were bandied about among the cards, and at a quarter to four tea on a trolley was wheeled in by Aggie.

Tea was composed of two kinds of sandwiches, thinly cut, biscuits, small cakes and a large cake to be freshly cut for the occasion. Everyone admired the quality of the baking and a hearty tea was eaten by all four ladies who then resumed their game. The trolley was wheeled out into the kitchen and the remains of the feast was fallen upon by Joyce and me as we waited, poised like vultures, for this moment. Aggie issued us with glasses of milk and we sat swinging our legs at the kitchen table and demolishing all the food with the gusto of the Children of Israel having their last meal before the Exodus.

When we had eaten we were expected to appear before the ladies. Aggie saw that our hands and faces were washed and our hair brushed before pushing us through the drawing room door where we were greeted by looks of feigned surprise and clucks of astonishment at how much we had grown. We wriggled with embarrassment at these remarks and made our escape after being clutched to the scented bosoms of the visitors and kissed, being scratched in the process by their pince-nez.

Occasionally Mama invited a few of the neighbours in to play bridge, most notably Miss Violet Ring. Miss Ring, as she was fond of telling everyone, was the daughter of the late Colonel Ring of the Indian Army. She lived just over the road with her mother, who was ninety-five and bedridden. The other members of the household were a maid called Keziah and three male pug dogs called Algy, Benjy and Chummy. Miss Ring wore tailored coats and pork pie hats, black in winter and pale grey in summer, and she was plump and excitable. She spoke in a high-pitched voice with an English accent, which in itself was unusual to our ears.

There were always three dogs. If one died another took its place and assumed the name of the dead one. They were all cross and crabby, probably because their sex life was nonexistent on account of the cloistered life they led. They took their daily exercise with Miss Ring, who drove them like a three-in-hand before her with one long lead dividing two feet from the bottom into three branches, each ending with a smooth-haired, curly-tailed dog.

Two things about Miss Violet Ring fascinated me. First, the dogs were all cast in her image, apart from the fact that she wore a monocle. Secondly, the poor lady was subject to fits. Mama, having been a nurse, was not at all put out at this, and always coped coolly with any medical crisis, so that if any other neighbour invited her to "make a fourth" she really had to make a third, as Mama had to be invited also in case Miss Ring passed out at an exciting part of the game. I longed to see her in one of these fits, and did indeed happen once to be in the drawing room when, dropping her cards quietly, she began to tremble violently and slipped beneath the card-table. The other ladies rose instantly from the table as though Jack the Ripper had suddenly appeared on the scene, but Mama calmly took charge and to my chagrin dismissed me from the room in tones which brooked no protest. After half an hour or so I peered round the door again found that all had been restored to serenity and that the cards were being dealt once more by the cause of the commotion. But, because Miss Violet Ring was indeed and without doubt, a lady, her foibles and disabilities were accepted and barely commented on. There was an unspoken rule that people were allowed to be eccentric, especially if they were comfortably off. The only two dragons which reared their ugly heads were drink and sex, and sex was, as I have said, countenanced extra-murally if practised with discretion. It was not, of course, called sex, that word being mentioned only at the registration of the birth of a child and not in connection with its conception.

Mama belonged to a bridge club, which consisted of a small regular gathering of ladies each Tuesday afternoon, and took place at Miss Ida Frazer's house. Ida was a friend of Mama's from old times. Her father had been a Methodist minister in a country district near Mama's old home and this fact gave Ida a great air of respectability. She taught bridge and ran classes as well as her bridge club. Even when she was ill, which was not often, she would summon three friends to her bedside and, balancing a folded down card table on her knees and wearing a hat, propped up on pillows she would enjoy a game, criticising and analysing her friends' bids the while. One of her cronies, a teacher called Marshall Mark, used to twit her and say, "Shall we cut for places, Ida?"

Ida had the habit of telephoning Mama at meal times to discuss her recent bridge games. Mama would obediently leave the table and go to the telephone. Anyone passing the cloakroom at the time could see Mama sitting on a chair and holding the telephone receiver a short distance from her ear, and could hear Ida's loud voice shouting, ". . . and she had three spades to the Ace, King, Queen, and she bid three No Trump. Now, what would you have done with a hand like that, Anna?" Mama would give her opinion and this would spark Ida off again, with a whole volley of recriminations against the holder of the bridge hand in question, and her voice went on and on. Mama's tea would grow cold and congeal on the plate, but she could not escape from Ida's post-mortems.

Chapter 10

Down Town

It was always exciting to be "Going down town", with Mama in her fur coat in winter and I in my warm Sunday hat and coat. We boarded the tram just opposite the house and I wriggled with delight as I sat on the golden-yellow slatted wooden seats which ran from front to back on either side. It was rare to get into a tram without finding some friend or neighbour already there and there were always polite arguments amongst the ladies as to who should have the privilege of paying the fares. It cost two pence to go into town for an adult, but only a halfpenny for a child. The two-penny tickets were orange, the penny ones for shorter journeys were white and the children's tickets blue. The conductor extracted these from the small bundle which he carried fastened to a little board which hung from a strap round his neck, and then punched them with a "ping" from his metal punch which was also suspended from his neck.

Mama usually had several things to do in town and nearly always these included a visit to the Bank Buildings. This was an exciting shop, housed in a large and imposing building which dominated Castle Junction, the city Centre. It was well stocked and beautifully warm, a gust of heat meeting one when the door was opened. Just inside the swing door was the haberdashery department, its mahogany counters edged on the inside with brass measuring rules screwed to the wood. These were for measuring laces, ribbons, tapes, braids and silk fringing, all by the yard and in large variety and a huge kaleidoscope of colour. Satin ribbon, velvet ribbon, silk ribbon, in all shades and widths were sold here, cut to the customer's requirements and wound skilfully round the assistant's fingers in a figure of eight, then drawn off, wrapped in white tissue paper (which Father always called silk paper) and put in a tiny paper bag with a brown silk string slotted through the top and the name "Robertson, Ledlie, Ferguson & Co. (The Bank

Buildings)" printed across it in dark brown, from corner to corner.

Round the corner from the ribbons was the knitting wool department, for knitting was much in vogue then. Spools of thread were also sold, and further along the main aisle was the counter where we bought my socks, wool knee-length for winter, grey for every day and fawn for Sunday, and white cotton with a coloured border for summer. Silk socks were for summer Sundays and were white. Pink silk – shell pink was the exact shade which Mama liked me to wear – was required wear for parties, which always took place in winter.

Mama charged her purchases to her account, which disappointed me as I loved to see the little wooden spool-shaped boxes in which the assistants put payments zinging along the wire to the cash desk at the back of the store. They were unscrewed there and the money removed, the correct change put back inside and then, with the pull of a handle, "zing" back they came to the counter where the customer waited seated on a small high bentwood chair. The assistant extracted the receipt and the change, counted it out to the customer, who was then bowed out of the shop by a floorwalker, a tall gentleman in a morning coat. This method of payment was just one step ahead of the little railways and the wooden balls in Robbs.

Upstairs was the department called "Mantles" where coats were displayed, and "Gowns" where dresses hung in rows inside cases with glass doors lining the walls.

Salesladies in floor-length black satin dresses glided about this floor, as though on wheels, polite to every customer, no matter how difficult she might be. At the back of the store on the first floor, behind the Mantles and the Gowns, was the Toy Department which only seemed to blossom at Christmas. Then it was like fairyland, with dolls, dolls' houses, tricycles, fairy-cycles, games, dolls' prams and children's books in one great welter of delight. My parents had a friend who, every year, asked them to bring Joyce and me here to choose a present. No limit was put on our choice and this man seemed like Santa Claus to us. I still remember him with affection, a man of kindness, generosity and imagination.

Downstairs again, Mama and I wended our way through the men's department at the back of the shop, past all the racks of overcoats and suits and gentlemen trying on new shoes, to a pair of glass swing doors which led to the grocery department. This was the Belfast equivalent of Fortnum and Mason. It had an air of luxury with the aroma of freshly roasted coffee beans rising to the nostrils like incense. All kinds of good things were stocked here; cheeses, bacon, both smoked and pale, Limerick ham, boxes of biscuits from the choicest manufacturers in stands holding twelve boxes in rows of four with glass lids so that the contents might be seen and fully appreciated. Biscuits were sold loose by the pound or half-pound and were weighed out and put in white bags which were then given a quick twirl to close them, making a little white ear at each top corner before being handed to the customer. Biscuits in packets were almost unheard of.

Tea, sugar, flour and the usual range of groceries – but only of the best quality obtainable – were also stocked, but these could be bought elsewhere and were not of much interest in this establishment. There was a large glass counter with marble shelves underneath displaying all kinds of cold meats, and another with a large selection of cheeses. Mama had a penchant for Rathkenny butter which came from North Antrim and was stocked here, and although her normal order of butter was delivered twice weekly from Forster Green's with the rest of her groceries, now and then she treated herself to a pound of Rathkenny which she felt had a special flavour.

When she had bought her butter and perhaps made one or two other purchases, she would say, looking down at me, "I think we'll go to the Carlton," and I nodded my head in pleased agreement. Along Donegall Place we went, I keeping close to her side on the pavement and enjoying the splashes of colour made by the flower-sellers' baskets of blooms arrayed along the kerb on the far side of the wide street, outside Mullan's book shop and the Union Club. Sometimes we met one of her friends coming the other way and my heart sank, as I knew we were then stuck for ten minutes or more while the ladies exchanged greetings and gossip. When the conversation ended we continued on our way and as we neared the Carlton the delectable smell of newly baked bread and cakes met us.

The Carlton was not merely a restaurant. It was an institution. It was unique in Belfast and was much loved and patronised by my parents and their friends. The whole ambience of the Twenties was epitomised here. Once inside the glass swing doors one sensed The Good Life. Here, on each side of the black-and-white tiled floor were counters where freshly-made chocolates and confectionery, all kinds of bread and cakes of every description were sold. The paper bags in which the bread was placed after purchase, and the boxes for the cakes, folded with amazing dexterity and a flutter of flaps of cardboard by the assistants, were black and white striped, to match the floor.

Through the shop we went, to the restaurant. This was screened from casual shoppers by a glass partition, and just beside the partition was a small office, set between two glass walls. Mrs. Henry who, with her husband Fred, owned the establishment, sat here for most of the day. Her husband was a quiet man, not often seen, for Mrs. Henry was the moving spirit and this was her domain. Her word was law, and because of the glass walls in the office, if she had had eyes in the back of her head she could and would have watched all activities in both shop and restaurant simultaneously. As she only had the normal two eyes she managed very well. Nothing escaped her notice. I was afraid of Mrs. Henry, with her white hair, hard sparkling pince-nez and tight-fitting black dress. She never deigned to speak to a child in her rather harsh voice and I was mightily relieved at this as I would have been instantly struck dumb had she asked me a question. She did have a chat with Mama, though, and when it had been established that both ladies were in good health we were allowed to proceed to the restaurant.

Here we were in another world. William, the head waiter, pin-neat in his tail coat and stiff white shirt, greeted us warmly and conducted us to a table. I was highly gratified when he pulled out a chair for me and pushed me nearer the table, after he had seated Mama. Afternoon tea was ordered, with pink ice cream for me, and as we settled ourselves comfortably, Mama looked around. Several of her friends were usually there and they waved companionably to each other. Sometimes we had tea alone, just the two of us, and sometimes we joined forces with friends. I enjoyed sitting looking round while the ladies laughed and talked with animation, waving their hands around as they chatted and exchanged gossip about their friends and acquaintances. Their interests were not wide, and things like world events or social questions were huge blanks in their minds.

The tablecloths and napkins were white linen, clean and fresh and crisply starched. There was a small silver vase of fresh flowers on each table and a group of potted palms in the middle of the room. Looking-glasses with a pinkish tinge lined the walls and made each lady feel wonderfully attractive. Upstairs there was a balcony on three sides, with tables. I longed to sit just once at one of these balcony tables where I could look down at the pretty scene below, but Mama did not care for the idea, preferring to remain downstairs where she could see and talk with her friends.

Tea was brought, plentiful and hot, and also hot scones, thin rolled pancakes with sugar and lemon, sandwiches, chocolate biscuits and cakes, and my ice cream in a small silver dish. Carlton teas were excellent and Mrs. Henry ensured that they were always of the same high standard. As we ate we could hear strains of music floating down through the potted palms from the fourth side of the balcony where a trio of ladies played selections of light music in best Palm Court style.

On Wednesday afternoons, upstairs in the ballroom the Carlton had thés dansants. Only once had I the pleasure of being there, for Mama did not at her time of life take part in this sort of entertainment. However, a young friend of hers who was anxious to meet her sweetheart without the knowledge of her flinty-hearted parents, borrowed me one day to accompany her to a thé dansant in the Carlton. She told her parents that she was taking me to tea in town and they naturally enough felt that with a child to look after she would be perfectly safe from harm. I was charmed at the outing though I did not realise my role in the drama.

Helen, dressed in pale green, collected me in the early afternoon and we rattled down town in the tram, reaching the Carlton soon after three. She was a sweet, pretty girl with fair hair and grey wide-apart eyes, and she talked to me all the way there, even though her thoughts were elsewhere. As we entered the Carlton and made our way upstairs to the ballroom we met some of Helen's friends, young women like herself, beautifully dressed and coiffed: I was swept on in the midst of them, holding Helen's hand tightly and feeling like a small ladybird among all these pretty butterflies.

When we reached the ballroom we saw several couples already dipping and swaying round the floor to the strains of "I'll See You Again" from "Bitter-Sweet", and we sat down, Helen, two of her friends and I, on little gold chairs with cane seats round a table by the side of the dance floor. Soon we were surrounded by a bevy of young men buzzing around, laughing and talking, they having escaped from their nearby offices for an hour to meet the girls, and within a few seconds and before tea reached us, Helen's friends were fox-trotting to "Alexander's Ragtime Band" and "Tea for Two" waving gaily to friends sitting at other tables as they whirled past.

Helen and I sat waiting, I for the promised tea and she for her sweetheart. Soon both of these appeared and when she had settled me with my ice cream she and Philip danced off together, locked in a close embrace and gazing into each other's eyes. They spent the rest of the afternoon like this, she coming back to the table between dances to see that I was all right. Her friends talked to me and so, politely, did their young men friends, and I shyly and monosyllabically replied to their questions. They hardly seemed real to me with their tinkly laughter and silly remarks. I did not know that this was their version of the mating call.

At five o'clock it was time to go home and I put on my hat and coat over my green velvet dress. Helen and Philip, who was a pleasant and good looking young man, stood by the table, eating each other up with their eyes, the tips of their fingers touching. Helen tore herself away reluctantly, holding me by the hand and gazing over her shoulder. She called, "Well, that's settled, then?" to which he replied, "Yes," in a firm voice.

Helen delivered me back to Mama and Aggie, to whom I gave a blow-by-blow description of the thé dansant and the pretty girls I had seen there, and I produced the little black and white striped box of chocolates from the Carlton which Helen had bought for me. I went to bed that night feeling slightly bemused with excitement at my outing and the sense that things went on in the outside world that I did not really understand.

About a month afterwards Helen and her sweetheart eloped. Thunder crashed and storms rose and fell in her parents' house at this calamity. They had no particular objection to their new son-in-law, but his father and Helen's father were rivals in business who had run across each other on several occasions and had not been on speaking terms for years. It was Romeo and Juliet all over again, the Montagues and the Capulets to the life, everyone sighed romantically. It had a happier ending, however, and soon, when Helen became pregnant with her first child, all was forgiven by both families.

The Carlton, the Carlton . . . It had an air of elegance, of felicity, of élan, which never returned to Belfast after Mrs. Henry's death.

Joyce, Hilary and their mother in Royal Avenue, Belfast, 1932

Chapter 11

Viv and Kate

Vivienne and Katherine lived just over the road. Viv was a little older than Joyce and Kate just over a year older than me, and we were inseparable. Most of my spare time, except on weekday mornings when I visited the new babies in the nursing home two doors away, and spent time with the Aunts and Uncles next door, was spent with Kate.

Their house was well ordered and apparently ran effortlessly. Mrs. Marshall was a volatile lady who was devoted to her daughters and she liked us because we were quiet and, she thought, well brought up and unlikely to make the house untidy when we played, or teach bad words or habits to Viv and Kate. Mr. Marshall was tall and quiet, a grey, kindly man who sang both in the choir of St. Anne's Cathedral downtown and on the wireless. Sometimes we would hear him practising scales when the upstairs drawing room window was open on summer evenings. He had a flourishing business in town and was comfortably off. On Viv's and Kate's birthdays he was able, because of his connection with the B.B.C., to have an announcement made during Children's Hour, saying that if Viv – or Kate – were to look in a certain cupboard or drawer in the house she would find a present there. This seemed to me to be a miracle and I could never understand how the Auntie on the wireless could possibly know the arrangements in the Marshall household.

The family was rounded out by Alice, who was a Mother's Help. She was about twenty-five years old, from a good country farming family and not at all a maid, although she did not eat with the Marshalls in the dining room, but in the kitchen. She did not wear a cap and apron, but a pretty flowery overall. She was also different from most domestics in that she was a Protestant. Nearly everyone we knew, including Uncle Abbie and Auntie Jessie in the manse, had a Catholic maid, preferring it this way as Catholics were supposed to be kinder, better workers, and were not carried away with high-falutin' notions.

Comfort was the watchword with the Marshalls and I felt that this would be a safe place to stay, with warm fires and good food and comfortable beds and soft lights and books to read until all the nasty things had gone away. The house revolved entirely round the children, whom Mrs. Marshall called, affectionately when she spoke to them "Bird". "What would you like to have for tea, bird?" she crooned, and when this was decided upon, Viv always wanting sardines on toast and Kate consenting to be coaxed to a boiled egg, she rang the bell for Alice, who came bustling in from the warm kitchen to receive the news.

They had Veda bread for tea, as well as the sardines and eggs, with butter-balls made from the best Danish butter from the Jersey Dairy on the Antrim Road. All this was topped off with a slice or two of cake and a plate of Jaffa cakes. When the table was set and tea was ready, our game of the moment was drawn to a speedy close, our coats were put on and we were "put over" the road, in case a tram should knock us down, to go home for our own tea. We sometimes felt hardly done by in that our wishes and tastes were not considered by Mama and Aggie, but in our family no one would have thought of this and the very idea of a child refusing to eat what was put before it was beyond anyone's imagination.

Viv and Kate had bookcases full of books in their bedrooms, and when I learnt to read, Kate's bookcase was a magnet for me. She lent me all the fairy tales, apart from Grimm and Andersen, which we already had at home. She had French Fairy tales, German and Italian Fairy Tales, the Green, Yellow and Purple, Red and Blue Fairy Tale books, until I was seeing visions of Younger Sons and Damsels in Distress at every turn. If these things could happen to people in books, I reasoned, surely they could happen to me? Perhaps I was a changeling child, I thought, the daughter of some beautiful people, and had been left in a basket on my parents' doorstep with a note saying, "Look After my Baby. Her Name is Hilary," in best fairy tale fashion. I was quite carried away by these romantic thoughts, only to have them smartly knocked on the head by Mama, who was not a creature of fantasy.

After the fairy tale stage I progressed to school stories and thrilled to tales of the Chalet School, all the school stories by Dorita Fairlie Bruce and her contemporaries and innumerable Annuals packed with tales of school adventures. The Chalet Books were prime favourites. How romantic it seemed, that school so far away in the Bernese Oberland amid the snow in winter and the wild spring flowers and jolly Austrian people, especially as the girls never seemed to do any work and spent all their time socialising with the daughters of diplomats and other important people. How different from the dull humdrum life we led on the Cliftonville Road in Belfast. I waded through volumes of this endless saga, sighing enviously the while. Then I started on the Alcott books, weeping at the death of angelic Beth and agonising when selfish, pretty Amy got her claws into Laurie as soon as Jo's back was turned. Kind as Professor Bhaer might be, I still felt that Jo had been sold short.

My very favourite books were the Anne of Green Gables stories and I longed to be like Anne, an orphan who was brought up by two elderly people who loved her more than anything else in the world. This to me was an enviable state of affairs, for in our house things were beginning to change and the dramas of daily life and lack of money were now being acted out with monotonous regularity. The world-wide slump was beginning to bite, and things would not get better. I suppose I subconsciously felt that if I could only pack my suitcase and move next door with Aggie to look after me, to be the idol of the Aunts and Uncles, my problems, anxieties and uncertainties would disappear. I loved Mama and Father very much, but now, suddenly, things were happening which I did not and could not understand, and I was troubled.

Viv and Kate had beautiful and expensive clothes. Jaeger was always worn, pretty wool dresses and jerseys and skirts in winter and Liberty prints in summer. Our dresses were pretty enough, thanks to Jinny, but we knew that they were not quite up to standard when we saw Viv's and Kate's. In very cold weather Viv and Joyce wore long stockings which were made of fine, fawn wool, but Kate and I wore gaiters over our socks. Mine were of fawn stockinette and could be pulled on over my shoes, the buttons being stitched in a row on the outside of each leg. Kate's were of leather and had to be fastened with a button hook. It was hard to match the buttons to the buttonholes and the leather was stiff to work with, and Kate and Alice had many a tussle before the gaiters were adjusted to Alice's satisfaction.

On cold days, dressed in coats, woollen hats, scarves and gloves and gaiters, we were sent out to play if it was not raining. I was the youngest and found it hard to keep up with the others. In no time at all my feet were like lumps of concrete with no feeling in them and I trudged along as we made our way "round the square". The square was a block, and we were forbidden to go any further from home than this. In late autumn we gathered the gold and red leaves as they fell from the trees and sometimes took the most perfect and beautiful ones home to press between the pages of a favourite book. I have come across books, years and years later, which still held a leaf or two which I must have pressed, looking after all the years like brown tissue-paper.

At one of the corners of the block there was a stone wall, divided halfway up into little pedestals surmounted by a parapet. Between each two pedestals, which were painted grey, was a tiny box-like niche, just at my eye-level, and here we would place carefully, with cold woollen-gloved hands, our store of treasures. In mine there would be a few laurel leaves, perhaps a red leaf from the Virginia creeper which grew round the house inside the wall, a spray of two or three orange berries from a pyracantha or red ones from the cotoneaster which grew in the garden of another house, and if I were really lucky, an acorn. Acorns were rare and seemed like magical things to me, each fitting so perfectly into its tiny cup, the whole so pretty and smooth. I arranged and re-arranged these things until I had made a pattern which I thought pretty and then went a few apertures along to see what Kate had in hers. Joyce and Viv had elegant collections, beautifully arranged. Their quick eyes could spot a little fir-cone, an unusual leaf or a late flower and perhaps even the odd, shiny, brown horse-chestnut which I always coveted. If they had been lucky enough to find one of these, they allowed me to hold it and I took off my glove (connected to its fellow by a long piece of white elastic which went up one sleeve of my coat and down the other) to hold it lovingly in my cold palm, yielding it up again unwillingly and hoping that they would give it to me to keep. But glossy horse-chestnuts were rare and hard to come by, and no one was willing to part with one.

Indoors we played happily during the winter and our favourite game was "Swanky Ladies" which meant that we dressed up in clothes which had belonged to our mothers or aunts. Hats were large and richly decorated and were much fought over by us. Mrs. Marshall's beaded blouses were long enough to make dresses, the sleeves rolled up to allow our hands to clutch the handbags which completed the outfits. Scarves were long and Isadora Duncan-like. Complete scenarios were acted out by us, but I was shy and did not like to take a leading role. I trailed along in Kate's wake, for I liked to be of the company but not to be too much noticed, and the others were kind and allowed me to do as I pleased.

Kate had a cardboard box with "Harrods" written on it, which meant nothing to me, filled with small empty bottles of all shapes and sizes. She must have had at least fifty, all different. Mostly they were scent bottles – these were the tiniest – and then there were aspirin bottles, dark blue with silvery screw tops, essence bottles, small brown medicine bottles, no two alike. Kate and I sat on the rug by the fire on cold winter days and unpacked the bottles. Then we played "Bottle School". Each bottle was given a name and the name remained with it always, investing it with a personality all its own and never being forgotten by Kate who had a genius for devising interesting games. The bottles were sorted into sizes and then arranged into "classes". Two or three slightly taller bottles were the teachers and prefects and the "pupils" were marched about the hearth rug which marked the perimeter of the school. I suppose we acted out all our complexes and problems in these games, just as today child psychologists say children should do. I don't know if it helped, but I loved those games very much. Kate made everything come alive for me and I even forgot my stutter as I joined in.

Kate and Viv had two dolls, made of dark brown stockinette, with smiling red lips and boot-button eyes. Viv's was called Topsy and Kate's Chloe, and I suppose no dolls have been more cherished than these. They had distinct personalities and were given the power of speech in strange voices supplied by their owners. They were almost like real people and I loved them as much as did Kate and Viv. They were cuddled, talked to, slept with and played with constantly. They had sealskin hair, soft and furry, and when Chloe's hair wore off Mrs. Marshall replaced it with a piece left over from her fur coat. When Topsy grew bald there was no sealskin left; her new hairpiece was made of skunk, and this gave her the appearance of a black doll who had had an electric shock.

In summer things were very different. We went out to play in our summer dresses and white socks and crêpe-soled sandals, and in June, July and August we were allowed to wear "white shoes", in other words tennis shoes, which were carefully whitened each night for us by Aggie. I remember the joy of the first day each summer when we wore these and the sense of freedom and lightness that I had. In high summer we were allowed to play outside after tea in the long summer evenings and were not called home for bed until eight o'clock. Children were safe outdoors then and it was unknown for one to be molested or frightened.

Our playthings for outdoors were simple. We had tops and whips. The whip was a stick with a long leather thong attached to the end. This thong was wound round the spiral which was cut into the sides of the wooden top and with a flick of the wrist the top was released and unwound from the thong which was then used to whip it ever faster in a spin. I was never any good at this, lacking the eye and dexterity to connect the two instruments. We had large wooden hoops which we trundled along the pavement, hitting them with a small stick when the pace slackened. This, too, was beyond my ability and I usually ran after the others carrying my hoop over my shoulder and the stick ready in my hand. When they slowed down and I caught up with them I tried again, but no matter how I tried, it did not work. I could skip, however, and enjoyed this very much. Sometimes we each skipped with our own ropes, like boxers in training, and sometimes we played skipping games, two children turning the rope and others taking it in turn to "run in". Rhymes were chanted by all the children to find out what their fortune would be, and whether they would be lucky enough to have a "brown dress, a blue dress, a pink dress, or a yellow dress" and so on.

Every child had a new ball each spring. Sometimes, when we were very young, the balls would be fairly large and hollow, but these were considered to be babyish if one was more than six years old. After that age the ball had to be of solid rubber and was painted over in a swirl of bright colours like a twisting rainbow, red, orange, blue, green and white. Everyone tried to have a different predominating colour so that each child could identify her own. The really sophisticated thing was to have a tennis ball, but no one under the age of eight ever achieved this.

The side wall of Miss Violet Ring's house faced into Cliftonville Avenue and as it abutted directly on to the pavement, it provided an ideal surface on which to bounce balls. We played there for hours, throwing our balls up against it and catching them as they bounced back. I remember the rituals we went through. First we threw the ball against the wall and caught it as it fell, the second time the ball had to bounce once on the pavement before we caught it. Back we threw it again and clapped our hands before the ball reached us, and so on. There were about ten variations of actions that had to be performed as the ball was thrown, ending with a double twirl, turning completely round twice where we stood and still managing to catch the ball before it touched the pavement. We never tired of this game and were constantly inventing new trials which we hoped no one would be able to achieve but ourselves.

How maddening it must have been for Miss Ring and her mother to have the constant thud-thud of balls on the outside of their drawing room wall, but they never complained. We neither understood nor appreciated their forbearance and were not at all grateful. I cannot think how our parents could have allowed us to play against that wall, but the fact that it was situated so that we could be observed from both our house and the Marshall's, so that everyone in either house could check instantly that we were safe, made Miss Ring's wall the only possible place for us to play ball.

The Marshalls had a small, smooth lawn in front of their house and in summer it was used for two things. On a really sunny day a canvas awning known as "the tent" was brought out and set up there, chairs were placed in it and Mrs. Marshall could sit there peacefully reading her book and shielded from the gaze of passersby, or we could play our games in privacy but still benefit from the air. The other use to which the lawn was put was croquet. Each year about mid-May the large wooden box containing the croquet mallets, balls, hoops and posts was brought out and checked over, and when the weather turned warm the game was set up. It was really miniature croquet, for although the croquet set was the right size, the lawn was too small, though it served our purpose and we played happily for hours. Mrs. Marshall supervised us in the intricacies of the game as she sat in a gaily striped deck chair sunning herself and reading a novel. She read a great deal and hardly played bridge at all, so I found her very different from Mama, who played more and more bridge as time went on, perhaps as a means of escape from the increasing difficulties of life.

Viv and Kate went with their parents each year to Torquay for two weeks in September, to stay at the Belgrave Hotel. If they had set off to go a thousand miles up the Amazon it would not have seemed more glamorous to me than this yearly journey to Torquay. Great preparations were made for it and Viv and Kate were kitted out with new dresses and soft pretty pastel coloured party dresses to be worn for when they dined each evening in the hotel. A new store of cardigans, shoes and all manner of things were bought. Kate once had a party dress made of Liberty fabric covered with tiny flowers in fawn, amber, rust, brown and green, all on a beige ground, perfect to go with her red hair, and a dorothy bag to match. If I could only have a dorothy bag to match my party dress, I felt, my cup would surely be full and running over. I don't know why it caught my fancy so much, but for months I dreamed of this dorothy bag; but Jinny's imagination did not encompass dorothy bags and I had to do without.

Our holidays were not so glamorous as Viv and Kate's. During my first few years we went to Portrush or Portstewart and stayed in a boarding house, where Father joined us at weekends. We paddled, I in rubber paddlers which were a kind of large billowy multicoloured rubber knickers which pulled on over my clothes and were tightly gathered at the legs and waist, so that the marks of the paddlers left a red dent around my thighs when they were taken off. We bathed in cotton bathing suits bound with white tape at neck, arms and hem and rubber bathing caps the shape of shower caps and trimmed at the side with a large rubber chrysanthemum. Once, but only once, Mama and Father took a house at Portballintrae for the summer, after Joyce had been ill.

After that our holidays consisted of visits to our country relatives which cost nothing. In the beginning Aggie came with us to look after us and to see that we were cared for as only she knew how to do. This went on until I was six or so and then I think Aggie refused point blank to accompany us again. Loving us as she did, something dreadful must have happened to make her dig her heels in like this, and I feel she must have crossed swords with Aunt Etta, Mama's spinster sister, a bitter woman who lived with my dear Aunt May, and who claimed that we – especially me – were dreadfully spoiled children. Aggie loathed her and the thought of abandoning her darlings to Aunt Etta's far from tender mercies must have distressed her very much. After that we were sent off by ourselves, and while I was desperately homesick, especially at nights, Joyce doing her best to comfort me as we wept together in bed, we settled down after a few days and made the best of our country holidays.

We adjusted in the manner of all children and because we spent our Easter holidays in the country too, became part of both worlds, city children first, but country children also, familiar with the country ways and part also of Mama's childhood life. Things moved slowly in South County Derry and times had not changed much since she was young and happy there.

On holiday at Portballintrae, c. 1924 – Hilary aged 1½ in foreground looking away from the camera, being held by her father, her sister Joyce two to the left of her.

Chapter 12

Lame Ducks

Mama was an inveterate whipper-in of lame ducks. Nothing gave her greater satisfaction than solving other people's problems, which always seemed so much worse than her own. After all, she reasoned, her own greatest problem was the lack of money, and that was no one's fault. Father was not a good provider, but he meant to be, and because the slump was affecting his business so badly he had to be excused. He was never unkind to her or to us, and he never forbade her to do anything she wanted. He got used to the house being haunted by people who were down on their luck, or weeping women who had come to confide their marital troubles to Mama. None of them went away without feeling better. She listened, she comforted, she advised, she gave them tea. Her advice was always good, but cautious, for she knew that most troubles between husbands and wives healed themselves in the end, and if she gave any encouragement towards a hasty walk-out by a wife, she would have not only the breakup of a half-tolerable marriage on her conscience, but would most likely have a permanent guest in the house until the trouble was sorted out. Divorce was almost unheard of, and in the rare cases in which it happened the woman was always the loser.

The lame ducks were always around and we grew to accept them. One of these was Victor. Mama and her friends had a great fad for fortune-telling evenings. One of her circle would hear of a "good fortune-teller" who was willing to come to the house, and the hostess for the evening, who indeed was often Mama, invited her friends along and provided for them the usual supper of tea, sandwiches and cakes. Other ladies' husbands, stalwart pillars of church or business, solid Ulstermen all, pooh-poohed the whole idea and even forbade the fortune-teller the house, whereas Father did not mind at all, though he never had his fortune told, thinking it unmanly.

The fortune-teller was installed in another room, with the

tools of his or her trade, perhaps a pack of playing cards or, even better, a crystal ball set upon a square of black velvet. A few of these fortune-tellers were palmists, and they also were thought to be good. Each lady in turn went into the room set aside for the reading, had her fortune told and emerged again to go back into the bright, laughter-filled room clouded with cigarette smoke where her friends sat, sometimes shaken at what she had been told, and always eager to tell the others what had been forecast for her in the future.

Victor, whose psychic powers had been recommended by one of Mama's bridge friends, agreed to come to our house one evening. Mama set the wheels in motion for a fortune-telling session, always a sure-fire draw. When she brought Victor a tray with tea and sandwiches and cakes halfway through the evening, to resuscitate him after several fortunes had been told, he looked at her gratefully and said, "I haven't eaten all day." Mama was appalled and elicited the information from him that he was unemployed and was often hungry. He had, he told her, been a footman at Massereene Castle in Antrim and when it had been burnt down had had to jump to safety from the first floor, breaking his leg in the fall. When he had recovered from this terrible shock he was slightly lame and could not get a job anywhere, for he only knew the work of a footman.

Mama, after hearing this sad little tale, said, hospitably as always, "If you're ever hungry, come to this house and you'll always get something to eat." She meant it, but not quite as Victor thought she did, for he arrived at eight o'clock the following morning and stayed until evening, and continued to do this every day. He kept busy in the house during the day, helping Aggie, polishing shoes, silver and brass with equal enthusiasm and great expertise. He sat in a chair near the kitchen range between chores, for he was always cold, and smoked Mama's cigarettes, blowing smoke rings all around. We enjoyed having him in the house, for he read the tea-leaves in our cups every day after lunch. I could sense, however, that he could not see much in mine and took no interest in my readings – nine-year-olds were not really in Victor's scheme of things.

Victor was tall, thin and pale, with a shock of brilliant red hair which seemed permanently to stand on end. He wore wire-rimmed glasses and his red-edged myopic eyes blinked through them as he read the tea-leaves and told us of "A man, not too tall, well-shaped nose, hair well brushed back," entering our lives, or warned of, "A woman, big, with dark eyes and greying hair," who was not our friend, though she pretended she was. In the cups all manner of people drifted through our lives and were commented on in detail and their identities guessed at.

He confided to Mama that he lived in rented rooms in Roden Street with a friend called Francis. Francis was very temperamental, he said. Sometimes Francis would shut him out of the rooms and behave in a very arbitrary manner, saying unkind and nasty things to him. This made Victor cry, and Mama was for once at a loss to know what to say to comfort him as he sat sobbing by the fire, eating toast and marmalade and pouring out his troubles into her ever-available ear. "Victor, dear," she would soothe, "you'd be far better away from him and in a nice wee room of your own." "But sure I couldn't live without him", wept Victor, breaking into fresh sobs, and Mama, innocent as ever, thought he meant that his friend paid the rent. Later, in the evening, she would speak of the problem to Father, who sniffed and rattled his paper, as he always did when matters of this sort, about which he could do nothing, were brought to his notice. Victor became part of the household and we grew so accustomed to his being among us that we became quite fond of the strange presence in the kitchen.

One evening, as Mama and Father sat by the fire, she playing a game of patience and he reading the Belfast Telegraph, Father asked, "What's Victor's other name?" "Victor Collins," replied Mama absently, putting a black Jack on a red Queen. "Was he here today?" asked Father.

"No," she said. "He's gone to Ballymena today to see his aunt."

"Well, he never got there," said Father. "He threw himself off a train and was killed this morning."

Mama was stunned. Poor Victor, poor, poor Victor, she thought, and wondered what more she could have done to help him. "Victor had had a hard time – I wonder if his friend knows?" she pondered. "He'll be in a terrible way about him – and so well he might be," she continued, warming to her subject in indignation, "for he was nasty to Victor, and only two days ago he wouldn't let him make himself a cup of tea when he went home at night. Victor told me that and he cried terribly. He said Francis had pushed him away from the stove and bruised his arm."

"Well, he's gone now, so Francis can have the stove all to himself," said Father pragmatically. He had felt sorry for Victor, but he was never able to get into the problems of all the people whom Mama befriended, and he had sensed something not quite normal about Victor, a kind of madness. Truth to tell, he was rather glad not to have to face those glinting, accusing eyes and long pale face each morning when he came down for breakfast. He had the uncomfortable feeling that Victor was looking right into his brain and seeing things that Father would rather not have anyone know about. The rest of us grieved for our friend and wished we had been nicer to him.

Mama put on her black hat and attended the funeral service, but Father declined to accompany her, saying he had to go to Banbridge on business that day. She was one of only three mourners, the other two being Victor's aunt from Ballymena who was his only relative, and Francis. Mama reported back to us that Francis was tall, dark and shifty-looking and she thought he might be an Italian.

"What made you think that?" asked Father disbelievingly.

"I know in my heart he was," said Mama, "for he had hair like patent leather and wore pointy shoes and a bracelet. He cried, too," she added thoughtfully, "and so well he might, for the life he led poor Victor. I was polite when he spoke to me, but I told him that I thought it was all his fault that Victor was dead, and then he cried more. He wanted to come to our house just like Victor used to do, but I drew the line at that. I couldn't have that man sitting there in Victor's chair by the range. And I'm sure that he couldn't polish silver like Victor, nor tell fortunes either."

Victor's friend telephoned several times to ask Mama how she was and if she would change her mind and let him come to see us, but for once in her life she was resolute and said, "No." "Poor old Victor," she would say from time to time, "He was a good soul and it was a pity he ever met that Italian. People are far better never to get mixed up with foreigners," and she sighed heavily for her poor lame duck.

Chapter 13

Life Before School

A neighbour and dear friend of Mama's was Miss Riley, who ran a nursing home two doors away. I must have been about four when I realised that there, right on my own doorstep, was an inexhaustible supply of babies. I had reluctantly come to accept Mama's word that we would not be having one in our house, so each morning about ten o'clock, before visiting Aunt Emma and Uncle Tempy, I arrived on the doorstep of the Antrim House Nursing Home. I asked to see Miss Riley and was ushered into her sitting room by Ada, the Italian maid, who once told me in her broken English that she had a sore finger in her boot.

Miss Riley then appeared, dressed in a white coat, her stout figure sailing like a galleon into view and her dark hair and eyes seeming even darker against the white of her coat. She was the kindest and most patient of women and never by word or look gave me the impression that I was a nuisance or that I had called at an inconvenient time. Holding her hand I went with her into her pantry where she kept a glass jar of boiled sweets. I selected my favourite, usually clove rock, which was dark red in the centre and had red and white stripes on the outside and made my tongue burn pleasantly, and together we set off on our rounds of the patients.

We visited the new mothers first. I remember the still brightness of each room, with highly polished brown linoleum on the floor and rugs here and there. There were bowls of flowers and a coal fire burned cheerfully in the grate with a guard in front of it. In the high bed lay the new mother, cosily tucked in and smiling weakly but triumphantly from her high-piled pillows, and best of all, the heart of the whole scene, the wicker-hooded Moses basket which stood on the floor by the fire and which contained the baby.

Together we approached the basket quietly and Miss Riley

gently pulled back the coverlet, blue for a boy and pink for a girl, to let me see the small red wizened face of the newborn infant. I gazed at it solemnly and, when the coverlet was replaced, I went over to the mother in the bed and told her how beautiful it was and asked its name. Usually it was a dull name like Muriel or Doris, but once to my great delight I was told the baby's name was Marigold.

Marigold! It was like a name from a fairy tale. I hurried home that day to tell the family about the baby with the fairy name and wished that Mama and Hester had had such an inspiration when naming me.

Next day I made my usual rounds with Miss Riley and went in to see Baby Marigold. I told her mother how beautiful I though the name she chosen, and to my surprise there were tears in her eyes. She blew her nose and said that, well, her husband had come in last night and had decided he did not like the name Marigold. He thought Mabel would be a better name, more sensible and more suitable for his daughter. Besides, he had said, it was his mother's name, and in fact that was the best name for the baby. Crushed by this, and feeling delicate and weepy after the birth, his wife had no choice. Mabel it was, and somehow that baby never seemed as pretty as she did the day she had been called Marigold.

When we had seen all the babies, usually about three or four of them, Miss Riley and I progressed to the other patients. These were surgical patients and were in various stages of recovery from their operations. If they were well enough they seemed quite pleased to have a small visitor for a few minutes, but if they were poorly we did not go in, Miss Riley just putting her head round the doors of their rooms to check, I suppose, that they were still breathing. I did not enjoy visiting the lady patients who lay back palely on their pillows and seemed to suffer much, all having had what Mama called "Big Operations". The elderly gentlemen were much more cheerful and usually produced a chocolate or a piece of butterscotch to speed me on my way.

Last of all I peeped into the operating theatre with all its shining steel and its table overhung by a huge lamp. The smell of disinfectant and general hospital atmosphere was heady and exciting and I sniffed it eagerly.

When all the patients had been visited I went to the kitchen to see Lucy. Lucy was a baby who was always said to be "not well". Her mother had died when she was born, and I suppose her father could not cope. She was cosseted by Miss Riley, the nurses and Ada who adored her, and her basket sat on a shelf near the warm stove and away from draughts. She had smooth, soft cheeks, large china-blue eyes and that lovely baby smell. No one would ever lift Lucy from her basket so that I could nurse her like a large, living doll, but they encouraged me to talk to her and to stroke her little face gently. One day, after I had been on holiday, I came into the kitchen to see Lucy as usual. Her basket had disappeared. Lucy had gone away, I was told. She would not be back. I thought she had gone home at last, and indeed she had, but not to her earthly home. Lucy had had spina bifida. She was five months old.

Sickness in our family was treated with all the seriousness it deserved. I do not recollect Mama ever being sick when I was a child, and Father only once, when he developed pleurisy and was treated by having steaming hot linseed meal poultices applied to his chest. The doctor visited him twice daily, and with all this solicitude and Mama's excellent nursing, he soon recovered.

Joyce had tonsillitis every year, and each winter without fail. She was sick enough to be confined to bed for two or three weeks and the doctor came every second day to check on her progress. Mama painted her throat twice daily with some solution and she had to gargle with glycerine and thymol, but it was never suggested that she should have her tonsils out. Kate, over the road, had had hers removed at home. Mama had gone across to be present and help at the operation, which took place in the drawing room of the Marshall's house. The kitchen table had been scrubbed with disinfectant before being carried up and covered with sterile sheets for the occasion. Kate's tonsils had been kept for her, at her own request, and were on view for some time afterwards, preserved in a small vial for all to see on the nursery mantelpiece.

I was a healthy child, but caught the usual childish illnesses which meant that I had to stay in bed from time to time. If either Joyce or I looked at all off-colour Mama went into action at once. The thermometer was produced from the medicine cabinet in the bathroom and if our temperatures were even minimally over the regulation 98.4°F we were kept in bed. This meant in my case being moved either to Mama's and Father's room or to the spare room if no visitor was present or expected. Joyce was allowed to stay in her own room if she was sick. Mama called it being "laid up" just as though we were ships in dry dock.

The gas fire in the bedroom was lit and the bowl of water before it changed twice daily. Tempting little meals and treats appeared every two hours or so. Small saucepans of beef or chicken tea to strengthen the invalid simmered on the stove downstairs and were carried up by Mama or Aggie, like two ministering angels. Extra pillows were brought and plumped up behind me and I was not allowed out of bed even to wash my hands and face. Instead, basins of warm water and soap were carried to the side of the bed and set on a table on a thick layer of towels in case they should spill. Bedpans were the order of the day, to my great humiliation, and if Mama were called to the telephone when I was using one, I invariably ended up with a round red indentation on my bottom. Favourite books were placed on the bedside table. The black bed-tray with its four sturdy non-collapsible legs and the rim round three of its sides was brought out and used to do jigsaws on, or for playing patience, as well as accommodating trays at mealtimes.

Each night Father came home with a small present for the invalid: fruit, a new book, a comic, some sweets, a bottle of fruit cordial. Aunt Ruth, having heard on the bush telegraph which operated quickly and well in case of sickness, came to visit and brought calves foot jelly in a small jar. This was flavoured with either orange or port wine and was fed to the sick child on a teaspoon after each meal. If there was no improvement after two days the doctor was sent for. Antibiotics had not yet been discovered and nothing was left to chance.

Before the doctor's visit the room, though already spotless, was re-dusted and hoovered. Furniture was polished by Aggie even though it already shone like glass, clean linen sheets and pillowcases were put on the bed and a clean night-dress – pyjamas in later years – was laid at the end of the bed so that it could be put on just before the doctor entered the house. Mama ran the sickroom like a hospital ward and even kept temperature charts and notes of bowel movements. This was what she was best at, what she had been trained for, and she enjoyed it. When I was the centre of all this activity I was terrified.

The doctor, although a kind man and an acknowledged expert on children's illnesses, scared me half to death. When I heard his feet pounding up the stairs I shrank down in bed and wished I could die in the instant before he entered the room. He did not often speak to me directly, fortunately, but after a few words with Mama about my symptoms he advanced to the bedside, whipped his stethoscope from his pocket and planted its cold steel end on my chest. He ordered me, "Breathe, child!" and when I did so, he kept on saying, "Again! Again!" until I was panting frantically to keep up. The he ordered, "Say ninety-nine!" and, "Again! Again!" as he moved the stethoscope over my chest and back. Then he examined my stomach and after all this he placed the stethoscope back in his pocket, saying, "Hm...," and wandered over to the dressing-table, opening and smelling bottles of scent while he considered the problem of my illness. He walked back to the bed, sat down on the side of it and fixed me with a glance. "You have measles," – or chicken pox – or influenza, he would say firmly and decisively, having made an accurate diagnosis of my ailment. "You must stay in bed and take this medicine," and he produced his prescription pad and began to write out a long and complicated prescription. It was certainly not a question of writing down the name of a drug or pill which had been manufactured in some distant chemical plant. He tailored all his prescriptions to each patient, so much of this, so much of that, so much of the other. Nux vomica always featured in each one. It was personalised medicine and with careful nursing it was nearly always successful.

Patting my head in farewell, he went downstairs, a portly man with a smooth pink complexion and skin and hair which might have been polished. He would have gone to the stake for his patients and showed kindness, care and concern to all of them, but despite his expertise he could never establish a rapport with children. He treated them skilfully and well and they got better. That was all that mattered to him. He did not seem to think of them as people – small, nervous people – but only as patients.

Mama and he would discuss my illness and treatment in the hall below and then after instructions to "Keep her in bed until I come back," he would mention the day of his next visit, usually two days ahead. My relief at seeing him go was tempered with the knowledge that he would return, and was mixed with the horrible anticipation of the taste of the medicine which he had prescribed. It always tasted terrible and was only forced down my throat by Mama, who suddenly before my very eyes had turned into a professional nurse, with many tears and lamentations from me, by the promise of a piece of chocolate afterwards.

Back and back again came the doctor, until I was better, and then on his last visit he delivered the coup de grâce – the prescription for an iron tonic. This followed every illness as surely as night followed day and Mama and I had many a tussle before the bottle was finished, Aggie watched sympathetically from the wings and said, "Ah, Ma'am, don't make her take it!" with tears in her eyes. Mama never relented and the dreadful black tonic was administered with regularity.

Father believed that prevention was better than cure and each October and March he came home with a large jar of "Roboleine" to build us up. This was a most delicious mixture which had the taste and texture and appearance of melted caramel. There was a special long-handled spoon to eat it with, and the nourishing confection was dispensed twice daily. Sometimes we were allowed to have it spread on bread and butter instead of jam. We loved it, and the dark brown jar in its green box was always greeted with delight. Some unfortunate children known to us had to take tonics like cod liver oil and malt, which, thanks to Father's implicit faith in "Roboleine" never crossed our lips.

Before "Roboleine" entered our lives Joyce was dosed each March with treacle and sulphur, one spoonful daily. Mama felt it was a "great cleanser for the blood" and mixed the black treacle and the yellow sulphur powder in a large jar which was kept in the pantry. Her mother, Grandma Martha had given this to her large family every year, so Mama had faith in the old remedy. Luckily for me I was too young to have it, and when I was old enough Father had discovered "Roboleine".

Chapter 14

School

I started school when I was six. Until then my days had drifted happily by at a tempo of my own choosing, the time divided between the elderly adults and my afternoons playing with Kate. Kate had gone to school a year and a half before me, and as I listened to her talk of her morning there – for school only operated in the mornings until children had grown accustomed to the routine – I had been half intrigued and half afraid of what lay in store for me just after my sixth birthday. One part of me longed to remain always in my chrysalis, sheltered from the world. The other part was anxious to venture into a new realm where Joyce, Viv and Kate were already at home. The choice, however, was not mine.

The time had come for me to go to school, and after much talk of the cost of such things, a navy blue gym tunic, two white blouses, a school tie with black and gold diagonal stripes, a navy blue cardigan, two pairs of navy blue knickers, grey socks and black lace-up shoes were bought. I was overwhelmed by all this. These were the first new clothes, apart from coats, which were bought for me ready-made, other than the baby dress with the yellow chickens and an apricot georgette party dress which had been a present and was my pride and joy. Everything else had been made by Jinny or handed down from Joyce.

It was a great step forward to be taught by Mama and Joyce to tie my new tie in a neat knot and to make the same knot in the black braid girdle which went with the gym tunic, and to learn to position it neatly to one side. They showed exemplary patience, and success was evident by the fact that I could manage both these feats by the time my sixth birthday came, on December 29th. The school term began a few days later, and I was ready.

Aggie cried at the thought of her ewe lamb going out into the cold world of school, among strangers, and she was reproached by Mama who suffered no such qualms and was probably quite glad to get me a step further on in life. Having been forty-three when I was born, she was now in her fiftieth year and a child of six was more like a grandchild in the house. It must have been difficult for her but she did not show it. Her life should have been approaching a tranquil, non-abrasive stage, but instead she was entering what was to prove the worst time of all. Her children were six and eleven years old, the very time when they would prove to be expensive, the slump was fast affecting the life of the whole country, and hers also. Father's business began to go downhill, and as he could never at the best of times have been described as a go-getter, he did not know what to do to remedy matters. There they were, these two human beings, wanting and trying to do the best they could, but bound upon a collision course. There, too, to make matters worse, were two young children whom they loved and for whom they were responsible, together with Aggie who was part of the family. The sense of life slowly grinding to a halt and impending doom began to permeate the atmosphere of the house, and yet outwardly everything still appeared to be fairly normal.

The third of January arrived, the day my first term at school began. The morning, like all winter mornings, was dark and cold. Aggie came to waken me at seven-thirty and lit the gas fire in the spare room, where I was sleeping. My school uniform hung over the back of a chair, together with the tubular hand-knitted vest with silk ribbons straps for over the shoulders, made by Mama, and a liberty bodice. I eyed it all with a mixture of dread and distrust, lightly overlaid with excited anticipation. The fire hissed and popped and I lay for a few minutes wondering if I could persuade Mama to put off the start of my education until the weather was warmer and the mornings lighter. This thought was banished by the entrance of Mama and Joyce, the former to help me get ready and the latter to see that I was properly turned out for my debut. She was naturally anxious that I should do her credit with her friends and supervised my dressing with an eagle eye.

The night before I had been bathed and scrubbed clean by Aggie, who had washed my hair and, as always, carried me into the hot cupboard to be dried, wrapped in a large white bath towel.

The hot cupboard, or airing cupboard, was really a little room where the hot water tank was. Two people could stand inside it comfortably and there were three rows of slatted shelves around its sides. It was just beside the bathroom and on the shelves, which were covered by white shelf paper, were piles of towels and extra blankets and, on the lowest shelf, clean clothes, one pile for each member of the household. Linens were not kept there because they might turn yellow in the heat. A special cool, airy cupboard for linens was on the landing above, between the first and second floors, and Mama spent each Tuesday morning sorting and putting away sheets and pillowcases and tablecloths which had been washed and ironed by Aggie the previous day. The hot cupboard was almost like a sauna, except that there was no moisture in the air. It was warm and cosy and after my bath I sat on a shelf just over the hot water tank on which I warmed my feet while Aggie rubbed me dry and then with a smaller towel made an onslaught on my wet hair amid many protests from me. Then she combed my hair and parted it to one side, put on my clean nightgown and dressing-gown, sent me downstairs to kiss Father and Mama goodnight, shepherded me upstairs again and watched me say my prayers. She kissed me goodnight and switched off the light, leaving the one in the landing burning until I fell asleep. This continued until I was about eight years old, and I accepted it as my due. Alice was doing the same things for Kate over the road and it was all part of the pattern of life.

On this, my first school day, I was dressed by Mama instead of Aggie, who came up to admire me as I stood looking at myself in the long glass of the wardrobe door. I saw a small, shy, fair-haired child with timid hazel-brown eyes and an eager-to-please expression, wearing a slightly too long tunic, for Mama always believed in buying our clothes one or two sizes too large so that we could "grow into them". My knee-length grey socks disappeared under the hem of the tunic and my black lace-up shoes looked large and heavy and I could feel them hard on my feet. I knew that I would have a blister on my heel before the day was out because of them. My white blouse looked fresh and crisp and I was inordinately proud of my school tie, its large knot peeping out between the collar of my blouse and the top of the tunic.

I went into Father's room to show him my new clothes and he looked at me over the top of his glasses from his bed, where he was reading the Belfast Newsletter. Father never relished getting up early and liked the world to have set its course for the day before he joined in. He pushed his glasses further down his nose so that he could see me better. "Turn around," he said, and then, "You look like a real schoolgirl!" I preened at this praise and pirouetted again. He reached over to the small table which stood at his side of the bed, where he placed the contents of his pockets each night before undressing, and from a small pile of loose change he selected a shilling. He put the shilling into my tunic pocket, saying, "That's to hansel your new clothes." All new clothes, he felt, should be hanselled for luck. Usually the hanselling was done with a penny, but this was a special occasion. A whole shilling! I thought of what I could buy the next time Aggie took me to do the messages on the Antrim Road. I would go to Brady's the news agents at the top of Duncairn Gardens, where there was always a great selection of desirable things; rubbers, pencil sharpeners, jotters, pens and pencils. Father kissed me and said he hoped I would like school and that I was to be a good girl, and then he returned to the news of the day.

I went down to the morning room where Aggie had placed my porridge to cool on the table. This porridge was made of white Indian meal, for the ordinary kind brought me out in hives. She hovered over me before pouring out some party tea – milk with a small splash of tea to colour and warm it. Sugar was never added, as Mama did not have it in her tea and I grew up thinking it unladylike to put sugar in tea or coffee. I had already noticed that it was always ladled plentifully into the cups or mugs of the knife-grinder, the china stitcher and suchlike, which seemed to bear out this theory. Ladies and gentlemen, I believed, never drank tea with sugar, and the really sophisticated drank theirs with a slice of lemon instead of milk, though no one in our family did this. We never had sugar on porridge, either, but always a good pinch of salt.

Joyce was already halfway through her toast and marmalade and her school case was propped against her chair. In this were her school books, pencil case, gym shoes and two ginger nuts for the mid-morning break. I thought she was truly a woman of the world; she would be eleven years old in another week's time, whereas I was shy and gauche and could feel what seemed to be snakes beginning to writhe around inside my stomach.

It came upon me suddenly that I was to be abandoned to total strangers. Terror shook me. What should I do? How should I manage? What if they laughed at me? Tears sprouted in my eyes and that terrible burning sensation of grief descended from behind my eyeballs to my throat. I could scarcely swallow even the soft porridge. Aggie was watching me from the doorway and Joyce was giving a corner of toast to Jimmy the dog, who sat, tail wagging, waiting for the titbit. With a loud wail I got down from the table and rushed over to Aggie, clinging to her white apron. "I don't want to go to school," I wept, "I want to stay at home. I'm afraid." My throat closed over as I choked over the words, and Aggie's arms folded over my head, hiding and comforting me.

Just then Mama came downstairs, surprisingly for that time of the morning already dressed in her coat and hat. When she saw my tears she said brightly, "Now, you are a big girl and you must go to school. Everyone has to go to school. Joyce goes, and so do Viv and Kate. You'll like it when you get there, and besides, you'll be home again at lunch time. And look what I've got for you!" I removed my red face from Aggie's apron and saw that Mama was handing me a small attaché case about twelve inches by six, with a handle and two little silvery clicking fasteners so that nothing would fall out. It was made of some sort of fibre and to me it was perfect. A tiny key was attached to the handle by a short strand of red thread. My tears stopped as though they had suddenly been switched off at source and I reached out for this treasure. All at once I felt that with this case I could face if not the world, at least the kindergarten. I was wreathed in smiles as I kissed Mama.

It occurs to me now that our family were inordinate kissers. We kissed everyone in the morning when we got up, upon leaving the house and on our return. We kissed all visitors both hello and goodbye and no matter how many people were in the house when we were going to bed, we kissed them all. This custom was the norm in my father's family which was not perhaps very unusual as they were city people, but was also prevalent among Mama's relatives, which was strange, since country people in Ulster usually considered displays of affection to be a sign of weakness. However all Mama's family kissed each other on meeting and parting, and at the time it did not strike me as odd. Only in later years, when I realised how much this differed from other people, did I begin to appreciate the obvious affection they all felt for one another. No matter how they might argue amongst themselves, which was often, they rarely departed from the custom of a farewell kiss. If the current argument had not been resolved, the kiss might be perfunctory, but still the custom prevailed.

Inside the little case I found a red jotter with lined pages so that I could learn to write at once. Aggie came in from the kitchen and handed me a small parcel wrapped in a brown paper bag which was neatly folded over it. "That's for your first day at school," she said. I was delighted when I found it contained a bright blue pencil case fastened with a shiny gold button. When I undid the button I discovered two pencils, one green and one red, already sharpened, with points of needle-like fineness. There was also a blue pen holder and beside this a tiny tubular box containing two steel nibs. I knew I would not be using pen and ink for some time yet, but it made me feel very grown up to be the possessor of such a fine thing. The outfit was completed by a rubber, a fat, squashy, white rubber with the unmistakable rubbery smell. I threw my arms around Mama and Aggie in turn and said that after all I thought I would go to school, for one day at any rate. Two biscuits in a small tin which had once contained Allen and Hanbury's black currant pastilles were placed in the case beside the jotter and pencil-case and a new pair of black gym-shoes was put in, too, to wear indoors. Joyce was instructed to tie the laces on these when I put them on in the school cloakroom in case I could not manage it myself, and she kindly agreed to see to my needs.

My coat and velour hat with its school hat band were put on, making me look like a small black mushroom, my gloves, as ever threaded through my sleeves, were adjusted, Joyce was checked on and pronounced ready, and Aggie opened the front door for us and stood waving as we went out of the garden gate. Father had got out of bed specially and stood at the bedroom window waving to us. Mama accompanied us as it was my first day and I remember that she wore a dark red coat with a brown fur collar which fastened round her neck, and a dark red hat with a brim.

We did not have far to go. The school was in Brookvale Avenue which was just at the end of Cliftonville Avenue, about five minutes away. I thought, and began to hope, the walk would never end, in spite of the precious case which swung from my left hand. My right hand gripped Mama's left as we walked. She was adjuring Joyce to take good care of me and Joyce was saying, irritably, "But she is only going to be in kindergarten and I will be Upstairs with the Big Girls." I looked at her admiringly, envying the prowess of this big sister who had already withstood the traumas of school for five years. As we turned the corner into Brookvale Avenue and approached the school, some other children joined us, and after exchanging greetings with Joyce and shyly saying hello to Mama, they peered under the brim of my hat and began to coo over me. Little girls then were besotted with the young of families other than their own, and the ice began to melt from my heart when I saw that these Big Girls of ten and eleven were kindly disposed towards me.

We went through the front door of the school in a knot, the other girls dispersing after they had shaken hands politely with the joint headmistresses, Miss McBride and Miss Ferguson who stood in the hallway to welcome everyone on this first day of term. They bent to speak to me and I tried to hide behind Mama's red coat, but I was firmly drawn out by her from the shelter of her plump figure as though she were peeling a banana, and I was handed over to Joyce, who drew me on inexorably with the rest of the girls who were by this time sweeping towards the cloakroom like the rats after the Pied Piper of Hamelin.

Everyone seemed to know what to do; coats were removed like pods from broad beans, hung on appropriate pegs and topped with hats swinging by their elastic. The chatter grew louder as shoes were removed and put in wooden pigeon-holes. I stood wishing for death, every garment still in place and my small case clutched in my hand. I had no peg yet, and even if I had one I could not have got anywhere near it because of the crush of schoolgirls, the smaller ones smelling of scented soap and the older ones of perspiration.

Joyce removed my hat and coat and hung them on her own peg, ". . . in the meantime," she said. I forced off my shoes, unable to untie the double bows, and knelt on the floor amid the welter of satchels and shoe-bags and moving legs and feet to open my case and get out my new gym shoes. Joyce helped me on with them and tied the laces, whispering to me, "You'll like it – everyone does! Miss Mitchell is lovely." I looked at her beseechingly and she took my hand and led me out of the cloakroom and into the kindergarten, which was the largest room in the school. Prayers were held here each morning. I sat beside her and on my other side was Viv, who appeared as we filed along the bench. A bright orange head of hair popped up nearer the front of the room, and Kate's familiar face grinned at me as she waved with both hands.

Miss McBride and Miss Ferguson came in with the other members of staff. Joyce had talked of these ladies at home, so I felt I already knew them. Miss Ferguson, who took charge of these proceedings, announced the hymn, a senior girl struck up the tune at the piano and off we went into the familiar strains of,

"God is always near me,
Hearing what I say;
Knowing all my thoughts and deeds,
All my work and play".

This made me anxious once again, torn as I was between the thought and the hope that God was always near me, and worried in case He would be furious that I was thinking now only of the new case and its contents.

Brookvale was, I suppose, one of the last of the Dame Schools. There were about seventy pupils from kindergarten to sixth form and the educative process was conducted in a gentle way which made the establishment more like a large and extended family than a school. It was situated in a terrace house, which carried the illusion even further. Some pupils travelled by bus or train from places like Ballyclare and Greenisland, though most came from the Cliftonville and Antrim Roads. The children who travelled to school each day were usually related to girls already there, so that for them it was really a family place.

Miss McBride and Miss Ferguson, were remarkably avant garde in their ideas of education for girls. Children began to learn French at the age of six and were introduced to German at nine. This enabled them to listen to their own voices saying foreign words and phrases without embarrassment. I have since noticed that children who do not begin to learn other languages until they are perhaps twelve years old, have to overcome the hurdle of self-consciousness.

Miss Ferguson was short and stout with thick hair, pince-nez and piercing dark eyes. She usually wore dark red. Her personality was stronger than Miss McBride's and she was the decision-maker. She it was who presided at morning prayers and reprimanded anyone who broke one of the few school rules. She taught English and German and my late sister often recalled the enthusiasm with which she imparted her knowledge and love of English literature.

Miss Murdoch taught mathematics and Miss Shaw taught geography and science – this last in a large room called the Science Room which boasted counters, two sinks and several Bunsen burners, backed up by some racks of test tubes and two cupboards which held jars of what I thought must be magic potions of one sort or another.

Miss Shields, who taught art, was slightly deaf and wore a wig, never moved from the Art Room right at the top of the house from the beginning until the end of the school day. Agnes, the maid, who was large, old and stout, wore steel-rimmed spectacles, a black dress and a white cap and apron, was a fixture in her kitchen on the ground floor, where she sat reading a large black Bible all day. She was constantly disturbed by children asking for drinks of water and she usually offered them a verse or two of scripture with the cup of water, declaiming piously as she watched them drink, "I was hungry and ye gave me meat; thirsty and ye gave me drink; I was a stranger and ye took me in," or, "I will give unto him that is athirst of the fountain of the water of life freely," whereupon the child answered vaguely, "Oh . . . " thanked her for the water and ran off. This happened often if a child was bored in a lesson, or felt she might not know the answer when it came her turn to be questioned. No teacher could refuse a request for a drink of water or a visit to the lavatory. Small children under the age of eight were forbidden to lock the lavatory door. This ruling stemmed from the time that Kate Marshall inadvertently and through excessive modesty locked herself in. The key would not turn back and she had to stay there for an hour and a half, with Miss Ferguson shouting instructions about turning the key and telling her to keep calm, and Miss McBride in her quiet voice assuring her that there was nothing to be afraid of. Kate already knew this and only regretted that she had not thought to provide herself with a book to while away the time until a carpenter could be brought to unscrew the lock. When the door was opened, and her imprisonment ended, she was revealed to everyone still sitting on the polished wooden seat with her knickers round her ankles.

For my first two years at school I was under the care of Miss Elsie Mitchell. Miss Mitchell was a child's delight. She was soft and bosomy and had fair wavy hair cut in a fringe. I thought she was old, but she must have been about forty. She wore two-piece suits made up in pretty colours and shiny satin blouses, white or pink and her scent was lavender water. She adored children and at the slightest sign of distress she would clasp the afflicted one to her shiny bosom. She taught me to read. I had such a thirst for stories that it wasn't difficult. I found the first reading books easy and longed to get on to those which told a story. When I finally reached the peaks of bliss with "The Tale of Chicken-Licken" my joy was complete. After that I was on my own and the world of books was mine.

Our mornings drifted along happily like summer days which we think will never end. On two afternoons a week in my second year we returned to school after lunch. On Wednesdays we had "drill" with Miss Taylor, a middle-aged lady who, I felt most incongruously for one of her years, wore a cream blouse and an extremely short brown gym-tunic with a brown girdle, long brown stockings and brown flat crêpe-soled shoes which fastened across her instep with a buttoned strap. She was English, which made her instantly alien to us, and for her age she had boundless energy which was demonstrated in her amazing capacity for bouncing about as though she had a concealed spring beneath her. She was bossy and brusque and the complete opposite of Miss Mitchell.

She began the lesson by forming us into a line and barking, "Turn left," or, "Turn right", and for me, if I succeeded in being in the coveted position of Leader of the Line, this was a dreadful moment. I still have difficulty in distinguishing between my right and left hands. When I have to (usually on entering a dark cinema which confuses me even more) I am whisked back in memory to the time when, aged seven, I stood in the kindergarten at Brookvale at the Head of the Line, trying to remember that my left hand was at the side where the wall with the coloured frieze was and my right hand was at the side where the fireplace was.

Miss Taylor brought with her a lady to play the piano so that we might do our exercises with dumb-bells to music. She played marches like "Blaze Away", and bright tunes for country-dancing which Miss Taylor also taught during the drill lesson. I liked best of all to do the polka. I had a friend called Peggy Magill who was small and plump and dark-haired and light on her feet. She was my partner and together we careened up and down the room, skidding on the linoleum as the music ended.

On Friday afternoons we had "Singing" with Mr. Charles Lindop. He was a small and portly Englishman who must have suffered greatly at the noise made by children who had no aptitude for music. Some were tone-deaf and one girl, who nearly always sat next to me, droned loudly on one note all through the lesson and I was thought to be the culprit. We used the "Clarendon" song book and the Hebridean love-songs were great favourites. Mr. Lindop taught us Tonic Sol-Fa which was and still is as intelligible as Ancient Sanskrit to me. I could see no point at all in this doh, reh, me just as later I could see no point in calling what was, I thought, the main note on the piano "C" instead of "A" and naming the notes on the lines of a music stave E G B D F instead of A C E G I or even 1 3 5 7 9, and the notes in the spaces F A C E instead of B D F H or 2 4 6 8.

I fitted gradually into the pleasant routine of kindergarten for it was easy to be happy there. Miss Mitchell taught us spellings, tables and writing fairly painlessly. I say "writing" but it would be more accurate to say "printing". Each child was taught to print her letters in beautiful script, capitals and small. We never practised "joint writing" but instead joined the script together. This was unconventional but it was her way.

Miss McBride, who taught French throughout the school, had her own little room off the landing at the top of the first flight of stairs, and here she reigned supreme. A fire burned in the grate during the winter terms – all the classrooms had coal fires with great brass-bound fire guards before them – and the walls were decorated with colourful pictures of what she called, brightly, "La Belle France", showing sunny streets in Paris with little children playing outside small cafes, shaded by trees which hung over old stone walls. There were pictures of long, straight roads stretching into the distance, bordered with poplars, which were strikingly different from the meandering roads I knew so well in Country Derry.

Miss McBride had a gramophone which she wound up energetically to play us records of French songs. She played these over and over again until we could all join in and sing most, if not all of the words, as she enjoined us to, "Chantez, mes enfants – et encore, encore!" We sang "Quand trois poules vent au champ", "Il était un petit navire", "Alouette", "Elle était une bergère" with their rousing repetitive lines of chorus, "Au clair de la lune", and the very first and simplest of all French songs "Frère Jacques". She taught us to sing this as a round, the echoing of the "Din, din, don" dying away in wonderfully bell-like fashion as we finished. The charming "Ma Normandie" which still makes the back of my eyes prickle when I hear it, and last and most bizarre of all "Auprès de ma blonde". Miss McBride, an innocent maiden lady, had no idea that she had set a class of six-year-old children carolling a barrack-room song, but eagerly conducted us in its rousing tune, her red pencil waving in time to the music as she spurred us on.

She was a thin, nervous, shy lady who really loved children and who should have been married with children of her own to sop up the affection which was wasted. She wore a blue wool suit, and her rather thin straight hair was caught back in a bun. Her kind eyes beamed at us through her rimless glasses as we swung through our repertoire and she would sometimes go into a reverie and tell us of her days in Paris, long ago, which seemed to us like the Dark Ages. She and all our other teachers, like so many of Mama's friends, were the generation of women whose potential husbands had been killed in the 1914-1918 war. Life must have been a continual frustration for them, and a sadness too, knowing that they had little chance of marriage or escape from dealing with other people's children instead of their own. They sublimated their maternal feelings into teaching and it is sad that they probably never realised how valuable the taste for learning, instilled by them, and the happiness so long remembered, were to the children under their care. The impression I have of my early schooldays is one of innocence and joy, the feeling of being a person, someone who mattered to everyone else, as they did to me. The sense of belonging and knowing that one was part of an interesting and caring community made the school a happy one.

We went upstairs for forty minutes every Tuesday and Friday to Miss McBride's room to sing the French songs to the music of the gramophone and to learn French by means of phonetics. I have yet to meet anyone else – save those who went also to Brookvale – who learnt French in this way. We learnt to say our vowels properly and to roll them round our mouths, copying Miss McBride as she leaned towards us and made the sounds, twisting her lips in an exaggerated way so that we could see how she did it. I can remember the strange way we wrote our little French sentences phonetically, and yet it did not seem to confuse us when we returned to normal lettering downstairs with Miss Mitchell.

Miss McBride had an inexhaustible supply of coloured pictures, all cut from French magazine, which she stuck into our French copy-books to illustrate our songs, or what we were writing about. Once she pasted into mine a wonderful picture of a French baker's shop, with a fat baker dressed in white behind the counter among his loaves which looked like cumulus clouds and his batons of French bread which I though resembled elongated sausages. The whole background of the picture was pink, and it all looked delightful, the baker laughing and jolly and the customers, who had obviously been buying bread for large families, as their baskets were overflowing, smiling too. "Le Boulanger" she hand-printed in spidery characters underneath, and then had printed it phonetically also. I treasured this picture, so foreign and charming.

Suddenly my stutter improved and I became more confident and was able to take a speaking part in the plays which were put on yearly for the School Concert. They were written and produced by Miss Mitchell who, with love and patience, included every child in the Junior School in her efforts.

Sometimes missionary friends of Miss Ferguson, visiting Belfast on furlough from China, came to talk to the school. The very name of China made their adventures seem unreal and Aladdin-like. One lady missionary actually brought as a present to the school, of which she was a past pupil, a large red satin banner with a message in Chinese characters stitched across the red in black velvet. It was brightly decorated in greens, blues and gold around the sides and we all "ooh-ed" and "ah-ed" in a very satisfactory way when it was unrolled, and made a light mental note that possible – just possibly – the missionary life might be ours one day. One day, that is, in the far, the very far, distant future, and in my case only a possibility if Aggie and Mama could come, too. At the end of her talk the missionary lady sang "Jesus Loves Me" in Chinese, and although the tune was familiar, it sounded strange and tinkly. After that we all rose to sing loudly "From Greenland's Icy Mountains", giving special emphasis to the line which said "The heathen in his blindness bows down to wood and stone", feeling glad and virtuous in the knowledge that we could certainly not be lumped together with that poor heathen.

Several Jewish children went to school at Brookvale and these girls had a kind of exotic charm which made them seem different and infinitely delightful. Most Jewish families in Belfast then lived near the Antrim Road because their synagogue was in Annesley Street, near Carlisle Circus, and as the families were fairly orthodox they had to live where the men could easily walk to *shul* on Shabbas and the High Holy Days.

Most of the Jewish girls were dark-haired, with sparkling black eyes and olive complexions, full of life and gaiety. One or two were red-haired, with delicate pink and white skins and these were less vivacious than the others, quieter and more thoughtful. They were all friendly and pleasant, but in a way that I did not understand, they were subtly different from us. The most notable difference was that in school they did not join in morning prayers, but waited outside in the hall as we prayed, read from the Bible and sang our morning hymn.

The difference was more evident when we visited them in their homes. "Visiting" is perhaps too grand a word; we went home with them to play for an hour or two after school, if our mothers agreed. Their houses were comfortable and cheerful and their parents most welcoming. Sometimes their fathers spoke with a strange foreign intonation and often their mothers had an

English accent. They had relatives in London, Leeds and Manchester and cousins with names like Natasha, Sonia and Rilke, which sounded strange to our Ulster ears. They were very precious to their parents, who loved and indulged them in every possible way. Their toys were always of the most expensive kind and their clothes of the best, often being ordered and sent from London.

When we visited their houses we were made to feel more than welcome. The large bowl of fruit which customarily stood on the sideboard in their dining room was handed around, oranges were tenderly peeled and offered by their mothers to their daughters' guests. The food was delicious and in some indefinable way different from ours, and there was a special smell in these houses, of furniture polish, good food and foreignness. The menorah in the dining room and the mezuzah fixed to each of the door-frames, containing a tiny portion of the Torah, brought a strange, mysterious and romantic atmosphere to the notice of the visitor, no matter how young.

I was conscious that these Jewish families had a great sense of oneness, and that it would not matter to them where they were, in what country or city they lived, just as long as they were together. I did not know why they should feel that way, for they were not cousins, nor even related to each other, but they all seemed to belong, while we, though welcome guests, were somehow unreal to them and could never be part of their life.

On summer days at school, during our mid-morning break, we were allowed to play in the back garden, a small green patch surrounded by a wooden fence. We played "tig", ran short races and tried never to stand still for a minute during the quarter of an hour's freedom. If the day was really warm and sunny we had a lesson outdoors with Miss Mitchell. She sat on a chair with her pupils grouped round her, saying tables or spellings, or listening to her gentle voice as she read a story aloud. In summer we did not wear school uniform, so that our summer dresses of cotton or voile made a bright patchwork of colour as we sat clustered close on our little chairs, our attention riveted on Miss Mitchell, enjoying the warm bright sun.

Schools like Brookvale have vanished, but the children who attended them were privileged to have been part of a way of life which instilled old fashioned virtues and values into sometimes reluctant pupils. To belong to a school like this taught them to care, to know that each child had a place in the world, and the old ways of kindness and thought for others.

Chapter 15

Uncertainty

The slump cut ever deeper and the difficulties at home grew worse. Father seemed unable to pull himself out of the lethargy into which he had fallen. I am sure he tried, and I feel that to a great extent his failure stemmed partly from dislike of his business and the deadly boredom it engendered. He now knew that he would never be rich, never see the bright lights and the sparkling gay life again. He was trapped in a situation he could do nothing about and with a family to support and little means of doing it. His only escape was to read and this he did avidly and late into the night.

He continued to go to the office each day and to do what selling he could, but the depression was upon everyone and things grew more and more difficult. The house would have to be sold and when things had been settled up and debts paid there would not be much left. Now there would be rent to pay and five people, including Aggie, to support. To outward appearances everything was normal. We were adequately clothed, we ate plain but nourishing food, and Aggie and Mama kept the house clean and sparkling.

Mama asked Aggie if she would like to look elsewhere for a job, as it was doubtful if her wages could be paid for much longer, but Aggie demurred, saying that she would rather stay on with all of us, come what might. There was very little cash money, but when bills for rates, gas or electricity, or the telephone account, came in I was afraid. This fear has never left me since those early days and I still cannot see a brown envelope falling through the letter-box without feeling sick, and in a way guilty.

Loud words were spoken downstairs when bills came in, and I could sometimes hear Mama weeping and Father slamming the door of the dining room in frustration. I covered my ears with my hands, climbed on my bed and pulled up the eiderdown and went back to my stories. Reading on my bed became my form of dream-time and enabled me to escape from the anxieties and shadows which were closing in. I read voraciously and all was grist to my mill. When I had been harrowed by Uncle Tom's Cabin and Black Beauty, and had read Jessica's First Prayer, a Sunday School prize of Mama's, I turned to the lesser-known L.M. Alcott books, Under the Lilacs, An Old-Fashioned Girl, Eight Cousins and Rose in Bloom. Rose, the heroine of these last two had a wonderful time with two Great-Aunts and a special unmarried Uncle who were devoted to her and cared for and protected her when her parents died. Whilst I had no wish to lose my parents, I longed to be in this happy position with Uncle Joss, who, with Uncle Tempy, would have given me, I was sure, absolute security in every way. Aunt Emma and Aunt Annie would have taken the place of Rose's Aunts Peace and Plenty. I had the good sense to keep these fantasies to myself, but I brought them out from the pockets of my mind before I went to sleep each night and turned them over. Home and parents were dear to me, but the mantle of safety which had been over me was fast being eroded and was slipping away, and I was afraid. How lucky Anne of Green Gables had been, I thought again and again, to have fallen by chance into the pleasant places she did, and to enjoy the care of Matthew and Marilla who loved her so much. How fortunate, too, were the March family in Little Women to have Mr. Lawrence and Aunt March to rescue them from all their difficulties. We had no one. Mama and Father were good and loving parents, but they were helpless to remedy the situation. There was a world recession, they said, and this phrase meant nothing to me. Money was scarce, they said, and this did mean something.

The days passed. The bridge afternoons went on – but not so frequently - rather like the band playing when the Titanic was sinking – and gossip was exchanged. Father and Mama were rarely invited to parties now. There was still, however, a nucleus of old friends who stuck by them and continued their friendship, but many of their acquaintances dropped them socially, for they were becoming an embarrassment. These were the people who had received lavish hospitality in our house when times were good. Mama would hear reports of parties to which she had not been invited and would be sad and depressed by the news. Joyce and I were no longer invited to her friends' children's parties, and while we were not desolated by this, some of the glamour disappeared from life as the entrée to the large houses with the warm pink-carpeted bedrooms and the smell of money was cut off.

We accepted this, as children accept any fact, but Mama was hurt by it. Nothing succeeds like success, and Father had long since passed the point of no return. Success would never be his again, and by implication would not be ours, either. It was my first experience of social rejection. We were judged by our lack of financial status which was almost the only thing that counted. If Joyce and I had had the brains of female Einsteins, or if either of us had shown signs of becoming a second Marie Curie, or even if we had produced evidence of stigmata upon our hands and feet, it would have made no difference. The dice were loaded against us by our lack of this world's goods and nothing could remedy this.

Suddenly we were told that the house had to be sold and that we would have to move. I was petrified with fear. Where would we go? I had never lived anywhere else and could not imagine doing so. My heart turned to ice and all the joy drained out of me like bath-water when the plug is pulled. We were all living on shifting sands and who knew if we would ever touch firm ground again?

I could hear voices rising and falling downstairs when I went to bed at night. People who were still loyal and friendly came and went, giving advice and counsel, but by this time my poor parents did not know which way to turn and were incapable of reaching rational decisions. Aunt Sara came up from County Tyrone and tried to make some sense out of the mess things were in and I think succeeded to some extent. My parents listened to her, for her advice was always sound and while she had not much love for Father, who she considered to be ineffectual and a complete failure, Mama was her sister and was dear to her. I was glad to see her, for my world was falling apart and was never to be put together again. How I longed to be back in the old, safe, familiar way of life, but that had gone and it was "never glad, confident morning again".

The Aunts and Uncles next door were oblivious of our

difficulties and in any case would have had little sympathy, as they did not care for poor Father. They admired men of perspicacity, which he was not. They liked successful men, solid men, which he most certainly was not. His apparent lack of thrift, in his circumstances, did not endear him to them in the least. They continued in their affection for Mama and for Joyce and me, but showed not the faintest understanding of how, as children, we were being slowly undermined by the growing insecurity. Their lives went on, placid and undisturbed. The sun still shone in their garden and the fires burned brightly in the grates, but just next door our lives were slowly changing. Mama tried to keep things going as well as she could, but it was not as it had once been. It was not the same at all and it would never be the same again. We were set on a collision course.

As in a dream we heard that Mama and Father had rented a house in Eglantine Avenue on the far side of the city. All our furniture and possessions were to be packed and moved by Johnsons, which Father considered the only possible firm for removals and burials, mainly because they were so good, but also because he had gone to school with "the Johnson boys".

The day of the move was a typically grey and wet February day, cold and desolate to match our hearts. Mama made a large cauldron of soup so that she could feed both the family and the removal men, as well as one of "the Johnson boys" who came in around lunch time to check that everything was going well. Aggie, and her sister who came to help with the move, scrubbed the house from top to bottom. I stood in the hall, not knowing what to do nor how to escape from this nightmare which had come upon me, when the door opened and Jean Walton, kindest of women and a true friend to Mama and Father, walked in.

She had promised to drive us to our new house, and somehow the sight of her heartened us all, and her pretty face with her dark hair and eyes and fascinating maquillage brought the feeling that perhaps after all we had not been completely deserted.

"Well, darlings," Jean greeted us, "How has it all gone? Are you ready to leave?"

Mama was too upset to speak and Jean hurriedly swept Joyce and me into her car, saying that she would take us to the

Allen's house, near to our new home, and where we were expected for tea. Mr. and Mrs. Allen were also staunch friends, and never failed us. Off she drove with us, telling Mama that she would return for her and for Aggie. Father was already at the other house to receive the furniture when the vans arrived. Jean gave us each a stick of Toblerone chocolate and talked to us about nothing in particular, allowing us to sit in silence without feeling we had to reply.

At the Allen's house there was a warm welcome and a lavish table set for tea. Mrs. Allen, a tiny kind-hearted lady with jet-black dyed hair, put her arms around us and settled us in two armchairs by the fire, saying, "You must be cold! Some tea will warm you up!"

Jean fussed around us for a while and said she would go back for Mama and then come for us to take us "home". Home. Home was where I would never be again. I could not bear it any longer as I tried to keep back the tears which burned my eyes. Joyce had to keep up the conversation for both of us.

This day, the culmination of months of anxiety and fear, was to be burnt into my subconscious mind forever. I felt, as all children in like situations do, that this debacle must be partly my fault and this made me even more unhappy. However, I tried to behave properly, as Mama would have wished, answering Mrs. Allen's kind enquiries as well as I could, and trying to eat the sandwiches and cakes she pressed on me, though it was all I could do to swallow a morsel. Mary, the maid, and Sissy, Mrs. Allen's sister who was even tinier than she, drifted in and out to ask if we were well, and finding the atmosphere like a wake, did not prolong the conversation. I dreaded that Mr. Allen might come home, for I was nervous of all men I didn't know well, and was shy if one spoke to me. My prayers were answered, and Jean came back for us before Mr. Allen, who was really the kindest and most generous of men, returned home from his office. We climbed back into the car after thanking our hostess, who kissed us and stood waving as we drove off, saying, "Tell your Mother I'll be round to see her tomorrow!"

When we arrived at the new house, which I had not seen before, I found that it was in a dark and forbidding-looking terrace and had only a tiny patch of garden and a green painted iron railing between the sitting room window and the street. It was dark when we got there and I was just able to make out the railing and the iron gate by the light of the street lamp at the corner, a short distance away. No one had thought to pull the blinds and the curtains were not yet in place. Through the window I could see the light shining from three bare bulbs which hung, shadeless as yet, from the sitting room ceiling. Familiar pieces of furniture were there, but somehow they did not look the same as they had done in the old house, and even though Mama and Aggie had worked hard and long to make it comfortable, it did not seem like home.

Father and Mama stood talking to the furniture removal men who had finished their task and were standing around waiting for their tip. This received, they departed, and Jean ushered Joyce and me through the front door. She carried in her arms a large bunch of daffodils, wrapped in florist's paper and a bottle of whiskey, the former for Mama and the latter, received with tired enthusiasm, for Father. Glasses were brought out from a packing case, Aggie was called in, and the four adults toasted a new life.

Leaving them there I went upstairs to see if I could find my room. It was the second-floor return room and my only consolation was that the brass bed with the jangling knobs had been replaced by a wooden one. Everything seemed somehow makeshift and I longed for everything I had ever known, but most of all for security, and for the feeling that I was like a paper boat in a stream, to go away. It never did. Security was never mine again, in any way, and the next decade was full of pain and uncertainty.

After a time Aggie followed me upstairs and found me standing there. She put her arms around me and said, as she always did to comfort me, but crying herself now, "Ah, pet, don't cry, don't cry." She took a clean handkerchief from her pocket and dried first my tears and then her own, and hand-in-hand we went downstairs together.

64 Cliftonville Road
Belfast.

Dear Madam.
                    Just a line to
say I arrived safe with all parcels
the Bus was packed all the way
My Sister was waiting at the
end of the road so I got all up
at one time. She was delighted
& awfully pleased with what
Mrs Garvin sent her. Jim had
left the Office last night (before)
the Martin got there so it was a
thing Mrs Garvin posted the letter
every thing is alright. The Puppy

was very good there was'nt a
a sound from him. he is out
in the yard at present.
I hope you found Dr & Mrs Duffe
& Family quite well. How is
Hilary did she say anything
when I left. I hope she is better
tell Joyce I won't forget her
Papers. I will say good-bye
now. Send me Mrs Garvins address
love to all. Victor & Tommie
are away in Donegal. they went
on there Bikes & they went through
Magherafelt. So I hope the
Journey will do them good.
        love to all.   yrs Respectfully
                                A. Walsh

Letter written c. 1924/5 by Agnes Walsh to her employer, Hilary's mother, from the Todd family home to which Agnes had returned from the country in advance of the family.

135

FATHER'S FAMILY

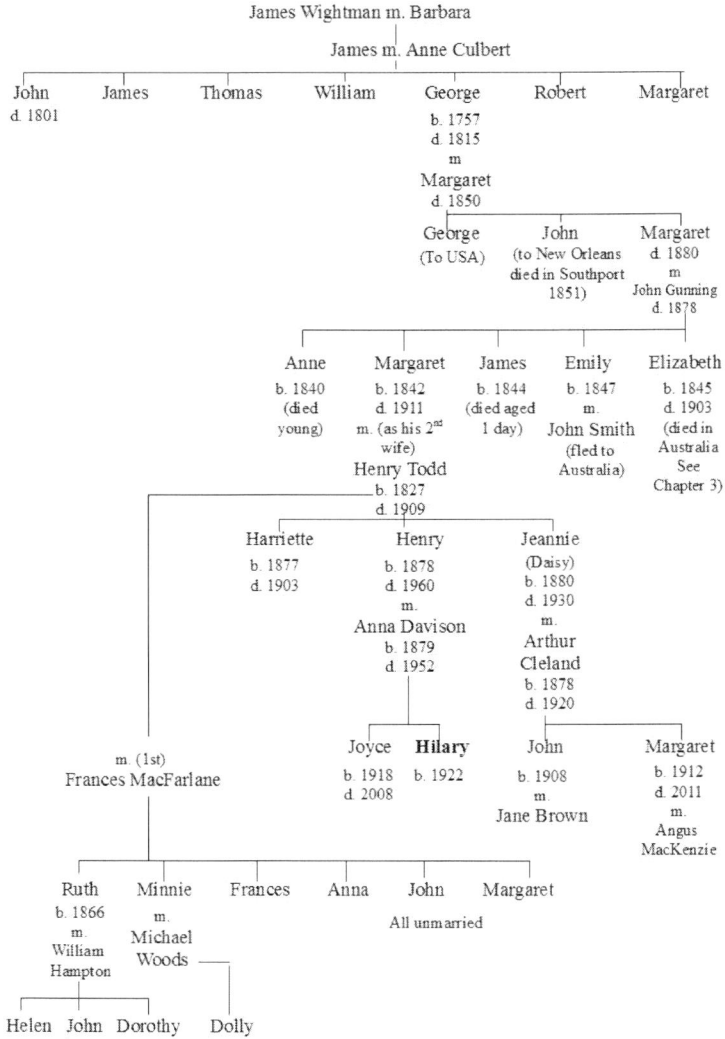

James Wightman m. Barbara

James m. Anne Culbert

John	James	Thomas	William	George	Robert	Margaret
d. 1801				b. 1757		
				d. 1815		
				m.		
				Margaret		
				d. 1850		

George	John	Margaret
(To USA)	(to New Orleans	d. 1880
	died in Southport	m
	1851)	John Gunning
		d. 1878

Anne	Margaret	James	Emily	Elizabeth
b. 1840	b. 1842	b. 1844	b. 1847	b. 1845
(died	d. 1911	(died aged	m.	d. 1903
young)	m. (as his 2nd	1 day)	John Smith	(died in
	wife)		(fled to	Australia
	Henry Todd		Australia)	See
	b. 1827			Chapter 3)
	d. 1909			

Harriette	Henry	Jeannie
b. 1877	b. 1878	(Daisy)
d. 1903	d. 1960	b. 1880
	m.	d. 1930
	Anna Davison	m.
	b. 1879	Arthur
	d. 1952	Cleland
		b. 1878
		d. 1920

Joyce	**Hilary**	John	Margaret
b. 1918	b. 1922	b. 1908	b. 1912
d. 2008		m.	d. 2011
		Jane Brown	m.
			Angus
			MacKenzie

m. (1st)
Frances MacFarlane

Ruth	Minnie	Frances	Anna	John	Margaret
b. 1866	m.				
m.	Michael		All unmarried		
William	Woods				
Hampton					

Helen	John	Dorothy	Dolly

Henry Todd senior with his second wife, Margaret, daughter Daisy on her knee & son Henry junior (Hilary's father) c. 1883

Children of Henry Todd senior c.1903, from left: Harriette, Daisy and Henry junior with their mother Margaret

MOTHER'S FAMILY

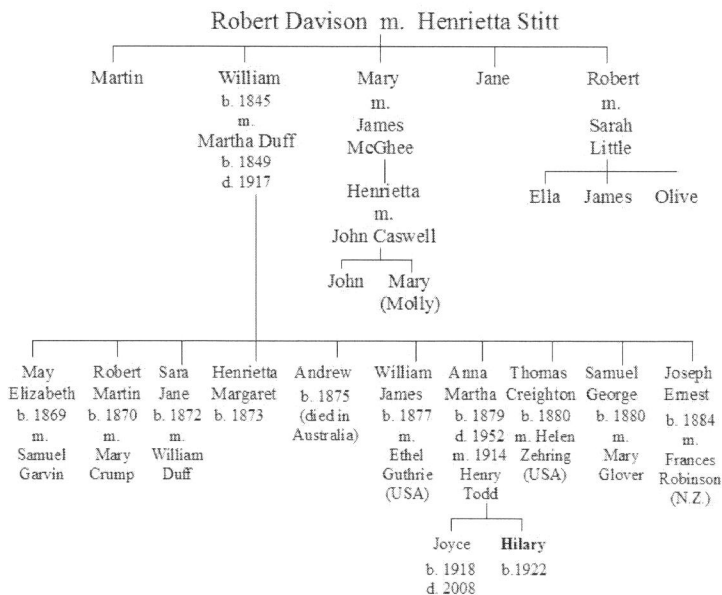

Robert Davison m. Henrietta Stitt

Martin	William b. 1845 m. Martha Duff b. 1849 d. 1917	Mary m. James McGhee	Jane	Robert m. Sarah Little

Mary
m.
James
McGhee

Henrietta
m.
John Caswell

| John | Mary
(Molly) |

Robert
m.
Sarah
Little

| Ella | James | Olive |

| May
Elizabeth
b. 1869
m.
Samuel
Garvin | Robert
Martin
b. 1870
m.
Mary
Crump | Sara
Jane
b. 1872
m.
William
Duff | Henrietta
Margaret
b. 1873 | Andrew
b. 1875
(died in
Australia) | William
James
b. 1877
m.
Ethel
Guthrie
(USA) | Anna
Martha
b. 1879
d. 1952
m. 1914
Henry
Todd | Thomas
Creighton
b. 1880
m. Helen
Zehring
(USA) | Samuel
George
b. 1880
m.
Mary
Glover | Joseph
Ernest
b. 1884
m.
Frances
Robinson
(N.Z.) |

| Joyce
b. 1918
d. 2008 | **Hilary**
b.1922 |

138

Left – William and Martha Davison, Hilary's maternal grandparents c. 1900
Right – Henrietta Stitt, Hilary's maternal great-grandmother (d. 1878)

William and Martha Davison, Hilary's maternal grandparents and 8 of their
10 children, c. 1900
back row – Thomas, May, Anna, Henrietta, William
seated – Robert, grandmother Martha, grandfather William, Samuel
front - Joseph with dog

Part II : The Country Child

"Like dolmens round my childhood: the old people"
John Montague

Farm Hill, c. 1905
Hilary's maternal aunts and uncles, mother and grandmother
(l to r) Aunt (Henri)Etta Davison; Uncle Tom Davison; Aunt May
Garvin (in doorway); standing behind; mother Anna , seated; Uncle Joe
Davison; grandmother Martha Davison and Uncle Sam Davison
(holding horse)

Chapter 1

The Old Home

When I close my eyes I see it all as it was, and smell again the scent of summer, the heavy languor of the meadowsweet in the hedgerows, the new-mown hay, the sharp acrid smoke from a turf fire. Time rolls away eighty years.

Once again I am back in the countryside of South Derry and I feel safe and loved, but those days have gone forever. The journey back stretches far away now, into the past, and for me it is the journey home.

"I'm going home," said Mama, when she went back to visit the house where she was born. It was always "Home" to her, even when it was occupied by her brother and his family, years after her parents had died. I spent most of my holidays every year here and grew to love it as she did, with a deep, defensive love.

Her mother, my grandmother, had died long before I was born, but Mama spoke of her as though she had only just gone to her long rest. I was steeped in tales of Grandma Martha, who, Mama intimated, was the next thing to a saint. She was a remarkable woman, who never cried defeat. She it was who had spun the safe cocoon of "Home" for Mama, a cocoon from which, when she was young, she had been eager to emerge, though later she would have given the world to be enfolded by it once more.

To the passerby Farm Hill was a smallish, low, whitewashed house which stood by the side of a small country road in South County Derry, in a dip between two little hills. When I knew it first it had a thatched roof, and when the thatching had been newly done, which was every few years, the bright gold of the straw shone in the sun and gave the place a picture-book appearance.

In front of the house was a small garden with two neat squares of grass, separated by a pathway and bordered by beds of old-fashioned flowers; wallflowers in season, with heavy yellow and brown heads, succeeded by lilies-of-the-valley with their sharp-sweet scent, snugly placed in one corner under the shelter of a double white lilac bush. In summer all the old favourites came into their own, lad's love, London Pride, lupins, mauve cup-and-saucer Canterbury bells, peonies in dark red, pink and white, the blooms hanging blowsily on strong stems and looking curiously exotic and out of place. The little garden was separated from the road by a white picket fence and a white painted iron gate. A tea-rose climbed around the door of the house, its creamy blossoms hanging in bunches against the white walls, the dark green leaves glossy and the stems full of long thorns.

The path from the gate led to the front door, which was also white, with a bright brass doorknob, letter-box and knocker. Hardly anyone except the minister used this door unless they came on insurance business, for my uncle was an agent for this, to supplement his small income. He took an active part in committee work to do with local government, and much preferred the ordering of things in the outside world to the work of the farm.

Family, friends and neighbours used the back door which was reached through the farmyard. This led through a scullery which contained a stone sink – always called a "jawtub" – into a stone-flagged passage and thence to the kitchen, the hub of the house. Everyday callers came into the house this way so that their boots would not mark the carpet runner in the front hall. They often came in as they journeyed to or from the fields where they were working and sat down to warm themselves by the fire, which burnt searingly both in summer and winter. They would ease themselves into a chair and say, "It's a brave day," or, "It's a saft day," depending on whether the weather was dry or wet. Then the conversation turned to the state of the crops, the price of cattle, the gossip of the neighbourhood and the lack of judgement on the part of the present Government.

The kitchen was a large, bright room which occupied one corner of the house. Two windows looked across the front garden to the road and another window faced the yard. This convenient arrangement meant that little happened in the immediate outside world which was not at once seen and commented on by the occupants of the kitchen. No passerby went unnoticed, the reason for his journey and his probable destination being freely speculated on. From the window looking into the yard, all movements of anyone working there, or of animals, could be instantly seen and if necessary rearranged. Children could also be checked up on and brought to book instantly by a sharp tap on the windowpane if they were thought to be misbehaving, which was often.

Four doors led off the kitchen, the one to the hall being reached by two steps – a kind of mild split-level. The hall was a long passage with doors leading to a bedroom and the drawing room. The bedroom was the spare room, stiff and starchy, with newish golden oak furniture, a patterned carpet of many colours, wallpaper decorated with bunches of unrecognisable pink flowers, a pink counterpane and a puffy eiderdown and pink curtains to match. The pink clashed with the golden oak, but no one minded. This room was kept swept and polished at all times, the bed always aired ready for a visitor, or for a member of the family if illness struck, so that they might rest and recover in comfort and peace. Also it meant that the doctor – and any visitor – could be ushered into a "good room" when he called to see the patient. The window was opened daily, except in wet weather, to keep the room from smelling musty – and propped with a block of wood, as the sash cords were not reliable. No one thought of renewing these – time enough to do this when one went "snap" and the window descended with a bang on some unfortunate's finger.

It was a small room, but it contained everything considered necessary for the comfort of a guest; a double bed, a wash-stand with a marble top bearing a large ewer and basin with gold edges and pink flowers, and a tooth-mug and soap-dish to match. There was a bedside table bearing a small paraffin lamp with a pink glass shade, a box of safety matches on a little dish beside it and a Bible with a bookmark inserted at the Twenty-third Psalm. The Bible was statutory bedtime reading, particularly this comforting psalm, and nothing else was provided. Reading in bed was thought to be a foible on the part of some people and not to be encouraged, hence the Bible. Even worse, a visitor – my father, for example, who was known for his idiosyncratic habit of bedtime reading – might fall asleep and knock the lamp over by accident, and then the whole household would be incinerated in their beds.

A dressing table stood in a corner near the window, covered with a linen runner with deep crocheted edges. My aunts, Mama's sisters, in their youth had spent hours making yards of crocheted lace in white linen thread, which was beautiful, intricate and delicate. It had been used on table-runners, pillowcases and white linen huckaback towels which were laid out for visitors on a mahogany towel-rail. Large corners of this exquisite crochet work were attached to squares of the finest linen to make afternoon tea and supper cloths. Everyone in the family had large, neat piles of these in their linen cupboards. It was the accepted thing. Linen sheets had deep borders of white hand embroidery and mitred edges at the top.

On the dressing table was a pink glass tray about six inches square and on this rested two silver-backed brushes, a silver looking glass and a comb with a silver edge to match. These had been Grandma Martha's and were never used, but they were polished brightly and glistened as they reflected the pink of the tray. Besides these there were two small pink glass jars with lids, matching the tray, and a pink ring stand. It was never used either. One of the small jars contained hair pins, lest a lady guest should run short during her visit, and the other was empty.

In the wardrobe was Uncle Sam's best suit which he wore on Sundays or to attend his beloved committee meetings, the hat which he wore only to Meeting and funerals and the Royal Ulster Agricultural Society's show in Belfast in early June, and a box which held Aunt Mary's summer hats of years past, which might possibly come into fashion again.

A small stiff chair stood in the corner, by the end of the bed and on the mantelpiece were two family photographs. One was of my grandparents, Grandma Martha and Grandpa William, taken when they were old. Each member of Mama's family had one of these prints displayed prominently at home, and it was regarded almost as a holy relic, rather like the pictures of the Sacred Heart in Catholic households. The second photograph was of my aunt and uncle, taken shortly after their wedding, he looking young and pleased with himself, and she, dark-eyed and timid, shy and slightly apprehensive.

On the wall hung a picture and an embroidered text. The picture showed two small children looking soulfully at their grandmother, who was handing them, rather meanly I thought, three cherries on a plate. How did she intend to divide three cherries between two children? The text, which hung over the head of the bed, was worked in bright wool on canvas and was framed in black. It stated ominously "Thou God Seest me". I wondered how anyone could possibly get undressed and go to bed with the thought of a Divine Onlooker staring them in the face, especially the women of Mama's generation. These were nearly all a buxom size eighteen, stout pink-corseted women. The corsets were all whalebone and dangling pink suspenders with metal clips which hurt when the unfortunate wearers sat down, and large pink brassieres which hooked on to the top of the corsets and encased their billowy breasts. Surely the Divine Eyes would have to close for a few minutes, for modesty's sake.

The hall passage ended at the drawing room door. This room formed the other front corner of the house and had windows at the front and at the side, the latter giving on the side garden of the house which was set into a hill. There was a damp smell here because of the siting. It was bright and pleasant, but was only used on Sundays when, with difficulty, a fire was lit in the grate, amid lamentations that the chimney did not draw well. At any moment a billow of sooty smoke might descend into the room, driving everyone out. Pieces of "colly" would float around in the air and settle lightly, the whole room would have to be dusted again and the chairs thoroughly brushed before they could be sat on.

This was truly a Sunday room. It was cheerful enough, but there was a prim stiffness about it. Family and visitors alike sat with straight backs in the chairs, and only in their best clothes. The sofa was covered in moss green velvet and the chairs had loose covers patterned with small sprigs of green leaves. The carpet was soft green with a cluster of roses at each corner and a wreath of roses in the centre. Tables by each window carried photographs of all the family, uncles unknown to me except by name, and aunts all known to me and part of my life. A small white bookcase stood by the door, filled with books of sermons, several Bibles of varying sizes and a few hymn books. There were old Sunday School prizes with pages browned along the edges because of age and lack of use. These had belonged to uncles far away in America and New Zealand.

The paint work was white and the walls were papered in a creamy paper. There were a few pictures in gilt frames. Visitors on

Sundays were entertained here – at least the ladies were. The men, uncomfortable in their dark Sunday suits and starched collars, sat uneasily for a few minutes, their hands clasped between their knees, and were then borne off by Uncle Sam to view his livestock.

Back in the kitchen another door led to a pantry, cool and dim. Jams and preserves were kept here as well as the things for baking bread – a daily task. Just at right angles to the pantry door, was the door to a bedroom. This, together with the kitchen, was the oldest part of the house, all other rooms having been added in haphazard fashion as money permitted and the size of the family grew.

Uncle Sam and Aunt Mary slept in this bedroom, which originally had been my grandparents' room, in a large mahogany bed covered with a turkey-red and white patchwork quilt, which had been quilted by Grandma Martha in the winter evenings long ago. Aunt Mary, who suffered dreadfully from migraine, tottered off to rest here when she had "one of her heads". All the children were bidden to be quiet when this happened and we flocked out of the house like a cloud of swallows taking off for the winter, to pursue our pleasures and games out of earshot.

Down the stone-flagged passage past the scullery was the dining room, a badly-lit room, its only window looking out on the yard and its dark-green walls giving the impression of an aquarium. Its dark furniture was polished to a high shine by Imelda, the maid, every week; the horse hair seats of the chairs were scratchy on bare legs, but we only ate here on special occasions – for example when the minister and his wife came to tea. Uncle Sam conducted his insurance business in this room, using it as an office and keeping his papers in the sideboard.

Another bedroom led off the dining room. This room was tiny, with a large featherbed and a wardrobe which must have been placed in position before the room was built, so tightly were they squeezed into the small space. The window looked out on the rising bank of the side garden, where in spring there were daffodils and apple-blossom, and the white walls reflected what light struggled into the room. The text above the bed read "Be still and Know that I am God" – surely a benison for restless sleepers like me. Joyce and I slept here when we visited, and later, when I came alone, I shared it with the cousin of my choice. Children never slept alone, for they might wake in the night and feel frightened. If this happened the bed companion would be instantly awakened to share the fright. This seemed strange to me, for at home I always slept alone. In the country I was instantly transformed into a country child, while at home I was a child of the town – a gentle form of schizophrenia.

Between the kitchen and the dining room, off the passage, a door opened to reveal a staircase. This led to two very large and airy bedrooms, each with two double beds. The children of the house slept here, and one side of one room was curtained off to make a private place for Imelda to sleep. This was sacrosanct to her and the children were not allowed to disturb her or to go past the curtain when it was pulled. She was like an older sister to them and they loved her, for she made them laugh and was never cross, no matter how much they teased her. She brought them news of another world – dances, boys, clothes, songs she had heard, and they listened to her eagerly, but they knew never to repeat any of it to their parents.

This house, which in Mama's childhood had accommodated a family of twelve – Grandpa William, Grandma Martha and their ten children - now held eight, my Uncle Sam and Aunt Mary, five children and Imelda. Tommy, the farm labourer or "servant man" went home at night to his own cottage and reported for work in the early morning before any of us were awake. He and Imelda ate their meals at the same time as the family, and in the kitchen, but at a different table and using different knives and forks. Imelda was a Roman Catholic, as were nearly all maids then. I suppose this was because Catholic families were usually large, and if a daughter could be placed as a maid or "servant girl" with a respectable local family, it meant one less mouth to feed and perhaps a small sum of money which she could contribute to her family. Imelda's religion made no impression on me at all, although I noticed she ate an egg for her dinner on Fridays, whereas at home Mama always bought fish for Aggie.

Chapter 2

Life at the Farm

The farm house was a busy one, with the usual farm work going on in and around it. As a visiting child, and "family", I was swept into the activity, doing all that my cousins did, though not nearly so expertly. I went with them each day to gather the eggs, although I was terrified of all birds, and hens in particular. A hen had pecked my finger when I was very small as I tried to stroke it – to the undoubted chagrin of the hen, which must have thought I was offering it a juicy pink worm. I watched in admiration as these younger cousins, the oldest six months my junior, firmly ejected the recalcitrant and indignant hens from their nests and sent them clucking and fluttering furiously out into the farmyard. The eggs were quickly and efficiently removed from the nests and placed carefully in a round brown willow basket which was kept specially for the purpose. When the rounds of the nests had been made the basket was carried into the scullery, where Imelda wiped the eggs with a damp cloth and dry salt to remove any marks.

Imelda had a relatively easy time. The children loved her and Aunt Mary was kind to her. Her job consisted of keeping the house clean and sparkling, washing dishes, helping with the cooking and feeding the hens. She did no other outside work as maids in many farmhouses were expected to do, nor did she bake the bread or do the washing. Aunt Mary baked the bread with great expertise and made the butter every week, and Mrs. Johnston appeared each Monday, like the genie of the lamp, to carry out the unpleasant task of washing the family's clothes, bed linen and anything else deemed used and washable.

She worked from an outhouse in the yard, where the boiler was kept. This boiler was a sullen-looking monster, black and ugly, but Mrs. Johnston knew how to tame it. Water was carried in buckets from the pump in the yard and poured into its belly, a fire was lit underneath, and when the water was hot Mrs. Johnston conducted the whole operation. Clouds of steam arose as she put load after load of clothes, towels and bed-linen into a large wooden washtub, rubbing them on a washboard with a wooden frame and a square of corrugated zinc set into it.

There was no washing powder, apart from a packet of Lux flakes which was hoarded like the elixir of life. It was kept in the pantry which led off the kitchen and no one was allowed to use it without first seeking Aunt Mary's permission. It was expensive, and was used only to wash her good blouses and lace collars, the fine linen cloths, or perhaps a christening robe made of delicate lawn, every stitch worked by hand, with finely pin-tucked bodice and lace edging. Lux flakes were not to be used carelessly, and the main washing was done with Finlay's Queen's Pale soap. Long yellow bars of it were kept on a shelf in the wash house to harden off, and then cut into chunks for use. This soap had a peculiar, pungent, though not unpleasant odour, and for some reason to me it was the smell of poverty, though everyone used it for washing, rich and poor alike.

When each load of washing was rinsed and finished, and the buckets of soapy water had been swilled around the yard, sending the Rhode Island Red and White Leghorn hens scurrying for shelter, Mrs. Johnston would call Imelda and together they would carry a large, two-handled oval washing basket to the orchard, where they hung the garments and linens on clotheslines strung between Beauty of Bath apple trees. Here the clothes dried quickly in the fresh breeze and were brought in at the end of the day by the two women with as much triumph as Hercules evinced when he finally got hold of the Golden Apples of the Hesperides. If the day was wet it was a different matter. Lines of clothing hung around the wash house and in the scullery, and it might be days before it dried.

Another task of Imelda's was the ironing or "smoothing". Each Tuesday she dealt with a mountain of clean clothes ready for her attention. The smaller kitchen table, the one by the window where she and Tommy ate, served as an ironing board. The iron was fuelled by methylated spirits, which was a vast improvement on the old-fashioned flatirons or box irons which had to be heated on the kitchen range and were liable to harbour lurking flakes of soot and so soil the clean linen.

Electricity had not reached country districts, and paraffin lamps were the only means of lighting, apart from candles. If one of the glass chimneys or "mantles" broke, it was a major tragedy, so the lamps were only lit by my uncle or aunt when dusk had well and truly fallen and it was difficult to see across the room. Bedrooms were lighted by candles and Imelda had the task of seeing that a certain number of white enamel candlesticks, one for each bedroom, shaped like saucers with handles, each complete with its candle, were left ready on the wide kitchen window sill in the evenings, together with a box of safety matches so that everyone could take a light to bed.

We children were not allowed to carry our own candlesticks in case we set the place on fire. This was always a worry, particularly in this house with its thatched roof. When bedtime came we were always accompanied by an adult as we went along the dark, cold, breezy passage to our bedrooms, the candle flickering in the wind as we passed the draughty scullery and casting shadows on the walls, making us quake pleasurably and talk of ghosts. We undressed quickly, gabbled our prayers with the speed of a tobacco auctioneer and jumped into bed, sinking into the feather mattress which in winter was marvellously cosy. In summer it was not so comfortable, and we felt just as lobsters must do when put into cool water and brought slowly to the boil. My boiling point was low and I spent hours lying in bed on long, light summer evenings, tossing and turning in the heat of the feather bed, scratching my hives until they bled. I was a martyr to hives and if I ate certain foods, like porridge, which I liked, I came out in large, red, itchy weals. Mama knew this and I was not given these hive-producing things at home, but here, in the hurly-burly of a large family and busy household, such vagaries were considered to be fanciful and indeed nonsensical, and rather than make a fuss I ate everything that was put before me. The fresh air of the country sharpened my appetite wonderfully and the good farm food was plentiful and delicious. Hives, I was told, were part of life and had to be accepted, like growing pains and every other ill which came upon children. I was told, comfortingly, by the adults that I "would grow out of it". They were right. I did grow out of it. Nowadays in such a case great talk of allergies would take place, and patch tests, allergy shots and all the rest of the medical ritual would be set in motion. I have no doubt that in the end the result would be the same. Things pass. Children grow out of childish complaints in just the way I did long ago.

The days floated past tranquilly. At night I was often homesick. I felt that home was far away and that everyone I loved would be dead before I returned there. I frequently sobbed myself to sleep, comforted by the cousin who was my bedmate. In the daytime I liked the country life, enjoying the fresh air and feeling that I had both feet on firm ground, missing only the books which my relatives considered a waste of time. There were a few Sunday School prizes which my cousins had been awarded for "good answering" in examinations, but they were all tales of pious – sometimes even dying – children, who had been "saved" before Nemesis overtook them. Saved from what, I wondered. They bored me.

Everyone was kind to me. I was always drawn forward and introduced to callers as "Anna Martha's girl" and in this way my identity was established. Nearly all the neighbours who came to the farm had known Mama when she was young and they remembered her with affection, though they might not have seen her for years. Memories are long in the country. I belonged here because of Mama. Nothing could change that. The great love of, and hunger for, land, and the acceptance of blood relatives, good and bad, under the family umbrella, characterised Ulster country men and women. Strangers might be suspect, but the blood ties were forever.

Chapter 3

Easter

Easter holidays meant pale, lengthening days, with grey-blue skies turning faint green and apricot in the chilly sunsets, daffodils, newborn lambs, yellow fluffy chickens, primroses and violets growing in the banks of the loanin's, bluebells under the trees in small woods or "plantin's", bird song, clear and sweet, and small streams in spate which could be dammed by children wearing Wellington boots and working with their hands like beavers. It also meant the glorious profusion of whin blossoms, brilliantly and gladly yellow, all over the countryside like large patches of saffron, ready to be picked by children for dyeing the eggs on Easter Monday.

Our Easter school holidays never lasted more than three weeks, but springtime in the country after the long winter days at home and the cold greyness of the city pavements made me feel that I was in an enchanted place. The country was as beautiful as ever. Everything was new once more. Newborn animals, especially lambs, were like toys, and while meeting a hen at close quarters startled me out of my wits and I avoided the high-stepping proud red rooster with his glistening blackish-green tail feathers and bright red comb which shook with fury when my cousins naughtily chased him, I was charmed by the sight of a plump brown Rhode Island Red mother hen with her flock of fluffy chickens round her like powderpuffs. I knew they would never approach me, but rather disappear like coins into a slot machine under their mama's wings if I drew near, the hen clucking indignantly, but not moving so as to keep them all safe.

We children tried to avoid the supervision of the grownups at all costs. The family gathered at mealtimes around the kitchen table, but children were not often spoken to and certainly received no encouragement to join in the conversation of the adults, whose every utterance was treated with the respect given by Jews to the

154

Mosaic Law.

As long as we ate it was taken for granted that all was well with us. If we did not eat, it was noted and we were understood to be sick and kept indoors. The prospect of this was so appalling in any kind of weather that a child would rarely admit to feeling poorly, and in the absence of a rash or a fever flush usually escaped detection. On would go our Wellingtons, compulsory wear for outdoors at this time of year, which had been jettisoned by the scullery door as we entered the house. Then off we ran, out into the road, carefree as newly-flushed birds, wondering where we should go next or what we would choose to do.

If it was not too wet underfoot we would make for the fields to see the new lambs and count them. Then we might be beguiled, our minds like thistledown, by the clumps of primroses and dark purple violets in the loanin'. We gathered bunches of these, the violets in the middle and pale, creamy primroses forming a broad border to the posies. We framed these with primrose leaves which looked like bright green crumpled tissue paper, and the ends of the stems were carefully wrapped in damp moss which we prised out from between the stones in a wall. Perhaps someone had brought along a skipping rope, and then we laid our small bouquets carefully in a damp hedgerow so that they would not wither, and repaired to the centre of the road to play our skipping games.

There was little traffic on the roads apart from horses and carts lumbering to and from the fields where men were working, or perhaps coming from Magherafelt where a farmer had gone to collect sacks of meal or feeding-stuffs from Job Logan's store. We were safe and played without a care our games of "Salt, Mustard, Vinegar, Pepper" or "Tinker, Tailor, Soldier, Sailor", screaming with laughter and excitement and hoping for the best of fates – to marry a rich man and certainly not a beggar-man or a thief.

Good Fridays passed virtually unnoticed by Protestants; this day of all days in the church calendar was considered a Papist holy day, not for "good Presbyterians" like us. Roman Catholic neighbours on their way to or from Mass, however, were acknowledged from the kitchen windows as they passed, and beckoned in for tea and hot cross buns. Aunt Mary bought these buns from Morton and Simpson's baker's cart which travelled all the way from Ballymena twice a week, when yeast bread – called loaf bread – was bought to supplement the home-baked, everyday variety. Uncle Sam liked toast, so the bought bread was kept mainly for him. Paris buns, dry and bright yellow inside, with a sprinkling of pieces of sugar on top, were also a specialty of Morton and Simpson, and were much enjoyed.

The laughter in the kitchen rose and fell with the conversation. Easter eggs, large chocolate ones which Father had sent for me and my cousins, were produced for the visitors to admire. They were truly striking, with their sugar roses and wide satin ribbons tied in a bow. These hollow eggs were made of dark plain chocolate and sometimes our names were written on them in pink icing, which made us feel very proud. Occasionally we had eggs wrapped in silver paper, which divided in two and were found to contain chocolates. These are commonplace today, but then they were really special. The silver paper was kept long after the chocolate eggs had been eaten, and smoothed out to a thin, creaseless sheet with great care, then placed between the leaves of a book for safe keeping. It was inevitably forgotten about, and in any case it was of no use, so that years later it was quite usual to find pieces of silver paper which had covered chocolates, or chocolate eggs, in bygone years, in children's books long since packed away in attics. The same thing happened with flower petals and with pretty leaves which after decades of being hidden in books, emerged like brown tissue-paper.

On Easter Monday it was time for the trundling of eggs. In the morning we would go out, armed with paper bags, to gather the golden whin blossom and bring it home to Aunt Mary, who placed it in a large black saucepan containing two or three eggs for each child. This was put on top of the range in the kitchen and brought slowly to the boil, then left to simmer for about twenty minutes, by which time the dye from the whin blossom had turned the eggshells bright yellow. Now the saucepan was drawn off the heat and the eggs were left to cool. When they were cold they were placed in a large basin and Uncle Sam carried them up to the sloping garden at the side of the house. We were each given eggs and began to play with them, throwing them up in the air and catching them, rolling them down the grassy slope until finally the shells cracked and broke. Then we peeled and ate the eggs. I never really saw the point of all this activity, but it was a ritual and I always joined in as everyone else seemed to set great store by it.

On Easter Monday afternoon it was party-time. Sometimes the party, for children only, was held at Uncle's farm, when we played games in the barn and had a special Easter tea round the kitchen table, Aunt Mary and Imelda hovering in the background. All the children were well-behaved, for the Easter party was a treat and they knew that if they were not, the story of any misdemeanour would reach home before they did and great recriminations would ensue. Sometimes the party was held at the O'Donnells', down the road, and sometimes at other houses. All the usual party games were played and we came Gathering Nuts in May and heard the Postman's Knock with as much enjoyment as ever. There were ten O'Donnells and six of us, as well as all the neighbours' children, making a total of about thirty. We girls wore our winter Sunday dresses and the boys sported their Sunday suits and we were en fête for the day. The party lasted until dusk and each child was given a small packet of sweets to take home at the end. These parties were much talked of in the days that followed, especially by the little girls who had been sought after by the boys in the game of Postman's Knock.

One year this game was given an extra fillip and excitement by the presence of a boy who was holidaying at his uncle's farm which marched with Uncle Sam's, and who came from Scotland. Hamish's dark, curly hair and brown eyes caused a flutter amongst the little girls – he was eleven years old – and they were all eager to go inside the barn to be kissed by him when their number was called. I, like all the rest, fell in love with him. I never saw him again after that holiday, but I remember his bright, eager face and the excitement he brought with him, and the strange beating of my heart when we met on the road to the village.

Chapter 4

The Ulster Sabbath

Sunday in the country, unless one was dead or in labour, meant attendance at church, or in the case of Presbyterians, Meeting. A Presbyterian who was asked if he or she had been to church that morning would reply sharply, "No, not at all – I was at Meeting." Presbyterians were credited with a certain independence of spirit and outlook not vouchsafed to their Church of Ireland neighbours, who were believed to be under the thumb of their Bishop. Roman Catholics attended chapel, and the words "meeting", "church" and "chapel" immediately indicated a person's religious persuasion.

The walk to Castledawson Meeting was just about a mile and we set off early, dressed in our Sunday clothes and hard shoes, to be there at eleven o'clock for Sunday school. We called it Sunday school, but it was always called Sabbath school in the announcements the minister made from the pulpit, which made it seem very grand and solemn. The morning service proper began at noon so that farmers had time to feed and water their animals and milk the cows before they got dressed in their good suits for the journey to Meeting, which in some cases was of several miles. Families who lived more than a mile and a half away arrived in a trap drawn by a pony. This relieved the farm horses, which had often been working all week and needed a day of rest.

Traps were cosy, with cushioned seats and a small door at the back and two small pedal-like steps to reach it. It was like being driven in a little brown, polished box, sheltered from the wind, but without a lid. Four people could usually sit comfortably in a trap, but if they came to a hill, either going up or down, the men of the party – and if the hill were really steep, the ladies – got out and walked, to save the pony. Uncle Sam owned a larger trap which held six adults. It had dark red cushions but no door. This made it rather draughty, so when we rode in it we were bundled up with brown and white checked rugs to keep us warm and a waterproof cover and large umbrellas in case of rain. Uncle did not use the trap to go to Meeting, but sometimes, if Dandy the farm horse had not been working too hard the previous week, we would set off on a Sunday afternoon to visit relatives who lived a few miles away.

When my cousins and I reached the Meeting in Castledawson we found the church all bright and bloomy with flowers, daffodils in springtime and other garden flowers in summer. We filed into the pew where, long ago, Mama had sat with all her brothers and sisters. When they had all been young and still at home, the Meeting and its activities had been the focus of their lives, spiritual and social, with prayer meetings every week, special missions which might last for a whole week, with visiting preachers. There were daffodil teas in springtime, each lady vying with her friends as to who had the prettiest table in the adjoining hall, with the nicest china and the most appetising food. Each lady who had a table invited a certain number of guests, who were expected to subscribe a sum of money for the privilege of being there. The hall and all the tables were decorated with daffodils and after tea there might be a concert by the choir. The money raised was given to missions. Grandma Martha always had a table, Mama said, and naturally hers was the best.

Now I sat in this pew, thinking of Mama and home, looking out of the same windows through which she had looked, with their small diamond-shaped panes of clear glass, taking part in the Sunday school lesson just as she had, and noting how the superintendent struck a tuning fork to give us the right note on which to start the first hymn. Off we would gallop into "All Things Bright and Beautiful" or "What a Friend We Have in Jesus", with Mr. Huston conducting frantically and trying to bring us all to the last note in unison. Then there was a prayer, usually a long one. I looked out of the window and wished that I did not have to sit through a church service, too. The prayer ended eventually and it was time for the saying of the Shorter Catechism. My cousins had learnt their answers and had rhymed them over and over again on the walk to Meeting, not understanding the meaning, but determined to be word perfect. As a visitor, I was excused from taking part in this. It was just as well, as my introduction to the Shorter Catechism did not come until I was eleven years old, when I found it just as incomprehensible as it had seemed when I was eight and sitting in the Sunday school at Castledawson Meeting.

Sunday school ended in just under an hour with the singing of another hymn. Those who were not already settled in their own family pews but had gone to be with their class in another part of the church, went back to where their families would join them for the service. We prepared for this by passing up and down our pew the paper bag containing boiled sweets which Aunt Mary had given us to sustain our strength and to keep us quiet through the long service.

The organist came in and began to play a selection of sacred music, pieces of hymns and psalms strung together, with a bar or two of Handel's Largo thrown in for catholicity. Now families began to arrive, the girls wearing Sunday clothes and looking self-conscious in their flower-trimmed or beribboned hats. Their brothers looked ill-at-ease and uncomfortable in their stiff suits and starched white collars. Their boots had been polished, but that type of heavy leather never shone; they had a sort of matt,grained finish and thick soles. A few young men wore shoes which did shine, and this was considered very smart indeed, though a trifle extravagant on the part of parents who allowed it. However, if their boots did not shine, their hair did. It was sleeked back with water and brilliantine, for a tin of this was kept in most houses so that men and boys could go with neat hair to Meeting, church and funerals.

The young of each family settled down in their respective pews and there was much flurrying and tossing of heads on the part of the girls, who thereby discovered who else had arrived for the service, who was absent and for whom they might yet watch. Life could be dull, and Meeting was the place to make contacts, especially with other people's brothers. When it came to hymn singing they applied some of the heavenly sentiments to their own earthly feelings and warbled soulfully, "I nothing lack if I am His and He is mine forever," batting their eyelashes at young men of their fancy across the aisle and satisfied if the objects of their attentions became embarrassed and turned turkey-red at these flirtatious girls' antics in the House of God.

Last of all into the Meeting came the men of the

congregation. They had stayed outside in the graveyard, or Meeting House Green leaning up against the tombstones and chatting, or in the stables where they unyoked the horses and ponies from their traps and left them in safety during the service. They usually loitered to discuss the state of their crops and the condition of their animals and the prices they had got for their produce at the last market. This was the only time during the week when they were able to meet their friends and neighbours casually and to discuss their problems and difficulties with those who were experiencing the same kind of thing.

Gossip, in the guise of news, was exchanged, and each man tried to glean a titbit of gossip to bring home to his wife. Young wives rarely came to Meeting except for special services like Harvest Thanksgiving, for they were obliged to remain at home to cook Sunday dinner, mind the house and look after the youngest children. Baptism of infants took place at home. Public baptism smacked of the Church of Ireland or even the Church of Rome and was never even thought of.

When everyone had settled down and adjusted hats or collars and ties, the organist began to draw his recital to a close as the choir filed in. Choir members carried important looking hymnbooks and rustled like a flock of pigeons round a stook of corn as they fluttered into their seats round the organ; the place where the choir sat was called the choir box, and indeed they were all boxed together in a very small space. The lady choir members in their Sunday hats smiled with pleased dignity at their friends in the congregation and the men busied themselves with their hymnbooks, looking grave and holy. Following the choir came the sexton, whose boots creaked as he mounted the steps to the pulpit carrying the Bible which he laid reverently on the Bible rest, from which hung a Presbyterian blue velvet pulpit fall, emblazoned with an emblem of the Burning Bush worked in gold thread. Most Presbyterians equated themselves with Moses receiving the Word direct from the Source. They felt themselves to be different, somehow...better, really...for theirs was a plain and simple faith with no frills. No one intervened between them and their God. No one would have got the chance.

Last of all the minister came in wearing a frock coat trimmed with silk braid and buttons. He sat for a minute or so with his head bowed, presumably in private prayer, but I feared he must be wondering what to do or say next and I was anxious lest he be at a loss. My worries proved groundless. He was always in complete command of the situation and for the rest of the service exhorted us to prayer, to sing psalms in metre and hymns, to listen to the Word of God as revealed in both the Old and New Testaments. Finally, and to our infinite boredom, he delivered a long sermon. Somewhere, tucked in amongst the hymns and prayers there was a children's address. This moral tale, or fable, nearly always had to do with a child of tender years who, like the children in the Sunday school prizes, we were told "came to God" through the medium of a simple act of kindness, or perhaps because of sickness or some such trauma. These angelic infants never seemed real to my cousins or me and we fidgeted irritably in our seats as we listened to the fanciful tale. It nearly always ended with the minister's voice rising in crescendo with the words, "...and now, boys and girls, remember...," as he pumped home the message to our reluctant minds and we shut off concentration entirely and began to leaf through our hymnbooks to find the next hymn. Without taking his eyes off the minister in the pulpit Uncle Sam stretched out his long arm along the pew in front of our noses to quiet us and stop the rustling of the thin hymn book paper. We subsided for a moment, rebelliously, and squirmed in our seats until the story of the unnaturally virtuous child had drawn to its conclusion.

When the long sermon for the adults was over we heaved a great sigh of relief and joyfully sang the last hymn, for it heralded our release. We stood with bowed heads for the benediction and then filed quietly into the fresh air, glad to escape after the two-and-a-half hour stint in the pew and thankful to stretch our legs on the mile-long walk home. Because Uncle Sam was with us we walked sedately in a long row across the road, all seven of us, Uncle in the middle with three children on either hand. There was no traffic. It was the Sabbath.

The table was set in the kitchen for dinner when we arrived home and Aunt Mary was making the gravy. The roast beef was resting in its tin at the back of the stove. Before we ate we had to take off our Sunday clothes and get back into everyday things in case we might drop something on our good dresses. Down we sat, conscious that this Sunday meal was a small occasion, marking a special day in the week. We bowed our heads as Uncle asked the blessing and then ate in silence broken only by the adults' conversation. The delicious beef and fresh vegetables were followed by a solid pudding, perhaps a steamed roly-poly oozing jam, or baked rice with raisins in a large white enamelled oven dish with a dark blue rim.

Imelda cleared the table when we had finished and washed the dishes before going home for the afternoon to visit her mother. Unless visitors were expected, Aunt Mary went to have a lie-down after her exertions at the kitchen range and Uncle Sam went to sit in the drawing room by the fire – to read, he said – but we knew that he too would sleep. All adult eyes being closed or occupied, we were free, and as long as we kept quiet and did not break the Sabbath silence too much and were not actually to be seen playing games on the Lord's Day we could do as we liked.

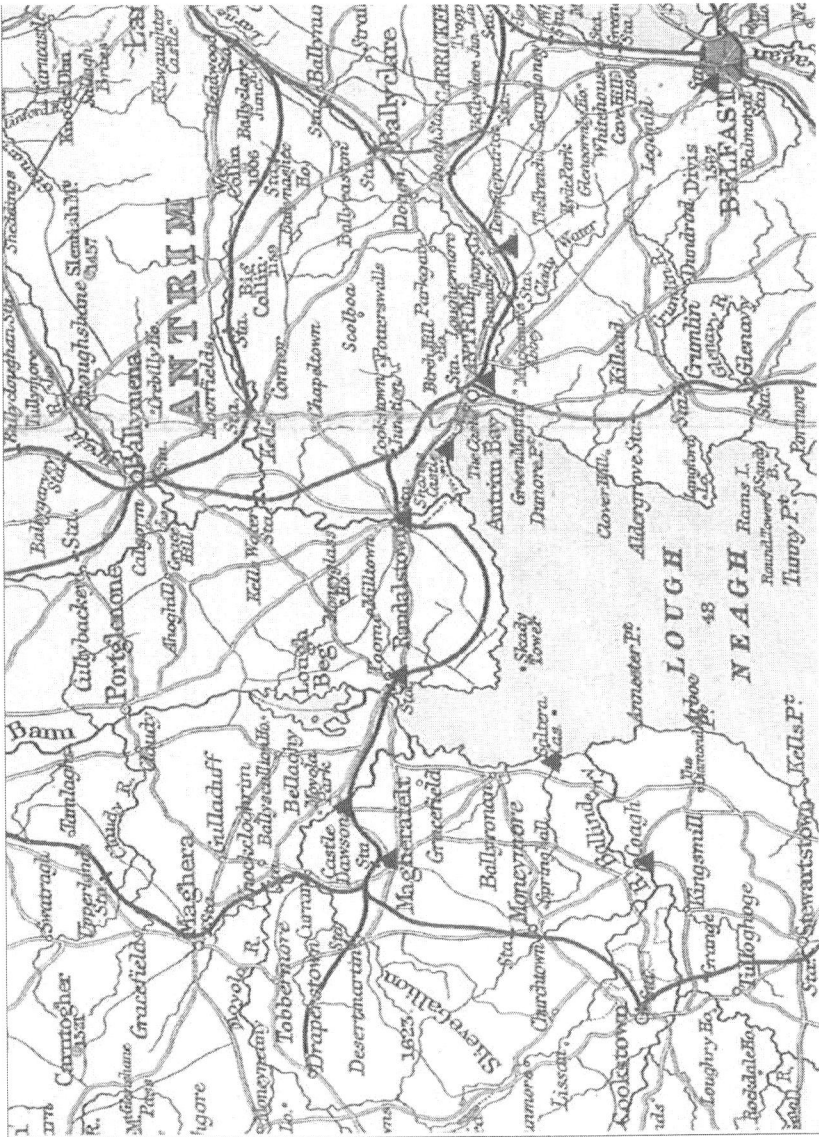

Map, c. 1900, of parts of Co. Antrim and Co. Derry, with places mentioned in succeeding chapters marked by black triangles.

Chapter 5

Summer Holidays

Summer holidays lasted for nine weeks and when the school term ended in the last week of June the long days of summer stretched interminably ahead. Two whole months of freedom! The first few days at home were pleasant and I was able to lie in bed late in the mornings reading. Aggie would bring breakfast to bed "to get it out of the way" she said. I would lie, lost in the adventures of some youthful and improbable heroine until the sun shining through the window drew me inexorably from between the sheets and out to play.

Soon Mama would "write to the country", meaning to Uncle Sam, Aunt May, Aunt Sara and to the McMaster family, who were her first cousins and who lived in a sort of Anne-of-Green-Gables-Land by the shore of Lough Neagh, to warn them that Joyce and I, and eventually as we grew older and Joyce's holiday plans were different, I alone, would be coming to visit. In Mama's family no one waited to be asked – they merely stated their time of arrival, or more often arrived without notice, expecting to be made as welcome as the flowers in May.

Visitors who were not family, however, imposed great strains on household arrangements and did not come without warning. Rooms, although always kept in pristine condition, were quite unnecessarily swept and garnished; mammoth cooking sessions took place, the object being to make the visitors think that the food was always as lavish and fancy as it appeared on the table during their stay. Chickens had their necks pulled and were de-feathered, cleaned, stuffed and roasted with great abandon. Hens were shooshed off their nests as soon as their eggs had emerged so that the latter might be made into mountainous golden sponge cakes and other delicacies; cream was whipped by the quart with a wire balloon whisk; at least three kinds of bread were baked daily, for bread older than one day was only thought fit for the hens.

Linen tablecloths were starched and ironed, linen sheets were brought out of cupboards for the beds, and in short the whole household was disrupted. These activities on the part of the women of the family drew great scowls of disapproval from the men. They liked to be left in peace to get on with the farm work and were furious each evening at having to shave, wash and change into suits and collars and ties before they were permitted to sit down at the table in the dining room with the visitors. They were tired at the end of a long day in the fields and had no desire for small talk, wanting only to doze by the fire in the warm kitchen.

Great sighs of relief went up when the visitors departed and the house was clear again, although they were always waved off at the front gate with cries of, "Come back again soon! Now don't be a stranger! It was lovely to see you!" and were sent on their way, usually to Belfast, bearing baskets of fresh eggs laid that very day, butter, a cake newly-baked and a large bunch of flowers from the garden. Everyone was so glad to see them go that they would willingly have sped the parting guests with the entire contents of the pantry if they could have carried it.

When the front door was closed, and only after the visitors' conveyance had carried them out of sight – the family rushed back into the kitchen like the bursting of a dam. The kettle was immediately put on to make tea and the women of the house would sit down comfortably to discuss in detail every aspect of the visit. It had been a success – a great success! How lovely the guests had been – how charming and kind. How much they had enjoyed all the lovely food which had been prepared for them! Wasn't that a beautiful dress that Mrs. So-and-So had worn, with the lace insertions on the bodice, and weren't her shoes smart? No matter that she could hardly walk in them, for she never went further than the garden. Aaahh . . . hhh they sighed, the whole visit had gone off beautifully and it had been well worth the effort expended.

After one or two cups of tea had been sipped, the euphoria would begin to wear a little thin. Mmmm, Mr. So-and-So was very fond of his food, in fact he was just the tiniest bit greedy. "He ate three helpings every day at his dinner," chimed in Imelda, and Aunt Mary said, "On Wednesday he ate the whole bowl of trifle, apart from the bit Mrs. So-and-So had. I only had a small spoonful, for I thought the rest of it would be a treat for the children. But when I turned round he had the serving spoon in his hand and it was fare ye well, Killeavy, to the trifle." Yes, he really was greedy. And his wife, now, she was a bit "near" and the small obligatory presents she had brought for the children were small indeed.

"A lot of trumpery," snorted Imelda, who had received nothing, not even half-a-crown when they left. And it wasn't that they didn't have plenty of money, mused Aunt Mary, as she felt her eyelids closing after all the stress of the visit. "Sure they have neither chick nor child, and they can't take it with them," Imelda said. But Aunt Mary was sleeping now in her chair and Imelda took her cup out of her hand and shushed the children out to play, saying to herself, "I trust in God that pair of heelers don't come back till Tib's Eve," under her breath. Now everyone could forget the fuss and bustle and the household corsets might be loosened. We were glad of this as we returned to our long outdoor days with the interminable games that children play when time is endless and the sun shines.

I travelled to the country by bus. Mama favoured the Independent Bus Company with its blue buses against the Belfast Omnibus Company, whose buses were green, and also their fares were cheaper.

There were no marked bus stops along the road. The bus stopped wherever a prospective passenger stood by the roadside with outstretched hand. The procedure for disembarkation was the same. The passenger would edge his way up the bus as it neared his destination before speaking in confidential tones to the driver. "Let me off at McGranaghan's loanin'," he might say, naming the place which was nearest to his house. The buses were rather like taxis, providing almost door-to-door service. The drivers were local men and knew nearly everyone who travelled with them and their reason for making the journey.

On the day I was to travel, Mama took me down to the end of the Cliftonville Road with my suitcase, I waving a tearful farewell to Aggie, who watched me from the gate till I was out of sight. As the blue bus chugged along the Antrim Road Mama put her hand out to stop it, handed me up and paid my fare to the driver. She then told him to look after me and where he was to let me off.

"Yes, yes," he would say, as I held on to Mama's hand, clutching it tightly, hopeful to the end that she would suddenly make up her mind to take me back home again or even, miracle of miracles, decide to come with me. "I'll let her off at the end of your Sam's loanin'." He looked at me kindly and asked, "Are you going to stay with your Uncle Sam for a wee while?" as we drove off, I nodding, "Yes," to his question and at the same time craning my neck to see, I felt dolefully, the last of Mama. I imagined that she might be knocked down by a tram or burnt alive or in some way disappear from my life before I came home again. I wept quietly for a mile or two and then cheered up as we reached Glengormley and the green fields, and settled down to enjoy the journey.

The road from Belfast to Antrim was flat and uninteresting and seemed to last forever. We drove through Templepatrick and into Antrim town where the bus stopped to leave off and collect parcels for other towns on the way. Through Antrim we went till we reached the Black Church, where we turned left on the road to Randalstown. We were led to believe that this church, a Catholic one, had been painted black by its parishioners, who said it would remain in mourning until Ireland was united. This was probably a fable, but my country relatives believed it and expressed the pious hope that the parishioners had laid in large stocks of black paint as they would be needing plenty of it for a long time.

On we sped, I looking in wonderment always at the long stone wall which ran the whole way to Randalstown, bordering Lord O'Neill's estates. I thought that in this place there might be dragons and unicorns rampant among the trees behind the grey wall, and surely there must be a tower with a fair damsel imprisoned in it. I was lulled by these thoughts and Randalstown was upon us before I knew it, with the seven-arched railway bridge looming to the left. The entrance to Shane's Castle looked as romantic as ever and I imagined a princess in a glass coach driving in and out of the gateway. Now we were through the small town and on the road to Toome. Across Toome Bridge we went, with the eel fisheries clearly visible, and straight on to a white road which led like an arrow to the Hillhead.

When the bus reached the Hillhead we turned left on to the Castledawson road, bordered on the right by yet another stone wall, this time enclosing the estates of the Chichester-Clark family, where in spring the old-fashioned double daffodils among the grass made sheets of gold. Castledawson came in a flash and I began to sit up straight and look out of the window with more interest as I saw the familiar shops and faces. We passed the Presbyterian meeting house with its unusual clock face which has, instead of numerals, letters spelling out the message "MEMORY FULTON", thus ensuring that the family of Fulton are constantly in the minds of the villagers.

I remember the unveiling of this clock when I was very young and all the talk there was in the congregation and the village about whether the lettering should be permitted or whether the clock ought to have normal Roman numerals. After much discussion, pressure and counter-pressure, the lettering was allowed, although the opposing faction felt strongly that a clock on the House of God should not advertise mortal man. There was a great tea party in the hall and much pushing and shoving by the guests and the congregation. This alarmed me because I was small and only reached the tops of people's legs and was naturally crushed and buffeted about.

I recall a small stout clergyman who shook hands with me as I hid behind Mama's skirts and saw my predicament. He drew us to the side and lifted me up on to a chair so that I could see properly, telling Mama that he would look after me for a while. Mama, nothing loth, abandoned me and dived into the fray once more and I could see her laughing and talking with friends from the old days. My new friend talked to me kindly and showed me his black flat clerical hat and how cleverly it was attached by a black cord to the top buttonhole of his frock coat so that the first puff of wind would not blow it away. He was just about to tell me a story when Mama came back to bear me off for tea – milk in my case – and cake, so I never got to hear what did happen to the princess who had been captured by a wicked green dragon.

Remembering all this, and by now wanting to stay in the warm, womb-like bus forever, I was borne on through the village, along the Magherafelt road and over Butler's Bridge, past the old house at Tamnadace where Aunt May and Uncle Sam Garvin had lived for a time after their late-in-life marriage. This house, Uncle Sam's old family home, from which they moved when I was not more than two years old, is only a vague picture in my mind, but it is a charming picture of flowery gardens and neatly clipped hedges in front and a farmyard with hens and ducks at the back. The lane leading to it was crossed by railway lines and I remember the hurried rush over, Aggie pushing me in a go-cart which lurched as we went, the frisson as the train whooshed past, the driver tooting the whistle in salute and the engine blowing out smoke. The sense of relief when we reached the house was totally out of proportion to the event, but the feeling of danger was omnipresent, although trains ran on the line infrequently. It seems to me now that Aggie took us out with the sole purpose of seeing the train, which always passed at noon, as she would never have placed us in any danger and would have gone to the scaffold rather than run any risks with either Joyce or me.

Now we were approaching the place where I was to alight, and the bus shuddered to a halt. My cousins, together with Imelda, were there to meet me as the driver handed down my case, and we eyed each other uncertainly, as children do after a separation. Soon we were at ease and the sense of kinship prevailed.

The pleasures of children in the country were simple but very satisfying in summer and we were never idle. With six of us around there was always someone to play with. One of the older children was deputed each day to go to Castledawson to collect the morning paper for Aunt May. One paper sufficed for the two houses. It was the Belfast Newsletter and Aunt May and Uncle Sam read it from front to back before sending it up to Uncle Sam Davison when Uncle Sam Garvin fetched the milk in the evening. Sometimes I would go to the village with the cousin who was on paper duty and sometimes I elected to stay at home to play with the others. I was allowed to do as I pleased.

Those of us who were playing near the house were frequently called on, after Aunt Mary's mammoth daily baking of griddle upon griddle of bread, to carry the morning and afternoon tea to the men who were working in the fields at the hay. We felt this was a great privilege, for it was a ritual and we the acolytes.

Two large baskets were fetched from their places on the scullery shelf by Imelda and set on the kitchen table. Aunt Mary lined one with a clean linen tea towel with a red stripe down the middle and a broad red border. In the lined basket were placed freshly-baked farls of soda and wheaten bread, split and lavishly buttered, and a large pot of homemade jam. No woman worth her salt would countenance bought jam in the house. It was thought in the first place to be inferior and unpleasant – made from turnips, people said – and secondly it was only to be found in the houses of clarts. A clart was a woman who took no pride in her house and was useless at cleaning or baking or cooking. There could be no excuse. If a house was not spotlessly clean, with all the furniture polished and gleaming and food cupboards and larders bulging and overflowing with homemade preserves, pickles, sauces and elderberry wine, fruit cake and madeira cake in case of callers, the woman in charge of it was a clart. One young neighbour had been found one morning, sitting down, exhausted, after a sleepless night with a new baby and glancing at the day's paper, by Aunt Etta who had called to sell tickets for a church social. She had discovered poor Matilda with her feet up on a stool and the unwashed dishes still on the breakfast table, and could hardly have been more appalled if she had found her in bed with the servant man – an unlikely event anyway, as he was seventy years old and married. Aunt Etta arrived back home full of the news. "Matilda Clark's nothing but a clart!" she declared delightedly to Aunt May. "She does nothing but read the paper from morning till night!" Neither Aunt May nor Aunt Etta could imagine the draining effect of a colicky baby on a new mother. Matilda Clark was slotted into the category of clart par excellence.

The baskets for the haymakers were got ready. The first was packed with food and the second filled with cans of hot tea and cold milk, together with a covered bowl of sugar. Cups, spoons and a knife to spread the jam, together with a small pink-and-white cloth completed the load, and four children were selected to make the journey, two to each basket.

Off we set, pleased at our importance and ready to share the tea with the men. Down the loanin' we walked, steadily so that the tea should not be spilt, setting down the baskets now and then so that we could change sides to rest our aching arms. On a warm July day the still air surrounded us thickly, not a leaf stirred and soft scents from the banks of the little winding lane of meadowsweet, honeysuckle and palest pink wild roses assailed our nostrils like incense. The lane became a kind of lotus-land and our steps grew slower as we sniffed the heavy, almost tangible perfume. Then we would remember our mission and off we would trot again as fast as we dared. We took care not to spill the hot tea in the lidded can, and soon we reached the main road, called the New Line, which was a flat tarmacadamed stretch of road which bypassed the hill where Uncle Sam Davison's farm lay. Over the New Line we went, across the railway bridge and along another short lane till we came to the reapers in the field. When they caught sight of us, four small brightly-clad figures coming through the gate, they stopped work, pushing back their caps and wiping the sweat from their foreheads with large coloured handkerchiefs or pieces of cloth. We set down our baskets, knelt down beside them and began to unpack the food.

The little pink-and-white cloth was spread on the stubble at the edge of the field, in a shady place, and the bread and jam, with the knife beside the jam pot, placed upon it. The cups were set out in a neat row and Uncle Sam Davison lifted the cans of tea and milk from the basket. He poured the strong brew into the cups and one of the children was trusted to pour the milk from the smaller can which had a pouring lip. One handed the bread and yet another carried round the sugar to the gathered men as they sat. Each man helped himself liberally, four or five spoonfuls for each cup being usual, for the sugar gave them energy. This sugar was not like our sugar at home, which was ordinary granulated. This was in coarse, clear grains, each grain being square and about two millimetres in diameter. It seemed sweeter than our sugar, and each grain could be lifted on a damp, licked finger and savoured for some moments on the tongue before it melted.

Aunt Mary always included four small cups for us and we had milk in these with a little tea to make it seem grownup. We sat, cross-legged, feeling important and listening to the men's talk and laughter, but not really understanding it, as it usually concerned the idiosyncrasies of the neighbouring farmers, always supposing of course that none of those so discussed were present.

This could be a tricky subject, for many people in the countryside were related by blood or marriage, the only division – and this as broad and deep as the Grand Canyon – being religious.

Relations between Protestants and Catholics were warm and friendly as far as individuals were concerned. They "neighboured" with each other, helping with seed time and harvest on each other's farms, and were always ready to offer what help they could at time of sickness, death or trouble. Intermarriage, however, was out. It just did not happen. Anyone who breached this great divide – and these cases were incredibly rare – had to leave the country, for they were not acceptable to either community. Their families, figuratively speaking, donned sackcloth and ashes and were treated by all with tenderness and concern, as though they had been visited by the Black Death. The names of the renegades were not spoken again, and the painful subject was avoided in conversation with the most extraordinary circumlocutions. Sermons were regularly preached, especially during Lent, by Roman Catholic priests, who warned their flocks strongly about the danger of "company-keeping" – danger number one being, naturally, keeping company with a Protestant, and danger number two being the loss of virginity. The second might possibly be coped with. The first could not.

Protestants were just as adamant about the purity of their faith and just as determined that it should not be adulterated by a Papist in the family. If a young man or woman showed signs of interest in a Roman Catholic, he or she was immediately brought to book by stern parents, and if this failed to achieve the desired separation the minister was sent for and a chastening sermon delivered, which usually cleared up the matter. One young girl who had gone to England to become a nurse, fell in love with a Catholic boy and when she came home on holiday felt she must break the news of her engagement gently to her parents. "I'm engaged to a lovely boy," she said, and was gratified at her mother's smile of approval. "But he'll not be going to the Twelfth!" she added hastily, whereupon her mother burst into tears and began to wail loudly. Anyone who did not attend the Twelfth of July Orange celebrations was by definition not a true Protestant and almost certainly a Roman Catholic. Lizzie married her lovely boy, but in England, and never returned home. Her parents never mentioned their beloved only child's name again and when they died they left their large and prosperous farm to a far-out cousin who was Master of the local Orange Lodge.

Otherwise, and leaving such regrettable incidents aside, everyone got along like a house on fire. One bachelor farmer, a Protestant, had an elderly Catholic housekeeper who had brought him up after his mother died in childbirth. Just before each Twelfth of July she washed, starched and ironed the great Union Jack which was flown each year from a tall flagstaff beside the house, and pressed his Orange Sash ready for him to wear in the Twelfth Procession at the head of his Lodge. She thought nothing of it and would have felt it a reflection on herself if William John had not been perfectly turned out to "Walk", and if the flag had not been in immaculate condition before being hoisted. This ritual was part of William John's life, and so was she.

Religion was not mentioned in "mixed company" lest feelings be hurt and umbrage taken. In the very rare event of this happening "one word would borrow another" and it could be catastrophic. Whole countrysides would be split down the middle for generations, with every syllable of the conversation which had caused the controversy being parsed and analysed, added to and taken from, according to which side was doing the telling.

After half-an-hour's break, the tea drunk and the bread eaten, and some of the men by this time lying on their backs in the sun with their handkerchiefs over their faces to shade their eyes, we gathered up the cloth and the cups and cans and repacked our baskets. As we started for home, with lighter burdens this time, the men went back to where they had left off work and waved goodbye to us. Uncle Sam left us to the gate, kissed us and warned us to be careful as we crossed the New Line on the way back. This warning was hardly necessary as the traffic was sparse and consisted mainly of farmers in their brightly painted orange and blue farm carts bowling peacefully along. When they saw us they raised an arm in salute as they sat, craggily hunched on a board at the side of the cart and called out, "It's a brave day!"

"It is!" we would chorus and wave in reply. Occasional buses chugged and snorted along and could be heard from afar off, so that we were never in danger. There were few cars.

On we walked, back to the loanin', where we set down our baskets and began to search with keen, bright eyes for wild strawberries, pushing aside the grass on the banks to seek out the tiny scarlet jewels. We did not eat them as we picked, but before starting to gather the little berries hidden among the grass, each child plucked a long-stemmed piece of timothy grass with a firm, not too sappy, end. On this piece of grass we threaded the strawberries, just as our parents had done long ago in this very lane, until the stalk was full and looked like a red bead necklace with a feathery end. It was the only way we could carry our treat home. To hold them in our hands would have squashed the strawberries, but this way they kept whole and separate.

When we had found enough ripe strawberries, and the older children had helped the younger ones to fill their grassy stalks, we lifted the baskets again and dangled the strawberries from our free hands and carried them home. There we unthreaded them on to dark blue saucers which were ranged on the kitchen dresser, their matching cups having been broken long since. We arranged the little scarlet fruits carefully in concentric circles on the saucers and this ritual took some time. Over them we poured thick yellow cream from a jug which was kept in the cool pantry off the kitchen. No sugar, for the berries were sweet enough and sugar would have spoilt the delicate flavour. We did not offer any to the grownups, nor did they expect us to. Wild strawberries were precious, magical things, perfect and tiny, and were made for children.

Another job for the children was that of bringing the cows home from the field for the evening milking. They were fetched by Tommy each morning, and arrived in record time, for they knew better than to challenge his authority. He addressed them sternly and they obediently plodded quickly and quietly in front of him as he drove them with an occasional touch of his stick to hasten their steps. In the afternoons he was busy in the fields and it fell to our lot to "go for the cows". Two children always went on this errand and sometimes three or four, depending upon what other entertainment or game offered a rival attraction.

Around four o'clock we were despatched to the grazing field which was a ten-minute walk from the house. We played guessing games and "I Spy" as we went busily along the "wee road" which was really a cross between a road and lane. There was never any traffic on it. We passed the house where Mrs. Murtagh lived. She was a tiny, grey-haired old lady who had lived for forty years in America, and when she came to fetch her milk each evening from the farm she always came into the kitchen to have a chat with Aunt Mary and Imelda. Her slight American accent sounded strange to our ears, superimposed as it was on that of her native South Derry. She had married Johnny Murtagh, a boy from the next townland, when she was a girl of nineteen and he was twenty-one and they had gone to New York. She told us marvellous tales of skyscrapers, moving stairways, coloured fountains and bright lights. She and Johnny had been caretakers in an "apartment block" and she told us wonderful stories of the rich people who lived in these apartments, their furs, their jewels, their limousines, their servants. We wondered why, if these people had so much money, they did not have houses of their own and instead lived in what seemed to us just "rooms" in someone else's house. But Mrs. Murtagh told us that in New York everyone lived this way and that often they had country houses, too, with large grounds and gardens tended by armies of gardeners. This was beyond us to understand or even imagine, but we loved to hear the stories and asked for them over and over again.

She had had a "wee girl" once, but the child had been delicate and had died young. She had wanted to come home then, but Johnny wanted to stay in New York, so she agreed. When, just before he was due to retire, Johnny was knocked down by a streetcar and killed, she said the heart went out of her. With the compensation money she received because of Johnny's death she was able to come home and was glad to be able to live quietly in the house where she was born and the gentle countryside she had missed so much all through the long, lonely years of her exile.

Sometimes, when she came for the milk, she brought a treat for us, for she loved children and was a good cook. We loved to see her walking up the hill carrying a small basket, for we knew she had been making something for us. Strawberry shortcake and cherry tart in season, apple pan dowdy, coffee fudge and a rich dark chocolate cake were her specialties, and though the quality of homemade cakes and pies in all my aunts' houses was high, this American cooking had something different about it, something rich and tasty that we could not quite define.

As we passed her house on our way to get the cows she would be sitting by the window, busy with her knitting, and would wave to us, lay down her work and come to the door, the top half of which was open, caught back against the wall of the kitchen by a bar. "Where are you off to?" she would call to us, though she knew the answer already.

"To get the cows – it's nearly milking-time," we answered.

"Well, for Heavens' sakes!" she would say in her slightly sing-song American way. "How the day does fly! Now, you children just wait a minute. I've been making cookies." She would disappear into the little house where the clock on the wall ticked the time away – time that no longer mattered to her, for her days slipped by with nothing to mark them – and then reappear with a large raisin biscuit for each child, golden and fruity. We stood for a few minutes, eating and talking, sensing her loneliness.

"Well now, you children had better fetch the cows. I'll be up later for the milk."

She waved us goodbye and returned to her seat by the window, picking up her knitting again.

When we reached the field some of the cows were usually gazing moodily over the gate, but others had strayed right to the far end of the pasture and stood stupidly gazing into space. We broke light branches from the hedge, green and leafy. Armed with these, and carefully closing the gate of the field behind us, we called with great gusto, "Get up, there!" which was our equivalent of "Oy – toro!" in the Spanish bullrings. We advanced upon the stragglers who gave no sign of seeing or hearing us until we were within a few yards of them. Then they gave a loud "mooo-ooo-ooo" and tossed their heads, rolling their navy-blue eyes sideways so that we could see the white shining milkily in the corners.

Nothing daunted by all this false bravado on the part of the animals, we went round behind them and gave them a smart switch with our branches on their hindquarters, driving them to join their sisters at the gate. We had to be careful not to rush them too much lest we make them fall or upset their milk yield, and this warning was always impressed on us before we set out from the house. In the event we had about the same effect on these slow-moving stately beasts as a gnat would have on a hippopotamus. The cows moved because they knew it was milking-time and their udders were swollen. They wanted relief from their burden and willingly cooperated with our puny wishes. We felt mightily proud as we herded them together, then one of us opened the gate of the field, pushing in front of the cows to reach the gate-bar and slapping them on their noses and rumps with our branches to keep them from trampling us. Back would swing the gate and out into the road ambled the cattle, looking this way and that until a child, stationed by now in the right place, drove them in the direction they were meant to go. Once the lead cow went in the right way the others followed without trouble.

Uncle Sam Davison had names for the cows, flower names like Buttercup, Daisy, Pansy and Primrose. Once he had promised the children that they might choose the name for a new heifer calf and to his dismay they had chosen to call it Georgina after the minister's wife. He could not go back on his word, but as long as Georgina was on the premises he felt he could not, in honour, invite the minister to view his herd.

We drove the animals back along the "wee road", past Mrs. Murtagh's house once more, she waving and smiling at us as we went. Each child acted as a whipper-in, keeping them on the move and not allowing them to dally in the lush green grass by the roadside, until we reached the farmyard gate. In skipped the cows, straight to their places in the byre, like dancers taking up their positions for an eight-some reel. Tommy and Uncle Sam were there to chain them in place, speaking soft endearments and patting them lovingly in a way I feel sure Uncle never did to Aunt Mary nor Tommy to his sweetheart.

Then the milking began, and a kind of sensual calm fell on the byre and pervaded the air. The two men, hands washed in a bucket of water and disinfectant, sat, each upon a small stool by the side of a cow, a bucket between their knees. They leaned their heads against the soft brown side of the animal pulling gently on the full udders to draw out the milk in thin, white streams, the silence enhanced by the soft sss-sss-sss as the jets of milk reached the pails. Gradually the buckets filled with the warm, foamy milk and we children stood in the doorway watching the age-old rite, gazing in silence at the daily miracle.

One summer, after I had been ill with some childish ailment, Mama thought I was run down. When I arrived at the farm her letter had got there before me, with a request that twice a day I should be given that old-fashioned sovereign remedy "a glass of milk straight from the cow". This was taken literally. Everyone else drank milk, water and tea from either a cup or a mug, but now a heavy glass tumbler was brought specially from the dining room cupboard and taken to the byre at milking-time by me. Willy-nilly I had to stand there until Uncle Sam came to milk a special cow whose butterfat yield was good, then he would call me over after he had milked a pint or so into the pail, and milk me a glass full right there as I stood. I had to drink it in his view, to the accompaniment of much face-pulling by my cousins, who thought this the most revolting thing they had witnessed. Warm, foamy milk straight from the cow! Dreadful! they thought. However, his sister Anna's wishes had been carried out and Uncle felt he had done his duty. Twice a day during my entire visit I drank my tumbler of milk and I speedily regained my strength. Whether it was due to the fresh cow's milk or the country air I do not know, but there were roses in my cheeks again and instead of wanting to stay languidly indoors with the grownups all day, I was out from morning till night with the other children.

The best time of all in the country was hay-time. The weather just had to be good for the hay or the farmers were ruined. Many years it must have been wet and the hay lost, but when I think of hay-time I remember only the hot sunshine and the dry dusty roads and lanes where the rick-shifter wobbled and swayed along under the green trees.

First the hay was cut and stooked and then it was made into small haystacks, the stooks being forked up to the man on the top as the stack was built. The builder of the stack had to be strong and highly skilled, for it had to be balanced perfectly. Then when the hay had been dried off in the stack it was brought home to the hay-shed in the farmyard to provide for the needs of the animals during the long winter months.

The rick-shifter! That, to the children, was the most exciting, satisfying vehicle in the world. Its charm lay in the rarity of its use – only at hay-time – and its simplicity. It was a low, completely flat conveyance, two-wheeled and without sides, made of smooth wooden boards worn grey and shiny with use, exactly the right size to hold and transport a haystack. In front, just beside the shafts for the horse, there was a sort of ratchet-cum-winch by which the stack, girdled around by stout ropes, was pulled slowly on to the rick-shifter which had been tipped towards it to make a ramp, until it sat firmly in place like a golden steamed pudding on a plate. Then it was secured again with ropes and Dandy, the chestnut horse, began the slow plodding journey home. The children, who enjoyed these days more than any others in the year, clambered on at the back and sat trailing their sockless, sandalled – or sometimes bare – feet in the dust as they went.

Sometimes Tommy allowed a favoured child to sit up in front with him. This was bliss. The chosen one sat queening it in state, enjoying the honour, breathing in the sweet scent of the new hay, the smell of the hot horse and the mixture of sweat and Lifebuoy soap from Tommy's strong arms. She wanted to be where she was, but paradoxically she also wanted to be with all the other children who screamed delightedly and jumped on and off the rick-shifter like beads falling off a string. They were all lightweights, so they did not upset the balance. At hay-time the farmers "neighboured" as with any other harvest, so that children could visit several farms nearby during the short hay season and share in the pleasure. No child who knew the joy of it could ever forget the sheer bliss and happiness of riding the rick-shifter in hay-time.

When the farmyard was reached and the haystack wound down from its platter and the men in the hay-shed began to fork it neatly into place, the best time came. Now the rick-shifter was empty, and when Dandy had had a long cool drink from the water-trough in the yard, the return journey to the field to collect another haystack began. On to the smooth flat boards, as slippery as any ballroom floor, jumped the children, the older ones standing upright and balancing like skaters on an ice-rink as the wheels lurched over rough parts of the road, the little ones sitting down and keeping well into the middle, hands clasped round their knees, so that they would not slide off. No Lord Mayor's Show ever had a float which gave more pleasure than this old grey vehicle. No matter how many times it set out on its journey to the hay field, it always had a full complement of children and the driver never complained. He remembered when he had been a child and it had been his delight to do the same thing. Times changed little, and children's pleasures were still rooted in the same old simple ways. Sometimes he would warn them, "Mind you don't fall!" if an argument broke out amongst his passengers, but no one paid any attention. The sun was shining and the hay, the first harvest of the year, was good, and time stood goldenly still.

Haystacks at Salter's Castle Farm beside the ruins of Salter's Castle, c. 1930

Chapter 6

Neighbours

A short distance down the road lived the O'Donnells. Owen O'Donnell was a small farmer with a family of ten pale, fair-haired children who looked as though they had been brought up in the dark and had never seen the sun. They were all perfectly healthy and strong, with the exception of Geraldine. Geraldine was beautiful but delicate, with dark blue eyes and golden hair and the flushed cheeks of the tubercular child. She stayed closer to her mother than was normal for a child of seven, and when we went "down to the O'Donnells" which was almost every day, to play with any available members of that large brood, Geraldine did not often join in our games. "I'll just stay and watch Mammy," she would say. She stayed in the house and lay on a sofa in the kitchen, covered by a blue checked rug, watching the activities of the house with her delphinium eyes.

Mrs. O'Donnell, pale also, with fair hair pinned up in a knot on top of her head, plied her with little, tempting treats, a fresh egg warm from the nest, lightly boiled and served in a rose-pink cup with salt, pepper and butter, or a small round cake of fresh soda bread specially shaped for her and baked on the griddle at the end of the day's bread-baking session. This was split while still hot, lavishly buttered and sprinkled with crunchy sugar and handed lovingly on a flowery plate to Geraldine as she lay quietly by the fire. "Come on, pet," her mother would coax anxiously, "eat it for Mammy!" Sometimes her sisters would bring home the precious wild strawberries, carrying the grassy stalks on which they were threaded carefully and unstringing them into Geraldine's special little dish with the large "G" in gold on the bottom and blue flowers to match her eyes round the rim. This had been brought back by her mother from Portrush, when Mrs. O'Donnell had gone there on a rare day excursion the previous summer.

There was a red votive lamp forever burning in a corner of

the kitchen, and pictures of the Sacred Heart and the Pope looked down from the kitchen walls. The house was always clean and well kept and Mrs. O'Donnell worked hard for her large brood, but it was not easy when money was scarce. The welcome to all callers was warm and the children were happy and loved. Mrs. O'Donnell's tired anxious face, even when she smiled her slow sweet smile at us when we arrived, was tinged with sadness. I did not understand why, but the combination of not much money, endless pregnancies and a sick child to look after had made her an old woman. She must have been only in her late thirties, but she looked twenty years older. The struggle had begun for her a long time ago.

She had married Owen O'Donnell when she was twenty, a young lively, bright-eyed girl. Owen was ten years her senior and he had put off marriage, as so many Ulster farmers did then, until his parents were dead, not wanting to bring another woman into the house in his mother's lifetime. Owen lived with his elder brother Michael, who was almost stone deaf. Michael O'Donnell's deafness was the result of an illness he had had at age twelve and he had taught himself to lip-read, but none of his neighbours really believed that he could do this, and communicated with him by roaring at the pitch of their lungs, so that poor Michael was never able to conduct a conversation with any degree of privacy. He was unable to judge the volume of his own voice, and so anything he said outside his own house was heard by all the neighbours. He loved children, any children, and always kept a bag of toffees in his pocket to share with any child he met on the road.

Shortly after Mrs. O'Donnell had married Owen, a matter of weeks after the ceremony, she was standing one afternoon in the large kitchen baking the day's bread and busily casting a few grains of flour on the griddle to test its heat. The griddle hung from a hook supported by the iron crane over the open fire. Owen and Michael sat idly by, watching her supple and graceful movements as she turned from baking board to griddle and back again. It was a warm day outside, with soft rain drizzling down, and they could not get on with their work in the fields.

Suddenly a face appeared above the half-door which was shut to keep the hens out of the house. It was a young woman, beautiful and dark-eyed, her face swollen with crying. Her black hair hung damply round her shoulders where it had escaped from its mooring hairpins and in her arms she carried a small baby about three months old. Owen leapt to his feet as though he had been stung by a bee, looking guilty and nervous. Mrs. O'Donnell moved hospitably to the door, opening it and saying, "Come on in out of the rain. You'll be soaked to the skin and catch your death of cold, you and the wean."

"God save us, Bridie, what brings you here?" bleated Owen as the young woman came towards him.

"You know well what brings me, Owen, and may you never have a day's luck again. This is wee Sean, and you're his father, as well you know. Mammy and Daddy have put me out of the house, and I've nowhere to go. You'll have to rear the wee boy, for I can't, and it's breaking my heart. I'm going to England the morra morn with my brother Gerard to look for work, for if I stay here wee Sean and me'll both starve. You've ruined me, Owen O'Donnell."

Everyone in the kitchen was frozen into immobility, like a tableau vivant, for a few seconds. Bridie kissed the baby fiercely, her tears falling on his head as he stirred in the thin shawl he was wrapped in, saying, "Och, och, och, my wee man. Your own Mammy'll never see you again, but there's no other way, God help us both." She tried to hand him to Owen, who retreated behind his wife with his hands behind his back. Bridie stood for a minute, not knowing what move to make next, and then turned to Michael, who had been lip-reading during the whole scene and had assessed the situation accurately.

Now his eyes flashed and his face reddened with anger as he shouted, "Owen O'Donnell and Bridie McNab! God's curse on the both of you for what you've done to this child." His face softened as the baby, frightened by all the shouting, began to cry. "Give the wean to me," he said more gently, "I'll rear him. I'll look after him." He held out his arms.

Bridie hesitated, but only for an instant, kissed the baby for the last time, gave a loud heartbreaking cry of despair and grief and then placed him, crying loudly, in Michael's arms. She turned and ran weeping out of the door and down the road, leaving Owen opening and closing his mouth soundlessly like a goldfish and Mrs. O'Donnell holding on to the bakeboard in a state of shock

184

and swaying back and forth, repeating feverishly, "O Jesus, Mary and Joseph; Jesus, Mary and Joseph; O Holy Mary Mother of God, pray for us this day; O Sacred Heart of Jesus, have mercy on us all," in a monotonous litany and crossing herself as though her hand was being moved by clockwork. Owen collapsed into a chair and began to cry. The baby wailed on and Michael began to croon to him tunelessly but in a surprisingly soft tone, whereupon the small hands ceased to flail, the angry little face turned from magenta to scarlet, to pink. Michael looked into the face of the child with the expression of one who has seen a miracle.

It was a miracle for Michael, who had never had anyone to love. He brought the child up, loving him passionately and standing in the place of a father to him. But, try as he might, he was unable to shield young Sean from being slighted in that house. Even though Michael idolised him and did everything he could for him, Sean was forever a second-class citizen, never given his true place as one of the family. His presence was a constant reproach to Owen, reminding him of his premarital infidelity and the girl whose life he had ruined; and possibly Owen thought to ingratiate himself with his wife by ignoring Sean. Mrs. O'Donnell would have needed to be a saint to accept Sean into the family without protest, and while she was a good woman, she was not a saint. Her own children came first and young Sean had to do the hardest work with no reward.

When Sean was about eighteen, Michael came to see my uncle, and after a long discussion and much heart-searching it was decided that the best course for the young man was emigration. The United States was still considered to be the land of gold, despite the slump, and it was there that Sean went. Michael had somehow scraped together the money for his fare and he accompanied this child of his heart to Belfast on the first stage of the journey.

They came first to our house as they did not know Belfast well and had time to kill before the Liverpool boat sailed, the ship which would take Sean to England to catch the boat for New York. Mama made them welcome, as she did all travellers from her old home, putting a hot meal before them. Neither of them could eat, and they barely spoke. Mama sensed Michael's wild grief at parting from his surrogate child and Father offered to go down to the boat with them, as they did not know the way. It was arranged, upon Mama's insistence, that he would bring Michael back to spend the night, for the last bus home would have left an hour before.

Father and Michael came home after the boat had sailed, both of them shaken to the core, and Father needing a stiff whiskey to revive him. Michael, who was a Pioneer, therefore a teetotaller, had strong, sweet tea. Father told Mama that Michael had clasped Sean to his breast, not able to speak, but heaving huge, soundless sobs. He had pressed into Sean's hand his dearest possession, the Rosary beads his mother had given him the night she died. Sean had cried openly and Father had had to separate them just before the gangplank was taken up. At that Michael had given one loud despairing cry and the tears had run down his cheeks in torrents. Father, who was easily upset, cried too, and they stood there together on the quay watching the figure of Sean waving to them and growing smaller, fading away as the ship disappeared into the dusk. Michael turned to Father and said, sadly, "I'll never see him again, my good child. But it's best for him...best for him," and he wept again.

Sean made his way to Philadelphia, to the large Irish community there. All his life accustomed to hard work, he got a job with a building contractor. In later years he started up in business for himself and did well. He wrote often, sending presents to Michael and urging him to come out to Philadelphia where life was good and he would look after him, but Michael could never bring himself to make the journey to a new life. He said he was better at home, where everyone knew and understood him. He was right about never seeing Sean again. When the United States entered the Second World War, Sean volunteered to join the army. He was killed in Italy. When the news reached his old home a Requiem Mass was held for him in the small Catholic church he had attended as a child. All the neighbours, Protestant and Catholic alike, attended it, for they had liked Sean and they wished to show respect to the O'Donnells. All the O'Donnells went, except Michael who stayed at home. The local schoolteacher, a newcomer to the district, was cycling past the O'Donnell's house at the time of the Mass and saw Michael standing alone in the middle of the farm yard with his hands held high above his head, roaring his boundless grief to the Heavens.

Ned O'Neill lived in a small cottage between Uncle Sam's and the O'Donnells. Ned I think was born an old man; even Mama could not remember his being young, although she had known his mother. Ned's cottage was small but cosy. It was whitewashed and a pink rambling rose grew against the gable wall. The door stood open at all times and few passersby did not step inside to pass the time of day with Ned and sit for a while by the turf fire which burned brightly on the hearth before going on their way. Ned's chair faced the door and he sat peaceably smoking his pipe and ready to greet any callers who might happen along. During the day these were mainly children, or men on their way to the village on an errand, but in the evenings it was a gathering-place for farm labourers who were glad to have a comfortable chair and a fire at which to warm themselves after the day's work. They talked of this and that, neighbours who had emigrated, and always of days past. Sometimes they just sat gazing into the fire and thinking of what might have been, what might yet be and what could never be.

Ned was a widower. When I was very young I remember his wife Susan, who was Mrs. Murtagh's sister. Unlike Mrs. Murtagh, Susan had never had any children and devoted her life to Ned. She bustled round the cottage, a diminutive figure in a brown shawl, keeping everything clean and tidy. Although the cottage had two rooms, only one, the kitchen, was lived in. The other, the one which should have been a bedroom, was used for storing wood, turf and coal for the ever-burning fire in the kitchen, so that the firing would always be dry and not make the kitchen smoky.

The kitchen was used for everything, but it was arranged in such a way that it did not seem overcrowded. Round the fire were grouped three chairs, one for Ned, one for Susan and one for a visitor. Against the front window there was a small table on which stood a paraffin lamp with a yellowish-green vaseline glass shade. By the door was a dresser with shelves full of delft, mugs, bowls with blue rings, plates bearing a brown design and a few cups and saucers with gold rims which were kept for visitors like the priest or friends visiting from America. Two buckets of fresh drinking water, newly filled each day and covered with wooden lids, stood by the dresser.

Against the back window there was a larger table covered

with oilcloth in a bright pattern where Ned and Susan ate their meals, and a chair for each. On the walls were pictures of saints wearing haloes, a photograph of the Pope and a holy relic in a small glass box. A tiny votive lamp burned beside these and a wall clock ticked the seconds away, but as in Mrs. Murtagh's house, needlessly, for time did not really matter.

In pride of place, and dominating the room, was a large four-poster bed complete with curtains of dark green. I was enchanted by this and thought what a splendid arrangement it was not to have to go upstairs into a cold bedroom to undress at night.

How very convenient, I thought, when one felt tired, to undress by the warm fire and with one bound be in the cosy bed, against the snowy pillows, under the red and white patchwork quilt, the lamp turned out and the firelight twinkling against the whitewashed walls with an occasional cascade of sparks flying up the wide chimney as the turf shifted and collapsed in white ash. If one should happen to be feeling poorly, how pleasant to lie there in bed with all the familiar things in the house around and a constant stream of visitors to talk to.

Susan died and had a splendid wake and funeral, attended by all her friends and neighbours. Afterwards Ned lived on in the cottage by himself. The cottage belonged to the O'Donnells, for whom Ned had worked in his active years and with whom he had been friendly. For some reason they had a great falling-out and all communication between the cottage and the O'Donnell farm, which was just a stone's throw away, was severed. Michael, however, refused to countenance Ned's eviction from the small dwelling and continued his evening visits to the warm fireside. This friendship was never shaken and the two old men talked endlessly of their youth and how they had "sported". Again, they might dream their private dreams. At other times Michael's loud shouts could be heard from the road, and Ned was obliged to raise his voice, too, in the evening dusk before the lamp was lighted, so that Michael could hear him.

Decades ago Ned had had brothers and sisters, three of whom had gone skating one hard winter when there was ice on a nearby pond. The ice in the centre of the pond had been too thin to bear their weight and they were all drowned. When the three small bodies were carried home that January evening on a farm gate,

Ned's mother had been so distraught that she was unable to weep or even speak, and Mama had heard that her face had "turned black with grief". She did not live long after this disaster and soon joined her children in the small graveyard beside the chapel.

We spent many sunny afternoons in this graveyard reading the headstones among the long grass and wallowing in grief and sentimentality over the little dead children. We saw so many. "Mary Anne O'Hara, dearly loved infant daughter of Gerard and Anne O'Hara, aged eight months. R.I.P. A flower too fair for earth". "Edward Pius Higgins, beloved son of Thomas and Eileen Higgins, aged three years. God is Love. R.I.P". The one I lingered at was that of a young girl of fourteen. My cousins had known her and related to me time and again at my behest what she was like and how she had died of tuberculosis and how pretty she had been with her dark hair and brown eyes. Her last words had been, "Hold me in your arms, Daddy," and at this I always burst into tears and was drenched with sadness as I stood by the small marble angel which kept watch over her. "Till the day break" were the words on the stone, below her name. I put a few wild flowers at the angel's feet before leaving.

One summer there was a special grave to visit. Geraldine O'Donnell had died two months previously. Her mother had fought for her in vain, in spite of the fresh eggs in the pink cup and the other delicacies. When she died, Ned was sent for. At a time of death in a Catholic household there was a tradition that all differences of opinion must be settled and all feuds wiped out.

Geraldine had had a small white coffin, my cousins said. They had gone, as was the custom, to see her when she was dressed for burial, and they dwelt with loving detail upon her delicacy and beauty in death. She wore a long white dress and her golden hair was combed into ringlets and tied with a blue ribbon.

I cried bitterly when I heard all this, for Geraldine, gentle Geraldine who was dead and who I would never see again. Mrs. O'Donnell looked thinner when I saw her, and the empty sofa where the blue checked rug lay neatly folded into a square, drew my eye inexorably. She stopped for a minute in her bread-making, and seeing my glance, put her arms around me and said, "Geraldine's gone," and held me tightly. Not knowing what to say I put my arms round her waist and as we clung together we both cried for a moment or two. The she loosened her arms and returned to the wheaten bread on the griddle. Soon she was pregnant once more and her days dragged on again.

Chapter 7

At Aunt May's

After a couple of weeks at the farm it was time for me to continue my visits. Now I would move down over the hill to where a quarter of a mile away, lived Aunt May and her husband, Uncle Sam Garvin, together with Aunt Etta. I understood this house and felt at home in it, despite Aunt Etta's disruptive presence. Once more I was safe among elderly adults and I adjusted perfectly to their tempo and their routine. My cousins were afraid of the aunts here, but Uncle Sam was quiet and kind and spent most of his time in his garden and workshop.

He had been a farmer, but had retired some years before, and while I suppose he was happy in his way, he rarely escaped from the eagle eye of the womenfolk. He was known to enjoy a glass or two or whiskey and if he went to Magherafelt his times of departure and return were noted by Aunt Etta, who faithfully reported them to Aunt May. If she smelt alcohol on his breath when he came home Aunt Etta would hobble into Aunt May's bedroom where she was having an afternoon nap, full of the bad news and bursting to impart it where it would cause trouble. "He's drunk again! I knew it! I could have told you! You can't let him out of your sight!" she crowed. Poor Aunt May was stirred to fever pitch by this news, not because she objected to Uncle Sam having a drink but because she felt she had to justify him to her vinegary sister, so she upbraided him severely for his lapse and forbade him to go to "the town" for the next month. After this scolding he would sigh heavily, hang up his coat and retire to his workshop where, amongst his tools and treasured possessions, he would fall asleep, dreaming no doubt of how one day he would get the better of his sister-in-law.

Aunt May had been a teacher for so many years that she found retirement difficult, without the interest of school to fill her days. She discovered in the end that the best substitute for this was ill-health and thereafter she devoted herself to being a semi-

191

invalid, although she always appeared to be hale and hearty and had the appetite of a horse. She did have a "bad heart" and coasted along for years with this complaint which was always called into play when a crisis arose, or a situation which was not resolving itself to her satisfaction. Several times Mama received a telegram in the late evening saying, "Come at once. May very low." and had at great expense and inconvenience taken a taxi the whole way to Castledawson. She had taken charge of the sickroom in her usual efficient way, only to find next morning that Aunt May had bobbed up to the surface of life again, like a cork, while Mama was tired and exhausted after the long night's vigil. Aunt Sara was not often sent for when Aunt May was sick, as Aunt May confided to Mama once that, "Sara won't let me moan," in vexed tones.

One summer my parents took a house in Portballintrae and Aunt May came to stay. I, aged one and a half, and just toddling, was tottering around the garden unsteadily and approached her where she sat sunning herself in a deck chair. She had a bag of her favourite sweets, buttered brazils, on her lap, and unthinkingly she gave me one, kindly unwrapping it from its paper so that I might enjoy the sweet at once. Hardly had I put it in my mouth and toddled off when I tripped on a stone and fell down, whereupon the buttered brazil shot down my throat and stuck fast. Mama and Father were out visiting friends, and hearing me choke and seeing me turn a dark blue, Aunt May leapt from her supine position in the deck chair and began to pound me on the back, but to no avail. Try as she might she could not dislodge the sweet. Aggie, seeing all this from the kitchen window rushed out from the house thinking I was about to die, threw her apron over her head and started to weep loudly. Aunt May knew that if I did die she would never hear the end of it. In desperation she lifted me by my heels and shook me violently, the buttered brazil flew out of my mouth into a clump of dahlias. I recovered my usual smooth pink complexion and resumed my voyage of discovery round the garden, while Aunt May, finding all this excitement too much, promptly had what she called a heart attack. It was really a bad shock, and she had to be put to bed by Aggie and given a glass of brandy. It was days before she recovered and in the meantime Mama vacillated between sympathy for her sister's illness and fury at the fact that she had nearly caused my death.

Uncle Sam had a green thumb and kept a garden which was the envy of everyone and was his pride and joy. At the front of the house he had a large rock garden which was divided into small rock-beds by tiny crazy-paved paths, just right for children to play "tig" round. They curved and crisscrossed and wove at the end to a point. Two roads – the Old Road and the New Line – joined at this point, so that anyone who passed on the way to Magherafelt could not go unobserved by my aunts. In spring the rock-garden was a mass of colour and became a landmark. Uncle Sam spent hours on his knees weeding it and keeping it trim – as much as anything to keep out of Aunt Etta's way.

At the back of the house he had a vegetable garden where he grew enough potatoes for the needs of the household. Peas, beans, spring cabbage which was called pamphrey, broccoli, onions, leeks, celery, brussels sprouts were grown and what seemed a vast amount of parsley. Always, and surprisingly, among the rigs of peas and beans he planted a rig of sweet pea, and in summer its pretty scented flowers of all colours cascaded riotously among the vegetables.

As well as all these vegetables he grew soft fruit, black-currants, red-currants, white-currants and raspberries, red and yellow, as well as gooseberries. I have not tasted yellow raspberries since those days, but I can still recall their sweet ripeness, not really a true raspberry flavour at all, but delicious when picked from the canes on a warm sunny day and eaten on the spot. Cream and sugar would have been superfluous. Uncle Sam also grew strawberries, but in spite of his constant attention to them and his assiduous placing of small straw mats to protect the berries from the earth and its insects, he never had a large crop. Every year he tried to improve the strawberry harvest, but it remained his one failure.

All this fruit meant that almost the entire summer, from the end of June onwards, was spent in making jam. Uncle Sam was the jam-maker here and hovered over his cauldrons of fruit and sugar with the air of an alchemist. Mama and her sisters never made less than fifty pounds of each kind of jam every year, so that they would have a surplus to give away to their friends.

Aunt May, who had not married until she was fifty-two and therefore had no children, failed to understand that it was not obligatory for her to have two hundred fresh pots of jam on her shelves each season. No matter how many jars she gave away to family, friends and visitors, all the jam used in her house was at least three years old, with lumps of sugar which had crystallised in the keeping, scattered throughout the jar. I hated this, as it meant one was in danger of crunching down upon a piece of this candied sugar just when one expected to bite upon a delicious piece of fruit. But still the jam making went on and the scent of boiling fruit and sugar hung in the air outside the little house every summer.

When the shelves began to buckle in the middle with the weight of preserves, and the new season's crop of fruit was being processed, the old jam was used with great abandon. Each morning a two-pound jar was produced, the grease-proof paper cover ripped off, the inside waxed circle which covered the jam removed, and then, more often than not, a rich winey odour pervaded the kitchen, making the whole place smell like a brewery. If the fermentation was too pronounced the jar was emptied on the compost heap, but if the smell was only faint and there was only a slight amount of mould on top of the jar, this was scooped out and thrown away. We then ate the rest of it on bread, on milk puddings which we had every day in some form, or perhaps on the upside-down cake which Aunt Etta had made for tea.

Mealtimes were strange and frequent here. We breakfasted, no two of us together, as and when we arose. Later we gathered round the kitchen table for ten o'clock tea in the morning, which meant tea, fresh bread and butter, the ubiquitous jam and perhaps a plate of plain biscuits – usually digestives. Midday dinner was eaten at twelve and consisted of two courses, stew or meat of some kind and then milk pudding, rice, sago, tapioca or semolina – with jam – topped off with a cup of tea and a piece of Aunt Etta's shortbread.

Tea, at two in the afternoon, consisted of tea, freshly made scones or pancakes with butter and again the jam du jour, but now we also had a newly baked cake. Aunt Etta spent part of each day baking, which, apart from embroidery, was her only form of creativity, and she produced from the Valor oil stove with its smoke-coloured translucent door and its two oil burners, not only bread and scones, but cakes of all descriptions. She took the People's Friend, a religious paper, every week, and sometimes tried out the recipes printed in the cookery pages.

At six o'clock we had supper, which was really high tea, with fried bacon and eggs and potato bread, soda and wheaten bread baked on the griddle or in the Valor, jam again – and by this time no one wanted any – and cake left over from tea.

At nine, just before bedtime – for everyone in this house, as they said "clocked up early" and I kept the same hours as the adults – we sat round the kitchen table yet again, this time to eat plates of freshly made porridge to sustain us against the approaching night's fast. Aunt May and Aunt Etta had cups of Ovaltine to wash it down and Uncle Sam drank a strong brew of cocoa laden with sugar. I was offered a choice of these and Horlicks was suggested, but I usually opted for a glass of milk. Milk was collected from the farm up the road by Uncle Sam, in a white enamel can with a navy blue lid and a wire handle to swing it by. He made the twice daily pilgrimage – almost his only outings – to collect the milk after the morning and evening milkings. He rarely went in to see Aunt Mary in case Uncle Sam Davison was there, as they did not get on very well together.

My milk was always served in a real glass, for Aunt May had a strict sense of propriety and a cup of milk was not quite the thing in her view. I even had a special glass. This had a pale yellowish tint at the bottom and widened at the top where a thumb-print design was pressed into it round the rim, and the glass itself took on a milky blue transparent look. It was kept in a special place on the pantry shelf beside the cups which were in daily use, and was known as "Hilary's glass" to the irritation of Aunt Etta who, in her dislike of me and thinking me a pampered child, frequently tried to palm me off with a plain Woolworth tumbler. I, however, had a favoured place in Aunt May's affections. I was called after her, so she never allowed this substitution and would quietly replace the cheap glass with the right one.

When the supper had been cleared away we sat round the table again for a short time in the lamplight. Aunt May would perhaps darn some socks, Aunt Etta worked on her coloured embroidery – usually a tea-cloth with a crinoline lady embroidered in each corner – while I played with a small puzzle or toy and

Uncle Sam Garvin would put on his glasses and read aloud from that morning's paper if it had not already been sent up to the farm for Uncle Sam Davison's perusal, or the latest copy of the Mid-Ulster Mail, locally know as the Mid, which contained all the news of the neighbourhood in great detail.

Uncle Sam wore his glasses perched on the end of his nose, and they often fell to the ground when he dozed off after reading. Even if they broke it did not matter greatly, for he always had a spare pair or two in his dressing table drawer. These spectacles, which Mama bought for him in Woolworths in Belfast, were ordinary magnifying glasses with imitation tortoise-shell rims. They cost sixpence a pair. Frequently Mama would receive a letter from Aunt May in her beautiful copperplate handwriting giving her the family news and ending with the words, "Please send Sam two new pairs of glasses. Money enclosed. He likes the dark-coloured rims best." The next time Mama went to town she did as requested and posted off the spectacles wrapped in a piece of corrugated cardboard underneath the brown paper wrapping, to prevent breakage.

Sunday meals were slightly more elaborate, and poached eggs replaced the usual boiled ones at breakfast. Michael O'Donnell was a regular visitor on his way home from Mass and joined us at ten o'clock tea, shouting all the local news and gossip at my aunts as he ate. Dinner, always roast beef and then jelly and tinned fruit, which was considered to be a great treat, was not set out until two on Sundays, because of Meeting being at midday. Neither of the aunts attended, for the distance was too great for them to walk. Uncle Sam Garvin was Church of Ireland, which Aunt May felt was a pity but could not be helped, and he did not go to church either. However, the gesture was made. No meals were eaten while Divine Service was in progress.

Tea on Sundays was at four, and frequently there were visitors, who might come unannounced, so everything had to be prepared in case of such an eventuality. Tea would be laid on the dining room table which was decked in a white linen cloth with embroidery and mitred edges which had been worked by Aunt May in her young days. Aunt Etta's Saturday baking was enjoyed and praised by everyone so that she felt all her efforts had been worthwhile. Supper, after the visitors had gone, was at seven, a lighter meal than on weekdays. At nine o'clock, instead of porridge, we had bowls of eggy rice pudding studded with raisins and served with a large jug of creamy milk.

In the spare room, where I slept, there was dark oak furniture. A print of "The Thin Red Line" hung over the fireplace, and I could almost smell the smoke of battle when I looked at it. There was also a picture of a father and mother bending over the cot of their child with the caption "More to be Desired than Gold". I did not know what this meant and thought nothing could be more desirable than gold and that in any case they looked as though they were sickening for something.

Aunt May's bathroom was minute, but remarkable in that it was there at all, as bathrooms were not by any means common in the country. Water had to be pumped by hand for use in them and this chore fell to Uncle Sam, who groaned every time he heard anyone flush the lavatory.

A large medicine chest hung on the wall and I spent many idle hours poring over its contents, although I had been warned on pain of death that none of the bottles in it must be opened.

There were bottles of red pills and bottles of black pills and small round black cardboard boxes with white rims containing white pills of varying sizes, some like little round balls and others of the normal flat shape. There were patent medicines of all kinds too, mainly laxatives, for like most elderly people the Aunts and Uncle Sam were much obsessed by the inactivity of their bowels. They almost never drank water, which probably accounted for this state of affairs. Most of the bottles and boxes bore either the name of "Badger" or that of "Flatley", both chemists in Magherafelt. Aunt May patronised both establishments, but for anything really esoteric she sometimes had to send a message to Mama, who bought whatever was needed in Grattans the Chemists in Cornmarket, Belfast. Every medicament imaginable could be bought in Grattans, which was the crème de la crème of chemists, or so Mama and the Aunts thought.

The things which interested me most in Aunt May's bathroom were, firstly, a bottle labelled "Eeel Oil" in her beautiful lettering. She must have had a moment of mental aberration as she wrote this, for she was an excellent speller, but the label with the three "E's" remained on the bottle until she died. Oil from Lough

Neagh eels was saved carefully for it was reputed to have wonderful powers to cure sprains or strains. In another jar with a tightly screwed lid on top was the skin of an eel, dried and rolled up carefully if anyone should have the misfortune to sustain a broken wrist or ankle, the break would be wound round with the eel-skin and would soon mend. A third jar bore the legend "Goose Seam" and this was the rendered down fat from inside a goose. It had a horrible stench but was used to treat muscle pains, when it was well rubbed in and the sufferer was careful not to sit near the fire, as the aroma grew stronger in the heat. Aunt May believed in keeping all her options open – as well as her bowels – and paid lip service to folk cures as well as patent medicines and doctors' prescriptions.

Visitors to Aunt May's were many and brought news to brighten her days. Sometimes former pupils would call to ask her advice, to tell her how they were progressing and what they had decided to do in life. The pupils she had taught in her younger days all looked to me like elderly men and women, and exceedingly staid and dull at that, while the children she had taught in Senior Infants class in her later years were at school-leaving age. Many intended to emigrate, for they could see no future at home, and they came to say goodbye. Aunt May had probably also taught their parents and knew, as she said, "...all about them – seed, breed and generation." She was always glad to see them and was touched that they remembered her. Sometimes as they drank the tea and ate the cakes which were always produced, no matter what time of day it was, she would disappear from the room for a few minutes and then return again to preside over the silver teapot which had been a wedding present to her from her pupils of that time. As the young visitors said goodbye in the hall she would press a pound note into their hands with a whispered, "Say nothing!" and a nod towards the sitting room where Aunt Etta sat like a malevolent spirit. There would be tears in her eyes as she waved them off from the gate, but she hated to think we noticed and would brusquely ask me and any other child around to clear the tea dishes and take them into the kitchen.

Old fellow-teachers came to see her sometimes and they spent hours remembering the days of their training in Marlborough Street in Dublin at the college there and pondering on what had happened to some of their fellow students. School inspectors of that time were talked about, their quirks and foibles sending the discussion group into gales of laughter.

The doctor came often. He came to take Aunt May's blood pressure and sound her heart and generally keep an eye on her health. This doctor was tall and thin and wore a tweed suit. He greatly admired the cut glass which she kept in her sideboard cupboard. He was usually given a nip of whiskey when the examination was over, and Aunt May tried to arrange that when this happened Uncle Sam was not in the house, but either fetching the milk or working in his garden so that she did not have to include him in the treat which might, she felt, "set him off" once more.

Time went on and on each visit the doctor grew more and more effusive in his praise of the cut glass tumblers. One day Aunt May parcelled them up in white tissue paper and gave them to him. Aunt Etta and Uncle Sam were beside themselves with rage when they discovered this, for the doctor's bills were known to be large and were sent in regularly. He was very different, the whole countryside mourned, from his predecessor, "the Old Doctor", who had practised in that district for as long as anyone could remember, and beside whom, it was felt, all doctors from Hippocrates onwards paled into nothingness. Old Dr. Thompson had held the lives of the people in his hands and had seen each family in the district through every crisis which could be imagined and many which could not.

He rode around in a large black car when I remember him in his last years, but before that he had had a large trap drawn by a spirited horse. He did not drive it himself, but had a driver who looked after the horse while the doctor made his visits. The two men would set out in all weathers and at any hour of the day or night if word came that the doctor was needed. It did not matter how poor the family was or that his bill had not been paid perhaps for years. When the need was there so was the doctor.

Tales were told and retold of the relief in a house with a sick child or a woman in labour when the wheels of the doctor's trap were heard in the yard, and if as often happened the weather was cold and wet and the night was dark, the door of the house would be thrown open so that the light would shine out and someone would rush with a lantern to open the stable door so that the horse would have shelter and warmth and a rubdown by his driver before he, too, made his way into the warm kitchen where the doctor would have thrown off his oilskins before going to the patients's bedside. Dr. Thompson seemed to have a special affinity with children, coaxing them back to health if they were only mildly ill, but seeming bodily to drag them back from the edge of the grave if their illnesses were severe.

Mama remembered him weeping when Aunt Mary's first child was born and found to be hydrocephalic. It had been a long labour and a difficult birth and he had used all his skill and experience to produce this child alive. When he saw it, as Mama described it, ". . . a beautiful little girl, but with a swelling on her head the size of an orange...," it was almost more than he could bear. The child died within a week of its birth and the doctor, when he came to the house at the time, thanked God, which mightily relieved the feelings of everyone else.

During his absence from home one day, at a wedding, a call came for him to visit a child in the village who, in the irritating way children have, had pushed a dried pea up one of his nostrils. No one realised for a time that he had done this, and as he was very young he could not tell them, but suddenly his breathing became difficult and other symptoms became alarmingly apparent. Distraught, his parents sent for the doctor, only to find he was away. Then they sent for another doctor – a vastly inferior specimen, everyone agreed – who lived some distance away. He tried everything he knew to dislodge the pea, which by now had swollen in its warm, damp nest, but only succeeded in pushing it further up. The child was now in considerable pain and after much deliberation the family decided that a specialist – the name at that time for a consultant – should be sent for from Belfast. This specialist would have to make the journey by train or car at vast expense. However, so frightened were the parents by this time that expense did not enter into the question at all. The eminent doctor made the journey, examined the child and then said in lofty tones that of course he could do nothing there and the child must be brought to hospital in Belfast, where he would have to be operated on immediately. Panic ensued and the minister was called in to see if perhaps the power of prayer could intervene between the child and the knife.

Just as the excitement was at its height, the child red-faced and in pain and the mother hysterical, the Old Doctor appeared on the scene, still dressed in his wedding clothes. His white hair which flowed to his shoulders and made him look like a Biblical prophet was dishevelled because of his haste. Greeting the other two doctors monosyllabically, he drew the child to the window, peered up its blocked nostril and called to the mother, "Bring me the pepper-pot!" She thought he had taken leave of his senses, but in a daze she took the pepper-pot from its shelf and handed it to him. He shook some pepper into the palm of his hand, covered the child's eyes and blew the pepper up his nose, whereupon with an almighty sneeze the little boy dislodged the pea which fell into the doctor's hand. Calling for soap and water to wash his hands, Dr. Thompson bade them all a quick farewell and left the other two doctors standing open-mouthed and discomfited.

In his last years he continued to practise, with the back seat of his car made into a sort of bed where he could recline as he was driven on his rounds. He still had long, white hair, and this was his dear eccentricity, it was thought, his trademark. Then one of his daughters was to be married and he was to give the bride away. The excitement in the district was great. The wedding of the Old Doctor's daughter interested everyone, for most of them had watched her grow up, and the church was packed to overflowing. The bride, wearing white satin and a long white veil, carried the traditional bouquet of arum lilies. She and her escort were halfway up the aisle to the tune of the Wedding March when the onlookers gave a gasp of disbelief. They were shocked to see her on the arm of a stranger. Then realisation dawned. It was the Old Doctor himself, but with short hair! The congregation felt as though this latter-day Samson had been betrayed, not by Delilah this time, but by convention and his daughter's reluctance to walk up the aisle with someone who looked like Old Father Time.

When he died it was like the end of the world. The practice of medicine in the district became mundane and the patients could never again rest secure in the knowledge that the doctor cared enough for them to do battle against death itself.

Farm Hill: Hilary's mother, maternal grandmother Martha Davison and uncle Joseph Davison on leave in his Anzac army uniform c. 1916

Chapter 8

Grandma Martha

Mama's mother, Grandma Martha, was an intelligent and strong-willed woman. When her children were young things were difficult and money was scarce, so she decided that only some of her ten children, six boys and four girls, could be educated past primary school stage. She selected one son who showed promise and sent him to the Rainey School in Magherafelt, and he eventually emigrated, becoming a pharmacist in Chicago. Two daughters were sent off to teacher training college, one to Dublin and the other to Edinburgh. Grandma was anxious that Mama should also become a teacher, for she felt strongly that women should be independent and be able to earn their own living, but Mama decided that teaching in a country school for the rest of her life was not what she wanted, and she elected instead to become a nurse.

Nurses were not accepted for training until the age of twenty, so she had to wait a few years when she finished school. She whiled away the time by assisting Aunt May, who was teaching in the village of Tobermore, a few miles away, travelling there and back in a small trap drawn by a white pony called Snowball. Aunt May was glad of Mama's company, for she was young and was afraid of some of the larger boys in the school who were bigger than she was. In photographs of the large family taken around that time, in the 1890s, I see Aunt May looking rather stern, and Mama seems gentle and soft-featured, with kind eyes and dark wavy hair.

Aunt Sara was Mama's second sister. She became a teacher in the village of Coagh, near Cookstown, County Tyrone, before marrying her second cousin, a kind man some years older than her.

My other aunt was Aunt Etta. She was insanely jealous of Mama and was not my favourite aunt. I was not her favourite niece, and from earliest days I regarded her warily, knowing she would make trouble for me if she could. She adored a cousin of mine, Uncle Sam's eldest daughter who was six months my junior, and she resented me greatly as she felt me to be in some way a threat to this child – for no good reason as we lived thirty miles apart and only saw each other during the holidays.

Aunt Etta had had poliomyelitis, then called infantile paralysis, as a young child, and amazingly enough, and entirely due to Grandma Martha's tenacity and determination not to lose any of her ten children, she survived, but her feet were deformed by the illness and she had to wear surgical boots and long skirts to hide them for the rest of her life.

Mama and her sisters, May and Sara, had a great love for, and rapport with, each other. Etta could have been happy with them, too, but chose to be otherwise. Her carping, lacerating tongue was dreaded and they shrank from listening to her caustic comments about them, their children (in the case of Mama and Aunt Sara), their husbands (in the case of Mama and Aunt May) and most of all about the way they chose to live their lives without asking her opinion or consent. If they had any small occasion for rejoicing, the pleasure was taken out of it by Aunt Etta when it came to her ears. Her remarks had the same effect on the spirit as a spoonful of unsweetened rhubarb in the mouth. I suppose she could not help it, and she must have been embittered by the effects of her early illness, but it was hard for the family to accept this irritating woman in their midst. Uncle Sam, after she had subjected him to a particularly wounding tirade, rolled his eyes heavenwards and said, to her departing back, "I know everyone has their cross to bear, but ours is made out of barbed wire."

Mama and Aunt Etta were especially at loggerheads. Mama, in her young days, was pretty and jolly and always in demand. Later, much later, when she married, Aunt Etta was displeased. She was displeased because she did not like my father, who in turn heartily detested her. She was then displeased because she felt that her sister Anna was having a gay time in what she felt were the bright lights of Belfast, and that she, Etta, should be at hand to criticise and bring her down to earth from time to time.

Mama's irritation was much inflamed on one occasion when, thinking to please her family, she brought with her on a visit home a quantity of first class daffodil bulbs. These, she suggested, might be planted in Grandma's garden in the grass under the trees, and arranged to spell out the names of members of the family. Aunt

Etta, who had special responsibility for the flower garden, made no reply to this suggestion, but went up to sit in the autumn sunshine in the little summer-seat cunningly set into a hawthorn hedge which formed an arch round it. After a time and much consideration she returned to the house and ordered Uncle Sam to carry the sack of bulbs up to the garden. No one thought any more of the project and the matter of the daffodils was forgotten.

Next spring, round about Easter, which was late, imagine everyone's surprise to find that Aunt Etta had indeed planted the bulbs. Not only that, but she had actually planted them as Mama had wished, marking out names of the family on the grassy slope under a William pear tree. First she had made the name E T T A, then came M A Y, then S A M. The final one, and the coup de grace, was A N A. Etta had realised that she could not leave out the donor of the daffodils, yet she did not wish to honour her, so, having used up most of the bulbs on the first three names, her own first and foremost, she planted the barb by perpetuating her sister's name wrongly spelled and thereby diminished.

Mama never forgave her. She laughed about it afterwards, but it rankled, for she knew it had been done to hurt her. The names are still there, spelled out in yellow daffodils every springtime after all the years. E T T A, M A Y, S A M, A N A.

The pattern of Ulster life then was for one son to inherit the farm and support his parents in their failing years, and provide any unmarried sisters with a roof over their heads. This often meant the kiss of death to any marriage plans he might have.

If he did marry, his new wife was forced to accommodate herself to the whims of his family. Purgatory would have been preferable, and yet this situation had to be accepted by countless women who could not escape from their own homes in any other way, and who were at least spared the ignominy of spinsterhood and near-slavery when their own brothers married and took over the family home. Once a woman married, her status in the community was instantly raised. Right up until her wedding day she was known and called by her Christian name by everyone, but the day she walked back down the aisle as a married woman she was instantly transformed into "Mrs. So-and-So" by the same people who the previous day had greeted her as "Mary" or whatever her name was.

Uncle Sam Davison married Aunt Mary, a gentle, doe-eyed woman quite unfitted to stand up to Aunt Etta's tirades of temper and black looks. Uncle Sam took little interest in the quarrels of his womenfolk. He worked on the farm with Tommy, the servant-man's help, but the world of local committees and politics was his great interest. He was a member of the local Rural District Council and a Poor Law Guardian, a Freemason and an Orangeman. He kept up with all the political news by reading the Belfast Newsletter right through as soon as it arrived from Aunt May's in the evening. Every cell of his body oozed True Blue Unionism, although he was on the friendliest terms with his Catholic, therefore Nationalist, neighbours.

Uncle Sam and Aunt Mary had six children in quick succession, all but the first surviving, and after the second was born Aunt Etta packed her things and left, fearing that she might be required to do too much for the infants. Aunt Mary must have heaved a great sigh of relief at this, but her sister-in-law did not go far away and was still able to note and comment with acerbity on all the doings at the farm. She went to live with Aunt May and Uncle Sam Garvin, and from that time onwards she succeeded in all her endeavours to make life difficult for this unfortunate pair until she died some twenty years later.

Her death, when it happened, caused little grief and much relief. Aunt May had been ill, as she so often was, and the doctor was in regular attendance. Seeking, as always, her share of attention, Aunt Etta took to her bed with a slight head cold. She complained that she could not sleep, and the doctor, a young man from a neighbouring practice who was standing in for the usual doctor who had gone on holiday, left a sedative for her. A local practical nurse, who was looking after Aunt May, administered the dose which had been left, and next morning Aunt Etta was, as Mama put it, "in Kingdom Come."

Great ripples of shock and excitement went through all branches of the family at this occurrence, but no post-mortem was held, and it was all smoothed over because Aunt May was ill and no one wanted to upset her, and besides they all felt that Etta had got her final comeuppance for crying "Wolf" over all the past years. The only thing which upset Aunt May was the fact that when Aunt Etta was laid out the undertaker forgot to put her false teeth in place, which did not improve her appearance.

Grandma Martha had not had an easy life, her mother having died when she was very young. Her father, my great-grandfather Thomas Duff, had remarried and provided his children, two boys and two girls, with a stepmother who mistreated them. The boys were kept at home because they were needed to help with the work of the small farm, but the girls, Martha and Sarah, were swept up and carried off by a maiden aunt who lived some miles away at a place called The Flush when she saw their great unhappiness. The children grew up there happily enough, but deprived of the company of their father and brothers. Their devotion to each other, however, remained constant all their lives.

Grandpa William in his youth had enlisted in the British Army, joining the Queen's Own Life Guards. Apparently he looked wonderful – six feet two and handsome – in the uniform and enjoyed army life. His great claim to fame was that once, when on duty in Buckingham Palace, he saw the Kaiser smoking in a corridor after sunset. This was forbidden by express order of Queen Victoria and Grandpa knew it. Up he stepped and asked the Kaiser to extinguish his cigar. Caught by surprise at Grandpa's temerity the Kaiser did as he was asked, giving Grandpa a cigar to mark the occasion. Whether he smoked it or not I do not know, but the story passed into family legend, and was really Grandpa's only claim to fame. Shortly afterwards Grandpa's stepfather died and his mother, Great-Grandma Henrietta "bought" him out of the army because she needed him at home to run the farm.

Grandma Martha and Grandpa William married after a courtship of six weeks, just after he came home from the army. Grandma, after the wedding, at which she wore a pearl-grey dress and bonnet and carried a posy of pink moss-roses which grew in her aunt's garden, came home to live with her new husband and mother-in-law.

Grandma Martha was small and blue-eyed, with brown curly hair and a sweet smile, and doubtless using these wiles she soon made it clear to Grandpa that all decisions during their married life would be made by her. He, who had grown up with a domineering mother and had survived a spell in the British Army, accepted this edict and settled down happily with Martha, whom he adored, and his children.

This mother-in-law, Great-Grandma Henrietta, was not perhaps the easiest person in the world with whom to set up housekeeping. She was a strong-minded woman who had made the best of many a difficult situation. Her first husband, Great-Grandpa Robert, had had a farm at Bellaghy. When his children were young he fell ill and his doctor, according to medical practice at the time, decided to bleed him. He opened a vein in Great-Grandpa's arm, and when the bleeding had started satisfactorily, he went into the kitchen "to talk to the womenfolk" it is said. The talk must have been long and interesting, for shortly afterwards Mary, the eldest child who was then aged thirteen, went into the bedroom and found her father dying "with his arm in blood on the bed". History does not relate the recriminations which must have taken place when the doctor was taxed, as he surely was, with negligence. Fortunately Great-Grandma, who was herself a "healer" in that she made up herbal cures and curative ointments for skin and other ailments and was always sent for by her neighbours when anyone fell ill, was made of strong stuff. She had a backbone of steel and she survived the tragedy, caring for her five children which was not an easy task for a widow left in those circumstances at that time.

Gathering her brood together, within a short time she married a man called Joseph Waugh and moved to his farm between Castledawson and Magherafelt. There were no children of this second marriage, and Joseph had not been married before, so the farm passed in the end to Henrietta's son William, who was my Grandfather. His elder brother Martin, having fought in the Crimea and lost an arm there had emigrated to New Zealand and his sister Mary had married. Jane, his younger sister, died young and Robert, his other brother, had married Sarah Little, a sister of the dear aunts and uncles who lived next door to us in Belfast, and lived in Stewartstown, where he conducted a prosperous business.

When Grandpa brought Grandma home as a bride, Henrietta was not elated. Although she liked the young Martha well enough and recognised that William needed a wife, and she believed that Martha would make a good wife and mother, she recognised that she, too, had a will like cast iron. Henrietta resented any threat or challenge to her own authority in the house. Her premonitions were well founded, and the two women were set on a collision course from the start.

Thursday was market day in Magherafelt and Henrietta was accustomed to driving there in a trap drawn by a grey pony called Diamond, to sell her butter and eggs, the traditional perquisite of every farmer's wife and the only cash money she was ever likely to handle. Honeymoons were not common among small farmers, who did not hold with spending money unnecessarily and contented themselves with a large party for their neighbours and friends on the night of the wedding. The Thursday morning after the wedding Henrietta dressed herself as usual in her bonnet and tippet, black as became a widow, and appeared in the kitchen, ready to board the trap which stood ready in the yard, Diamond's reins being hitched to a convenient hook on the wall. Grandpa, however, blocked her way.

"Out of the way, William," said his mother in matter-of-fact tones. "I'm late for market already."

Grandpa stood with his tall figure between her and the door. "You won't be going to market today, Mother," he said. "Martha is my wife. She is the mistress here now, and she will go to market."

Henrietta's face turned to stone. She did not reply, but turned on her heel and went back to her bedroom. She did not reappear for two whole days. Grandma Martha, meanwhile, dressed for the occasion, adjusted her bonnet, stepped lightly into the trap, blew a kiss to Grandpa, took Diamond's reins in her hands and drove off, her first victory achieved without any effort on her own part.

On her return she was wise enough to bring her mother-in-law a present, a Paisley shawl, very soft and fine, the best that Grandma could find in Magherafelt. It had cost a great deal of money, but it was worth it. This shawl was not only a present, but a silent message. It was time now for Henrietta to step back from the action and sit with her shawl around her shoulders. In short, she must take a back seat. This must have been a bitter pill for her to swallow, but it was the pattern of life and of the time, and she had to come to terms with it if life were to be bearable in the house. At least, she felt, William would have someone to look after him when she was dead. In the end she was kept exceedingly busy, as Martha and William produced ten children and Henrietta helped to look after the first six.

Mama was the seventh child, born in December 1878 and, it was said, she developed whooping cough when she was only a few days old. I doubt that it was really whooping cough at such an early age, but she was certainly very ill. She was so ill that when Henrietta, who had been ailing for some months, died, William and Martha seriously considered postponing the funeral for a few days so that the baby Anna Martha could be buried at the same time. Mama, however, had inherited her grandmother's strong constitution and lived on. Henrietta was borne to her grave in solitude and life on the farm returned to normal.

Martha was an indomitable woman. In times when it was rare not to find a few "infants, who died young" marked up on family tombstones, she brought up all of her ten children in good health, with the exception of Aunt Etta's bout with poliomyelitis. Martha had seen this killer disease before and had never known anyone to survive it. She prepared for battle. As her child grew weaker and more feverish and approached death, she sent to Belfast for ice. I do not know how the ice was transported, for unlike Caesar who had relays of runners bearing ice from the Alps to cool his wine, her resources were limited, but she did not let that stop her. I seem to remember Mama saying that she had heard that it had arrived "wrapped in straw". It must have been sent by train to Castledawson where it was probably collected by Grandpa in the farm cart. The ice was then broken up and put in makeshift ice bags round the dying child to break the fever.

The life of the farm ground to a halt as Martha waged her private war with God. Neighbours took over the daily chores, baking the bread and looking after the children. The doctor came twice a day and departed after each visit shaking his head as much in amazement at Martha's tenacity as in his fears for Etta's life. He was wrong. God must have dozed off or had His attention distracted for a split second, and in that time Martha dragged her child back into life just as the Pearly Gates were about to slam shut with Etta inside. God had underestimated Martha Davison and when he saw what had happened, yielded to a worthy adversary.

Grandma loved a challenge. I remember, once, meeting an old man who shook my hand and told me, gravely, "Your grandmother saved my life," and went on to relate how, as a young boy, he went to Castledawson to visit his bachelor brother who was the Presbyterian minister there.

One day he and his brother were out walking and called to see Grandma and Grandpa. The boy, George, looked unwell, so Grandma Martha felt his forehead and decided that he was feverish and must go to bed at once. No, she said, to his brother's mild suggestion that they should go home first, he could not go back to the manse where there was no one to look after him – for the minister was not married. "You'll stay here and I'll nurse you," she told the young George, who truth to tell was feeling queasier and more peaky by the minute. His brother had his sermon to write for the following Sunday, she said, and besides that the manse housekeeper was a slut and a bad cook – in short, a clart. The minister knew when he was beaten and thankfully gave in to Grandma's steamroller tactics. Grandma could never have been a Quaker, for friendly persuasion was not her way. She believed in laying down the law at the start and seeing that it was acted on instantly. George must stay with her, she decreed, and be nursed back to health, hopefully before Sunday, so that he could attend Meeting and sit in the minister's pew where he could be admired, fully restored, by the rest of the congregation.

Grandma's plans and hopes were dashed, but not completely. George grew sicker and she was forced to send for the doctor, who diagnosed typhoid fever. Here was a challenge indeed. Typhoid! People died of this, she knew, but she brushed this thought aside as she would a marauding mosquito, and installed George in the little bedroom off the dining room at the end of the long cold passage leading from the kitchen. A sheet was wrung out in carbolic and hung over the dining room door. All the family were warned, on pain of death, or – worse still – Grandma's wrath – not to go beyond it. Behind the sheet, beyond the dining room, in the little bedroom, Grandma Martha duelled once more with death. Needless to say, she won. The minister liked to think that perhaps the fact that he and the congregation had offered up special prayers to the Almighty for George's recovery had helped. Grandma knew that it was her nursing through the long days and sleepless nights which had turned the tide for George. God might have helped a little, she reluctantly allowed, but mostly it had been Grandma Martha.

During the first World War my Uncle Joe, who had

emigrated to New Zealand and had later joined the army to fight with the Anzacs at Gallipoli and at the Somme, came "home", for it was always "home" to all its scattered children, to see his parents. When he left to go back to the trenches in France, Mama and Father were at the farm. Father told me that it was heartbreaking when Uncle Joe held his mother in his arms and kissed her goodbye and was then driven off in the trap to the station by Grandpa and Uncle Sam, to see Grandma Martha, small but ramrod-straight, waving them off, her head high and a smile on her lips. As soon as the trap crested the hill and disappeared from sight Father said that Grandma Martha threw her black apron over her head and wept, crying aloud, "My last-born, my last-born . . . " She felt that she would not see him again, but a year later, when she was dying, he was granted compassionate leave from his regiment and sat by her bedside, holding her hand in his as she passed away.

Father always cried when he told this story, and so did Mama, no matter how many times he told it, for they were both tender-hearted and they had never seen this small, great-hearted woman weep like this before. Now, when I tell this story to my own children I find the tears rising in my eyes, though it happened six years before I was born.

Grandpa's brother Robert died before I was born. He was a forthright character, with much more get-up-and-go than Grandpa. He was a Liberal, while Grandpa was a staunch Conservative, and at election times Grandpa, who owned a small property in Stewartstown, hitched up the pony and drove off to "cancel Robert's vote".

Mama spoke of Robert with affection, and he seems to have had style and panache, with an air of opulent wealth about him. After conducting his flourishing business in Stewartstown for some years he set off for the United States, taking with him his wife Sarah and his three children, Ella, Jim and Olive. Ella, his favourite, was a delicate child, and hoping that the sea air on the voyage might do her good, he bought her a tiny rocking chair, with a caned seat and back, upon which she rocked herself on deck all the way to New York and back again. I do not know why they went to New York. Perhaps it was to visit relatives. Perhaps it was to see to one of his business ventures. Whatever the purpose of the journey it did not in any way diminish Great-Uncle Robert's fortune. He returned home, bought a large, low ivy-covered house and lived there in comfort for the rest of his days.

Poor Ella died when she was nineteen, and later, much later, when my sister was born, Great-Uncle Robert gave her his darling's rocking chair.

His son, James, known as Jim, became a bank official, from which occupation he retired immediately upon his father's death, feeling that now he had no need to work, for his father's fortune was indeed large. The family then moved to Bangor, County Down. Jim never married, but lived with his mother, who towards the end of her life went blind, and his sister Olive, a spinster who was very strange indeed. Mama told me of her great alarm when, in their young days, she and Olive were out driving in a trap, with Olive at the reins, when she turned to Mama and told her that she should be happy to drive with someone who had blue blood in their veins and was related to the Duke of Argyll! Certainly the name Campbell cropped up somewhere in her family, but I think that was probably the only connection. This was the first of many romantic and bizarre delusions on Olive's part. Mama used to say, "She's away in the head." Great-Aunt Sarah must have had a wretched time in her last years, for her children refused to have any dealings with the outside world and she herself could not see. Jim drank heavily and Olive grew more and more odd.

After their mother died Jim and Olive lived together in a spacious house, but were not on speaking terms. They breakfasted, lunched and dined upon boiled eggs, washed down in Jim's case with Scotch whisky. Olive spent her days lying on a blue velvet chaise longue in front of a gas fire which burned day and night, summer and winter. The bills for the household were sent directly to a solicitor, who paid them. When they eventually died there was no one to mourn them, as no one had seen them for years. The grass grew shoulder-high in the garden of the house, the hedges were like those in the Briar Rose fairy tale, and the eggshells were ankle deep in the kitchen.

Hilary's maternal Aunt Sara Duff, her husband Willie & their daughter Muriel,
c.1926

Chapter 9

Aunt Sara

Grandma Martha's strong will and ability to see things through to a satisfactory – to her – conclusion was passed on to Aunt Sara. More than any other of Grandma's children she had strength of character and a clear mind. She, like Aunt May, was a teacher and she felt it was up to her to see that her pupils made good in life. She chivvied them ever onwards and upwards and would brook no excuse for any laziness on the part of a child who she thought could do better. The genuinely weak, however, knew that she was their friend. No bullying ever took place in her class, and wrongdoers quivered at her glance, thinking she could see right into their minds. She lived in the village square and kept a strict eye upon all occurrences in the village.

She was strong-minded, stiff-necked and high principled, the sort of woman who, if she had been in America at the time the west was being won, would have faced wild beasts and Indians alike and would have survived hardships beyond imagination as those Pioneer women did. She would have made sure that hers was the first covered wagon to reach California and would have pitched her tent on Nob Hill in San Francisco before building herself a log cabin to serve as an office from where she could run the entire city. She was made of sterling stuff and her life in County Tyrone was, as far as her abilities were concerned, wasted. She had the strong backbone of the Ulster Scot, the refusal to accept "No" for an answer and the direct honesty and straightforwardness which made this Ulster breed such a power in the United States when they fought for freedom and independence. George Washington said, "If all else fails in this great fight I will die with my own Scots-Irish in Virginia." George could have depended his life on Aunt Sara if she had been there, for she was of that same invincible breed. She was unfortunately caught in the trap of a small Ulster village. Realising this too late she, ever a pragmatist, conformed. Had she been born into another culture, another métier, another land, she would have been foremost in any

215

fight for justice and would naturally have espoused the cause of the underdog.

As things were, she played the cards which had been dealt to her. She was a fount of good sense and balanced judgement in the village, setting things to rights as she saw them, giving advice where she felt it was needed and keeping an eye on the doings of her present and past pupils, whose behaviour was not always impeccable. My early awe gave way, as I grew to adolescence, to a deep and abiding affection for Aunt Sara. She became my friend and much loved adviser, kind and generous to the end. I felt safe when I was with her.

When her husband, Uncle Willie, died of cancer of the throat, an agonising death, she remained a widow for the rest of her life, never coming completely out of mourning. She wore black relieved with touches of white for years and then graduated into various shades of mauve and violet, but I never remember her wearing anything else. In appearance she was tall and striking, with beautiful legs, and she always wore the finest grey silk stockings with clocks up the sides. She was immaculately groomed and had "presence", not an attribute common in countrywomen of the day. How frustrated she must have been, with her eager, questing brain finding nothing more to occupy it than teaching school and running her house.

When she decided that we had visited long enough with Aunt May, we were summoned to stay with her in Coagh, and the summons was a Royal Command. There was no gainsaying it. By this time I had got used to being at Aunt May's and did not want to change my quiet routine, but go I must.

In the early days we were accompanied by Aggie, and went by train to Moneymore. There we were met by the mail car which was one of the few motor vehicles in the countryside. This car was used to collect and deliver the mail sacks from the train to the village a few miles away. It also carried passengers, for a consideration. The driver, Robert John, once a pupil of Aunt Sara's, would never have refused to transport us, and we were packed in, dressed in our Sunday coats and hats, among the parcels and mail bags.

We chugged along the road, crushed together in the back seat. The driver asked how we were and how was Belfast? Aggie of course could not hear him, but nodded brightly, and I was too shy to make any reply, so Joyce had to do her best to respond. He did not really expect an answer and was only trying to be kind.

As we drove over the bridge at the end of the village, which spanned the Ballinderry River, we peered over the driver's shoulder to catch the first glimpse of Aunt Sara's house, fronting on to the village square. It was large and double-fronted, painted sometimes pale grey and sometimes cream. She cared for her property and kept it in good repair, changing the colour of the house from time to time so that people would know it had been newly painted. There was a stretch of fawn and white round pebbles, thickly spread and scrunchy underfoot, brought there from the Lough Neagh shore, before the house, and the door was open, framing Aunt Sara as she waited for us.

She greeted us warmly and supervised the unloading of our suitcases with the assurance of a quartermaster-general, as she instructed the driver in reloading his car. He listened to her, like a rabbit in front of a snake, no doubt thinking himself back in the classroom, before climbing into the driver's seat and chugging off to deliver the rest of his cargo. We stood in front of the house, not exactly relishing the prospect of a visit here.

Aunt Sara was the kindest of women and the most generous, and I was not exactly afraid of her. It was just that she made me nervous because she was so self-assured. As I grew older I grew to love her more than any other relative, for her rapport was better with older children and teenagers, to whom she would talk for hours, her quick mind finding solutions for all their problems with ease.

When Aunt Sara was not at school, during her school holidays – which were much shorter in the country than in Belfast – things went smoothly and the days had a pleasant pattern, but when she was teaching and not at home, time dragged. At the farm I had had other children to play with, and at Aunt May's there were only the familiar adults who did not alarm me.

The cousins here were in their twenties, the wrong age for either Joyce or me. They led full and busy lives, gravitating between work, church, dances and the tennis club. Swimming in Lough Neagh, a cycle ride away, was one of their favourite pastimes, but until we were older, this was beyond us. They cycled here and there, doing this and that, taking part in the social life of the village.

Aggie usually went home after delivering us safely, and this parting was a great trial to me, for the safe, sheltering presence was gone and I felt I was at the mercy of strangers, though they were my cousins and were kind to us.

One consolation was that there were old-fashioned books in that house which we could read with pleasure. Some were picture-books for young children, and I liked these, but as the summers drifted past I progressed to Pixie O'Shaughnessy, a Victorian tale for girls about an Irish Ascendancy family, A World of Girls, Queechy, sad stories over which I wept, and Black Beauty, which made me cry even more. Some of the old Gene Stratton-Porter books were there, too, "Laddie", "Michael O'Halloran", "Girl of the Limberlost" and "Freckles", with their American backgrounds caught my fancy and I felt I would have liked that way of life. On wet days I read indoors, but when it was dry and warm I carried the books out to the garden at the back, through the red door at the end of the yard. There I sat on a garden seat, or perhaps lay on a rug if the grass had been cut, sunning myself among the flowers and getting up every few minutes to gather and eat raspberries which grew in rows far down the garden.

Sometimes I was called into the house to find Willie Charlton, the postman, cutting Aunt Sara's hair. This was Willie's sideline and after the mail had been delivered time hung heavy on his hands, so he took up barbering and went round his customers' houses trimming their hair. He could only cut hair in a straight bob – shingling was far too complicated – so that everyone who availed themselves of his services had to wear their hair in the same style.

"Now just a wee bit off this time, Willie," Aunt Sara would warn.

"Right, right, whatever you say, Mrs. Duff, but sure if I happen to take a wee bit too much off it'll do you the longer" replied Willie, snipping away and standing back from time to time to survey his handiwork. When I visited Aunt Sara I, too, had my hair cut by Willie, and when I went back home Mama would look sadly at it and say she wished Willie would stick to cutting his hedges, which he did with great art, shaping peacocks and swans at the corners.

Aunt Sara's house had a large, airy hall with yellow flagstones and to the right of the hall door was the dining room. This was used by her as a small sitting room, for we ate in the kitchen. It gave a good view of passersby, and if she wanted to speak to someone she saw passing, she could rise from her chair by the window and reach the front door before they were out of earshot. She would summon them imperiously and quiz them closely. She would have made a splendid lawyer, for her cross-examination technique was well-nigh perfect. She went round and round the point she was investigating until her witness had irrevocably committed himself, and then went for his jugular vein. Before he knew, and certainly against his will she had extracted the kernel of information she wanted, rather like the men in Africa who squeeze venom from unwilling snakes. Once she had gained the information she wanted, the informant was dismissed peremptorily, with an added rider not to stay out too late, or instructions as to how he was to look after his mother, if my Aunt thought he was shirking his duty.

Behind the dining room was the kitchen, with a small pantry and a scullery leading off it, and upstairs was the drawing room, the bathroom, several bedrooms and attics. The kitchen and scullery looked out on the yard, large and long, with many doors leading off it into "houses" – henhouses, a byre, a stable, and so on. One of these houses was a dairy, with a cool stone floor and slate shelves. The churn was kept here and the crocks where the milk waited to be churned stood upon the floor, terra-cotta coloured outside and black and shiny inside, with wooden lids, just the same as Mama had at home to crock the eggs. My cousin Muriel was in charge of the churning, and this took place each Thursday. She scrubbed her hands, poured the milk from the crocks into the churn, and then the work began.

Once the brown shiny barrel of the wooden churn was sealed up and the lid screwed on tightly, Muriel began to turn the handle and then there was no let-up until the job was finished and the butter had "come". It was rather like going into labour. Joyce and I quite looked forward to starting off, helping Muriel by taking turns at the turning of the barrel, keeping always to the same rhythm and leaping to our position at a word from her. Her arms were strong and she could turn the handle for a long time without flagging, but our arms were like boiled spaghetti and we tired after only a few turns. But we dared not stop, for if we did the butter would be spoiled.

On and on we turned as though we were on a treadmill. If a neighbour, male or female, should happen to call while the churning was in progress, he or she was roped in to give a turn or two to relieve us. We sang songs to relieve the monotony and to keep us going. Muriel had a strong contralto voice and sang in the church choir, and we joined in with our reedy voices. We sang "Onward, Christian Soldiers" and "Fight the Good Fight", "Show Me the Way to go Home", "Blaze Away", "Old Father Thames", and any other songs we could think of with a good swing. Then we launched into "The Isle of Capri", "Red Sails in the Sunset", speeded up to our tempo, for had not Jimmy Kennedy, who wrote these songs, lived in the village and gone to school with Muriel, her sister Eva, who now lived abroad, and their brother. It would have been a slight to Jimmy, Muriel felt, if we had not included his songs in our repertoire. She was also partial to all the old waltzes, especially "All Alone", "Always" and "What'll I Do?", but these did not fit in with the swing of the churn. When I was allowed to choose it was usually "When the Red, Red Robin Comes Bob-Bob-Bobbin' Along", and Joyce often chose "Love is the Sweetest Thing", so our tastes varied greatly according to our mood, for Muriel was temperamental, and if things were going well with her all was merry as a marriage bell, but if not we had to watch our step.

After what seemed hours the churn would be stopped and the little round window in the lid inspected. If there were flecks of yellow butter on it we could stop the work, but if it still looked milky, or if the curds were too fine, the work had to continue. Once it was seen that everything was right, the churn was hooked into the upright position, the lid removed, and leaving the yellow butter flakes floating in their buttermilk pond, we all went back into the house to have a long cool drink of homemade lemonade for us and several cups of tea for Muriel.

Our part in the churning was finished, but Muriel now had to make the butter. This she did with a great flourish, washing it time after time in a large wooden butter-bowl to remove the buttermilk, then squeezing the water out. After this, the wooden butter-pats in her flailing hands, she salted it and shaped it into oblong blocks, each weighing roughly a pound. The butter was either bright golden in colour, or creamy pale, depending on where the cows had been feeding and the lushness of the pasture. Two more large crocks were freshly scalded and filled with ice-cold spring water from the pump in the village square and the blocks of butter were gently floated on the water to keep fresh and cool and sweet. Then the buttermilk was poured into a clean enamel bucket, also freshly scalded out and rinsed with cold water, and was covered with a lid. The dairy was scrubbed out afterwards from top to bottom, and endless buckets of water – from the pump in the yard this time where the water was never used for drinking – were swilled round the floor. Once Joyce, obeying Muriel's instruction to "Throw it! Come on, throw it!" took the instruction literally, misjudged her aim and flung a whole bucket of icy water too high, soaking Muriel from head to toe. Loud recriminations followed and poor Joyce, who had only done as she was asked, was made to feel less than welcome for a time. Once the churn was scrubbed and scalded and the butter-bowl and pats restored to their pristine freshness, the dairy door was closed for another week, only being opened when milk, butter and eggs, which were also kept there, were wanted, or someone felt the need of a drink of good, fresh buttermilk. Buttermilk was thought to cool the blood and it was also used for baking bread. The byre was in the yard also, right at the end beside the door which led to the garden where the raspberries grew. Although her house stood in the centre of the village, Aunt Sara had land "at the top of the town", right on the outskirts of the village, and used one or two of the fields for grazing her cattle. This was usual. Most families had fields nearby and kept a few cows to supply milk for their own use. Morning and evening the cows were fetched for milking and it was a common sight to see perhaps four or five cows ambling down one of the streets leading to the square, switching their tails angrily and mooing indignantly as the person in charge, usually a young boy on a bicycle, rang the bicycle bell and shouted at them, herding them through the gateway leading to their own yard and byre.

Cows were valuable and the loss of one was a serious matter. I remember when one of Aunt Sara's cows became ill and she, for once, was helpless in the situation. She did not trust the vet and besides it would be very costly to bring him out from Cookstown at night. On the other hand the animal, if left untreated, might not live till morning.

After some deliberation and much lamentation, she sent for her old friend Willie Blackstock. Willie knew more about cattle than anyone around. He had a large herd of his own which he managed perfectly and he could diagnose an ailment in a cow within seconds, and, even better, he could treat that ailment. Aunt's cow was very sick indeed. Aunt was frantic. The cow had caught a chill, she thought, and would probably die. The outlook was gloomy indeed. But she had underestimated Willie Blackstock. No Sir Galahad, no knight in shining armour, had ever looked better than Willie when he appeared at the door. "What ails the beast?" was his first question, and he listened carefully to all Aunt Sara told him.

Now Willie took over the situation and everyone relaxed. Something was being done. Willie sent my cousins to get various necessities and asked my aunt for an empty whiskey bottle. Aunt did not drink spirits, so she sent across the road to McVey's pub to ask them to let her have an empty bottle, and then, in the kitchen lamplight, Willie mixed his magic potion, measuring carefully and talking calmly about this and that to Aunt Sara all the while. He gave the mixture a mighty shake and then opened the back door into the yard. Aunt followed him with a hurricane lamp, and we all trooped after her. I stood by the open door of the byre, wrapped in a cardigan of Muriel's against the night air and watched with fascination as the little drama was played out before my eyes.

One of my cousins held the sick cow's head to steady it, Aunt Sara stood perched on the edge of a manger, holding up the lamp to shed as much light as possible on the scene of action, and Willie stood silhouetted against the light in his riding breeches and leather leggings, his tweed cap pushed back on his head. He thrust the neck of the dark green bottle into the side of the cow's mouth and as the animal jerked violently against the draught trickling down its throat Willie and my cousin swayed together as they struggled to hold it still.

Finally the job was done, the bottle withdrawn, and Willie talked soothingly to the cow and to my aunt, who were equally distressed. Fresh straw was carried in for the cow to lie on, she was made as warm and as comfortable as possible, and we went back to the house and the warmth of the turf burning in the kitchen stove. Black currant wine was produced and served to everyone, even to me, though mine was diluted with water. Aunt Sara was a mighty wine maker and used anything she could lay hands on for this purpose – elderberries, dandelions, damsons, parsnips and black currants, which were best of all. I drowsed off after the excitement. The wine, the warmth and the drone of the voices in the kitchen were soothing and I slept soundly.

An hour or more passed, then a huge roar from the byre galvanised the entire company and woke me from my sleep. There was a mad rush for the door, and down the yard we all ran, the lamp swinging from Willie's hand this time. He threw the door of the byre open and the cow was revealed, standing up and roaring at the top of her voice. Her eyes rolled round to the light to observe her audience and she stamped her foot and switched her tail.

"She's all right now, but that was a near thing," said Willie as he felt her throat and stomach tenderly. "Just watch her and keep her warm for a day or two and you'll have no more bother with her. I must go home now, for I've a sow farrowing and I might be needed." Off he went, the carbide lamp on his bicycle shining wanly in the darkness, refusing thanks for his good turn, and we all went to bed exhausted after the fuss and the near catastrophe.

In a small stable in the yard lived Norah, a dark brown pony aged thirty-two years, who spent the summers happily in one of Aunt Sara's fields and the winters in her warm stable. She earned her keep by occasionally pulling the small trap which Aunt used to jaunt around the country when she went visiting. Norah was never required to travel far and she proceeded at a stately pace, only trotting gently when the road was flat. Aunt Sara, to my great delight, sometimes allowed me to hold the reins as we drove out sedately on a summer afternoon. I found it hard to understand why she only allowed me to do this when Norah was pulling us up a gentle hill. It was years before the truth dawned on me, but I felt as proud as any coachman riding up in front of the Irish State Coach. There was so little traffic that when we went up hill Norah did not walk in a straight line, but was guided by her mistress with a gentle tug on the reins in a zigzag pattern, so that the strain was removed. If the hill was more than a slight incline we – my aunt, Joyce and I – got out and walked. If we were not there Aunt went alone in the trap, the other members of the family going where they needed to go on their bicycles, which had high handlebars so that the rider sat as though he or she were playing the piano. Ladies' cycles, apart from their curvy "bar" had a fan-shaped arrangement of strings running from the hub of the back wheel to a series of tiny holes in the back mudguard, so that their skirts would not catch in the spokes of the wheel.

One Sunday in the summer of 1931 Aunt Sara came to visit her sisters May and Etta. I was staying with them, and we were all astounded to see Aunt Sara dismounting from an unfamiliar car. Aunt Sara told us she had bought it a few days previously and she proudly showed us her new possession. It was a Clyno, fawn in colour and with brown leather upholstery, and was driven by my Cousin Robert, Aunt Sara's youngest child, who was known as "Baby" until he reached the age of seventeen. This created a great sensation, and each Aunt in turn was spooned into it to be driven a mile or so up the road and back again. Aunt Sara, as befitted the proud owner, sat in the seat of honour beside the driver on each journey and refused to be dislodged from this position, in spite of Aunt Etta's querulous complaints that it made her feel sick to sit in the back seat.

"Please yourself, Etta," replied her sister. "Sit in the back or don't come at all." Aunt Etta scowled at her sister, but she could not resist the drive and pretended that she felt ill on the return journey. The car was an exciting addition to the family. Even though it had many drawbacks, such as bad springs and the windscreen wipers having to be worked by hand, it was felt that the family honour had been enhanced by its possession. The windscreen itself was rubbed on the outside when it rained with the cut surface of a raw potato so that the raindrops would run quickly down the glass and not obscure the driver's vision.

Aunt Etta, intensely jealous of Aunt Sara, immediately began to plan that from now on she would never travel anywhere by train or bus. Before Cousin Robert realised it, he had been trysted to drive her to Portstewart for her annual two weeks' holiday.

"Of course, Sara, I'll pay for the petrol," she declared, feeling magnanimous and hoping her offer would not be accepted. Aunt Sara, quite carried away by the impression the new car had made, agreed rather thoughtlessly to this arrangement, but we heard later that she and Robert had had sharp words on the subject on the journey home. However, she always had the last word, and her children, argue as they might, had to yield to her wishes with a disconsolate, "Och, Mamma!"

From that time onwards, each summer Cousin Robert had to transport Aunt Etta to Portstewart and fetch her home again when her annual holiday was over. His reluctance to be her chauffeur was compounded by his fear that she might be sick over the brown leather seats, for she always mentioned just before her departure that she was a "bad traveller" and carried with her two bath towels, a siphon of kali water and a tin of barley sugar, "just in case," she said.

Mama shuddered with laughter, her eyes behind her shiny glasses closing into slits, as always, when she enjoyed a joke, as I told her when I got home about Aunt Sara's car and Aunt Etta's proposed use of it. "That's Etta over the world," she said, but then added gleefully, "but Sara will be able for her!"

I was delighted to see the new car and hoped to share in the rides in this treasure, though I was relieved to hear that even though the Clyno had come upon the scene, my old friend Norah the pony was still in residence in her stable in the yard. She was too old, now, to pull the trap, but she lived happily until the ripe old age of forty-five, dividing her time between her cosy stable in winter and one of the fields "at the top of the town" in summer, where she grazed gently under the trees to her heart's content, troubled by no one.

Most families in the village rented a piece of the moss, which was a bog not far from the village, and here the men cut turf for the winter's fuel. This was done with a special spade which had a small blade protruding from the main blade at right-angles. The spade was long and thin and it was a real art to be able to cut and lift the turf into neat oblongs which looked like chocolate fudge before they were stacked and dried. This was hard work and no one enjoyed it, but there was great satisfaction later in the year when every house had a turf-stack in the yard, under cover and near the house.

Uncle Willie, Aunt Sara's husband, had been an undertaker as well as a farmer. When he died, Aunt, with the help of family, carried on the undertaking business in a small way. The coffins were kept in a large, dry outhouse, perhaps half a dozen of them at a time, in varying sizes. There were shelves around, on which rested cardboard boxes containing the apparel of death, shrouds, white stockings and even white gloves all ready to be used when someone in the neighbourhood was gathered to his forefathers.

Once, at dead of night, I had to go out with Muriel to the coffin house to find a pair of white gloves forgotten by my other cousin who had gone to lay out a corpse. He had sent a messenger post-haste by bicycle to collect the gloves for the dead woman. After much hmm-ing and ha-ing, Muriel reluctantly agreed to go out in the darkness to the coffin house in the yard, but she wouldn't go alone, she said. I, then aged seven, was in the kitchen at the time, and she stipulated that I must accompany her. She fetched a candle in a candlestick which she lit as we entered the dark doorway of the coffin house, and nervously we threaded our way, hand in hand, between the ghostly coffins. In the flickering light of the candle Muriel began to open cardboard boxes. The first few she opened were full of shrouds and she hastily jammed the lids back on again. At last she found a box of gloves, but they were for men and were too large, except for two smaller gloves which were both for the right hand and had somehow got into the wrong box. Frantically Muriel groped in yet more boxes as the candle guttered lower and cast shadows on the wall before the coffins. Still not finding suitable gloves, she finally said, lifting the two right-hand gloves, "These will just have to do. They'll not be shaking hands with her, and not a soul will know the difference. It's a wake after all, not a fashion parade!"

Out we skipped, slamming the door behind us, and ran back to the house. When Muriel handed her the gloves Aunt Sara, who had just returned from the house of mourning, was furious. "You're a right pair of straps," she declaimed angrily, including me in her wrath. "Lizzie Bowden was a decent modest wee woman all her days. She was always neatly dressed and wore a hat when she went out of the house, even if she did wear that navy serge costume for ten years because Jacob was too mean to give her the money for a new one. And now, when she does have the chance to be well dressed – and Jacob can't very well complain about the price of her grave-clothes – you expect her to meet her Maker – and dear knows who else will be there, too – in two right-hand gloves! You must be mad!"

"But Mamma," expostulated Muriel, "no one will see – Lizzie'll be in her coffin, and anyway I'm afraid to go out in that dark house again."

"See or not see," said her mother sharply, "when Lizzie rises on the Judgement Day I don't want her to look over at me in the graveyard and say, 'In the name of goodness why did you not get me a proper pair of gloves?'

The candle was lit again and this time all three of us went out to search for the match of the glove selected by Aunt Sara. The messenger, meanwhile, remained in the house drinking tea and eating marble cake. It was a long time before we returned to the kitchen, but when we did it was with a proper pair of gloves for Lizzie.

Aunt Sara had a dear friend called Jessie McAuley and when we were visiting Coagh we were always invited to tea at Jessie's house. Her husband Matthew, know as "Mattha" was notoriously mean and kept Jessie very short of money. They had no children, and Mattha had been heard to say that it was maybe just as well, for weans were costly items and you never knew how they would turn out. Still, Jessie was kind and cheerful and made the best of things. She always gave us a good tea, but we were always asked to visit her on a Fair Day, when Mattha would be away selling his produce and putting the money in the bank in Magherafelt.

One hot summer day we went to visit Jessie. Joyce and I wore pink voile dresses with puffed sleeves, socks and sandals, and Aunt Sara was in a grey dress with a mauve pattern and a black straw hat. Aunt Sara thought it was too hot to bring Norah and the trap, so we trudged the two miles to Jessie's, almost melting in the sunshine.

Jessie welcomed us and brought us into the cool parlour with its stiff furniture and damp, unused smell, and we sat, hands folded in our laps, while she and Aunt Sara exchanged pleasantries. Soon Jessie went out to the kitchen to make the tea and shortly afterwards called us to join her. The kitchen table was set with her good china – a wedding present from her mother – and she had put a pretty jug spilling over with honeysuckle in the centre. There was soda and wheaten bread, freshly made that morning, homemade butter and jam and a sponge cake, high, light and golden. An eggcup was set at each place and the eggs were boiling in a saucepan on the range.

Jessie poured the tea and spooned the eggs out of the saucepan into our eggcups. At that moment the dog barked and Mattha drove into the yard, the wheels of the cart grating noisily as he drew up. Jessie's face turned white, then deep pink, then white again and she hissed urgently at us, "Hide your eggs – here comes Mattha!" Obediently we tipped the boiling eggs into our laps – for there was nowhere else to put them out of sight – and quickly handed her the eggcups, which she whisked into a cupboard.

Mattha came into the kitchen and we all smiled in greeting rather falsely, for our thighs were burning with the heat of the eggs through our thin summer dresses. We jiggled around uncomfortably as Mattha looked at us gloomily and said, "That's a good day," casting a critical eye over the table to see what extravagance Jessie had been guilty of. Finally he said, "That's a good cake. Did you put many eggs in it?"

"Not at all, man dear," said Jessie airily. "Only a couple of cracked ones the black hen knocked against the edge of the nest when the cat frightened her. Sure they'd have gone to waste if I hadn't used them." This was a lie and we all knew it, for the cake had been made with at least five eggs, but Mattha could prove nothing and went out disgruntled, saying he had to feed the pigs.

The insides of our legs were red and sore by now, but Jessie dealt out the eggcups again and we all fell to demolishing the eggs before Mattha returned. Jessie said, "Never heed Mattha. His mother could have lived on the clippings of tin and he thinks I can, too. Dear help his foolish wit. When I sell the eggs and butter I keep some of the money back and never let on to him. I have a wheen of pounds by me now and when I have enough I'm bound and determined to go and see my sister Violet in America. I'll just tell Mattha she sent me the ticket and I be to go." Aunt Sara made encouraging noises as she took the top off her egg.

When we got home Aunt Sara retailed the story to Robert and Muriel, with actions, and they laughed, picturing the three of us with the burning eggs in our laps. "Mattha McAuley would skin a ghost under the bed for a ha'penny," said Muriel, and Robert added, "Hell will never be full till he's in it."

Hilary's cousin Robert Duff with his mother's, Sara Duff's, Clyno car, 1931

Chapter 10

Coagh

Sundays were strictly kept at Aunt Sara's. Everyone in the house attended Meeting. The Meeting House was one of the old "barn" churches of the earliest Presbyterian days. It was a large square building, painted, like Aunt's house, in either grey or cream, depending on the whim of the Kirk Session and the price of paint. The large plain glass windows were outlined in white. Inside, the starkness of the building and the clear, cool atmosphere made an instant and lasting impression. The windows were tall, but did not begin low down. They were constructed so as to ensure as little distraction as possible for the congregation, and all that could be seen through them during the service was the tops of the trees waving and swaying in the breeze and the great white clouds riding past in the sky.

Two of my cousins sang in the choir, and Joyce and I sat with Aunt Sara in her family pew. The pews were box pews with little doors, which meant that there was sometimes an anxious moment when a family trooped down the aisle and had to wait while their leader fumbled with the latch on the pew door, the rest of them standing, transfixed, willing the fumbler to prise it open. Once the door was opened they all fluttered in like hens to nesting boxes and sat like statues, looking neither to right nor to left. I sat beside my Aunt, my short silk-socked legs in their black patent Sunday shoes dangling loosely, until she noticed my discomfort and pushed over a hassock for me to rest my feet on.

The seats were high and uncushioned, not designed for comfort. The God who was worshipped here was not a comfortable or friendly God, but a rather querulous Being of uncertain temperament, always on the alert for small misdemeanours or infringements of His rules, and ready and willing to hand out punishment as a school prefect hands out lines. His was not the grandeur of the Old Testament which said majestically, "God was wroth," if anyone stepped out of line, but rather the spitefulness of a petty demagogue, having to be appeased at all times. I noticed that God in country Presbyterian churches seemed to be very different from God in our church at home in Belfast, but perhaps the emotional needs of a country congregation were different. At home He seemed to be more urbane and sophisticated than He was in the country, where he seemed to be very temperamental and acted in a thoroughly highhanded fashion over the question of good weather for the crops, survival of cattle and other rural matters. In Belfast He appeared to concentrate much more on the outside world and the calling of people to the mission field. For years I had a dread that I might suddenly hear this Call and not be able to gainsay it. Fortunately for my peace of mind there were no openings in missionary work for children of tender years, and by the time I was old enough my thoughts were on other things.

The service opened with a metrical psalm, and the old tunes like "Crimond", "Brother James' Air", "Rockingham" and others were sung with great fervour by the congregation, for God was indeed a Presbyterian God and was among them as they sang. I felt relieved to be among the numbered elect and was sorry for those outside the fold who lacked instant communion with Him. The prayers were long, very long and very detailed. God was thanked for everything in daily life, from the smallest daisy growing in the hedgerow to the condition of the crops at that moment, and was asked to look kindly upon the same crops during the coming week. The birds which nested in the trees were mentioned, as well as the butterflies which floated lazily past in the sunshine outside the windows of the church. Also touched on were those "who are laid aside upon beds of sickness" which sounded very grand and dignified and hardly appropriate for little children with measles or chickenpox.

I chafed at the length of these prayers, for the minister sometimes got quite carried away, but I was instantly quieted with a disapproving look from Aunt and a sweet, a small round white mint imperial, was pressed into my hot palm. I sucked on this until the next hymn or psalm was announced, when I hastily crunched the remainder of it so that I could join in the singing. The sermon was long and regarded as a penance which everyone had to endure for the sins they had committed during the preceding week.

Once, when we were singing the final hymn, which happened to be "Rock of Ages" and had reached the verse which starts, "While I draw this fleeting breath, When mine eyelids close in death," when, overcome by the summer heat and the length of the service, an adolescent girl fainted dead away. She was instantly scooped up and borne out of the meeting by her father and brothers, while the rest of us sang valiantly on, pretending that nothing untoward had happened. The hymn finished and the benediction was pronounced over a restive meeting, whereupon everyone streamed out into the sunshine in a great hurry to catch up with the latest development.

I thought that surely God had called the redheaded Minnie to His Presence at an opportune moment during the hymn, wearing her Sunday best. I was surprised and just a little disappointed to find Minnie laid out on the steps of the meeting, resting on her brothers' coats which they had gallantly removed to make her comfortable. It was the story of Jairus's daughter over again, I felt, just as I had often heard it in church – Minnie returned from the dead. Unlike Jairus's daughter, however, she blinked her pale eyes myopically and demanded her steel-rimmed spectacles which had been removed by her sister for safekeeping. As I watched, her family's trap drawn by a hastily-yoked skewbald pony was brought to the steps, Minnie was loaded into it like a sack of potatoes and driven off home. It seemed that God had, on a sudden whim, decided that He needed Minnie and had then changed His mind in a very arbitrary fashion.

The congregation went home to their large Sunday dinners and Minnie's sudden fainting fit, her general health and all matters to do with Minnie and her family were dissected and discussed over every table.

Sometimes we were taken to wakes, if we knew, or were even distantly related to the dead person. Of all the social gatherings in the countryside, wakes were considered to be among the best. That is, of course, for those who were not directly connected to the deceased and therefore were not emotionally involved.

Wakes were an occasion for meeting friends and neighbours, relatives from a distance who had come to pay their last respects to the dead, and those of differing religions and diverse political opinions. All these were present in the same house for a time, and all old animosities and differences were put aside, for the house was a house of mourning. It was a time of getting together, of closing ranks and of paying respect to the bereaved family. But if all old animosities were set aside, a wake was the perfect breeding ground for new ones. Umbrage was taken very easily and much care was taken not to offend those who were likely to be offended. However, no matter how the family tried to avoid it, often a lifelong feud was started amongst the grieving relatives. It was easy to know when this happened, for small knots of people could be observed in corners, talking in low tones and looking out of the corners of their eyes in case anyone came too near and heard the conversation which was not for their ears.

"And I said to her . . ."

"Yes, and do you know . . . ?"

"I never heard the like of it . . . "

"The cheek of her, and her not even a near friend – her mother was only related into the family in a far-out way, through her Granny . . . "

"Some people!"

"And what's going to happen to her linen tablecloths...and that blue china tea set? It should be our Mary's by rights!"

All these and other phrases could be heard as the quiet voices grew shrill with anger. Mainly the groups of complainers were women, and they were ready to criticise anyone and anything. All was grist to their mill, for what happened at a wake could make conversation for many long months ahead. Their neighbours were driven into taking sides, no matter how they tried to resist, for the constant babble of invective would not let them rest, and they found themselves, in spite of all aspirations to the contrary, saying something they had not meant to say and hearing it quoted loudly, "Did you hear that? Meta says . . ." or "Sammy Thompson says . . . and he's right!"

We loved wakes, for we heard all sorts of gossip. No one expected a child to heed, or remember, what was said, but it gave us an insight into people's lives and we found it fascinating.

When asked to view the corpse – and everyone, no matter how squeamish they were, was invited to do this – the bereaved family thought they were bestowing a great honour by leading small groups of people to the bedroom where their loved one lay in state. The deceased person was usually in a bed, for at that time no one was coffined until the funeral service, held in the house, was taking place, when the noise of the undertaker screwing down the coffin lid could be very distracting. The bed was decked out with white linen embroidered sheets with a white coverlet on top and white embroidered pillowcases. The white face and often white hair of the dead person gave the whole scene an unearthly appearance. It was difficult to know what to say, though of course children were not expected to comment, but just to look. We could hear the adults murmuring things like, "Dear, but he's like himself," or "Doesn't he look peaceful?" or, sadly, "God help him, he must have suffered," or even, "He makes a lovely corpse." Then it was back to the chat and the company in the kitchen or the "room" as the sitting room was often called, and yet another round of tea, sandwiches and cakes.

In the village of Coagh most people had pumps in their yards, but the water from them could only be used for washing or for the livestock. Drinking water had to be carried daily from the village pump which stood in the middle of the square. This was a most convenient arrangement for the houses in the square, but not so handy for those who lived "up the street" or "round the road".

There was constant traffic to and from the pump, and the water which flowed from it was clear, sweet and pure. It was easy to tell when someone was there, for the pump handle squeaked. It had the kind of handle that went round and round, over and up, not the kind that went up and down and had a knob at the end as smaller pumps in farmyards did. It was altogether a rather splendid pump with its wheel and great gush of water. Children loved to swing on this handle and wasted much water as they swung to and fro. We were not allowed to do this, but Aunt Sara provided us with small buckets – really large white enamelled cans – so that we might take our turn at carrying water for the house. She liked us to be neat and tidy before going to the pump. I don't think that anyone in the village was interested in two children fetching water, but she felt she had a position to keep up, and insisted on clean socks and newly-polished shoes or sandals before we issued forth from the house on our way to the pump.

Sometimes we sat on the garden seat in front of the dining room window, swishing our feet through the pebbles and enjoying the noise, and watching the water carriers come and go. I watched especially each day for Joseph. Joseph was a Downs Syndrome child about ten years old. Children like this were treated with great tenderness and kindness. If they strayed from home they were set upon their way by neighbours and they were never in any danger. They were accepted as naturally as the flowers and trees. Gentle in themselves, they were gently dealt with. "He's simple," people would say kindly, and all allowances were made for slight eccentricities of behaviour.

When Joseph came to the pump, which he did many times a day, he carried a white enamelled bucket. He stood for a long time considering the best way to hook its handle on to the pump so that the water would fill the bucket. When this problem had been solved he sat down on the pump handle, swaying gently to and fro, to watch the world go by for a time and recover from his short walk. Then he stood up and began to move the handle. His arms were not long enough, nor strong enough, to make the handle turn right round. It took the length and strength of an adult's arms to do that. Children could only swing it to and fro, causing the water to spurt out in small jets and not in the great whoosh which an adult could achieve. This did not worry Joseph, who had all the time in the world. His main concern was, first of all, to see that his bucket was clean and free from specks of dust. To this end he filled it time after time with clear, sparkling water, rinsing it round and then sluicing it down the street. He occupied himself with this cleansing operation until someone happened to come to the pump and dislodge him from his position at the handle.

The village square was on a slight slope and when Joseph really got going and had a long, uninterrupted session, a stream of water washed down towards the bridge at the end of the village. Everyone watched him with tolerance and no one spoke to him sharply. If someone else needed water, Joseph willingly stepped aside to give him precedence, and if his supplanter lived near Joseph's home Joseph would allow a few drops of water to remain in his own bucket and would accompany his neighbour on his homeward journey, swinging his bucket jauntily and chatting amiably as he went.

One summer Joseph fell ill and the whole village held its breath. He was prayed for, not only in the Presbyterian Meeting where his family worshipped, but also in the Church of Ireland and the Roman Catholic chapel, and after an anxious time he was fully restored to glistening health, much to everyone's relief. Once more his small, portly figure appeared at the pump, watched even more fondly now by the villagers as they contemplated the cascades of water flowing down the street. I think they saw in him the total innocence which had almost disappeared from amongst them.

Aunt Sara resembled Grandma Martha in her whole attitude to life, to bend it to her will and to swim, if necessary, against the current. This was never more apparent than when her elder daughter, aged then about fourteen, suddenly became ill. She was in great pain, and the doctor, who lived just a few doors away, was sent for. He felt the pain might resolve in its own time and advised bed-rest and warmth. The pain grew worse, and next morning Eva was feverish and obviously very ill. The doctor was called in again by the anxious parents. Eva was Uncle Willie's favourite child and he was growing more apprehensive by the minute about the outcome of his daughter's illness. Still the doctor procrastinated.

By afternoon Eva was moaning, her abdomen now so tender that she could scarcely move. Uncle Willie stumped angrily down to the doctor's house and demanded that something – anything – be done to alleviate the pain. Now the doctor was alarmed, and after examining the patient again he said he felt a surgeon would have to be sent for all the way to Belfast. Eva could not be moved to hospital there, she was now far too ill, so the surgeon must come to her. It would be costly, he said to Uncle Willie, who replied that he didn't care if he had to sell his farm and all he had, just so long as his darling recovered.

The surgeon arrived by car that evening, examined Eva and shook his head. She had appendicitis, he said, and the appendix was just on the point of perforation. It was, he feared, too late to save her.

"Why can't you operate here?" said Aunt Sara. He pointed out that without the proper hygiene and facilities of an operating theatre, Eva's chances were slim – one in a thousand. Also, it was growing dark and there was no electricity in the house, no proper light for him to see, even if he did operate.

At this news Uncle Willie almost went berserk, blaming the doctor for negligence and the surgeon for faintheartedness, and threatened all kinds of retribution if Eva did not survive. The surgeon, not a whit intimidated by all this bluster – for Uncle Willie was normally a mild and kind man – and seeing her father's distress, decided he would at least try to save her.

Now Aunt Sara took charge. The local police sergeant was sent for, and after she had a private word with him he led Uncle Willie back with him to the barracks, where he promised he would keep the distraught man occupied for a time.

The stage was set for the small drama. The dining room was cleared of furniture and the kitchen table was scrubbed down thoroughly with disinfectant and carried in. Light was the big problem. All the lamps in the house were gathered together, but the light was too diffuse. Concentrated light was needed. Aunt Sara cogitated on the problem and then sent word to everyone in the village who owned a bicycle that their bicycle lamp was needed. At least twenty of these carbide lamps were yielded up and brought to the house. Aunt Sara arranged them round the makeshift operating table on tables, chairs, anything she could find to hold them at the right angle to shed light where it was needed.

The surgeon, who was having supper with the doctor, was told that all was in readiness, and the two men walked up to the house. The surgeon's instruments were brought from his car and sterilised in boiling water, the now almost unconscious Eva was laid upon the table, and the operation began.

Aunt Sara sat outside the dining room door on a stiff hall chair, the rest of the family grouped round her, except for Uncle Willie, who had grown so frantic as the situation developed that he had had to be locked up in a cell in the police barracks. She had done all she could. If God was good, her child would live. She must live. If she did live, her mother promised God, she would never ask for anything else again. This bargain with God, the prayer of all mothers with sick children, went round and round in her head.

After a long time the dining room door opened and the doctors came out. They said the operation had been completed, but only just in time. They thought it had been successful, but they could not be sure till morning when they would be able to judge better. The surgeon would remain overnight in the doctor's house. Aunt Sara's pale face relaxed. At least there was a chance, some hope for Eva.

Next morning the news was good, for Eva had a strong constitution. Uncle Willie returned home to hear that if everything proceeded normally, Eva would get better. He shook the surgeon's hand tearfully and rushed up to see his daughter, who had recovered from the anaesthetic and was demanding sips of water. A few weeks later she was well on the way to convalescence and the household returned to normal. Aunt Sara was tired out, but she had triumphed, and like Grandma Martha, was well satisfied with her endeavours. God, she allowed, had been good after all.

Coagh Presbyterian Church
Founded 1708

Chapter 11

Salterstown

After two or three weeks with Aunt Sara the time would come for us to move on to the place Joyce and I loved best. This time we went to stay with Mama's aunt and cousins, two bachelor brothers and their sister, all middle-aged, who lived in what seemed to be a sort of golden dreamland, Salterstown, on the shores of Lough Neagh. This was the enchanted place I entered with joy and left with sadness that I did not understand, only knowing that in leaving it I was venturing out once more into a greyer world and leaving the sunshine behind. All happiness for me was encapsulated in this house, in this countryside. During the time I spent there over the years, I never heard a raised voice or an unkind word.

We caught the once-daily bus which passed through the village and stopped to pick us up at Aunt Sara's door. As we drove along I could see all the familiar landmarks. The little roads were shady with trees and bushes and my excitement grew with every hundred yards as the bus neared Salterstown. I watched for the church and saw the grave-digger digging a grave in the graveyard in a leisurely way. Who, I wondered, was the grave for? Who could have died? Who would I not see this year? Over Ballinderry Bridge we went, the water rushing underneath and foaming on the stones below. Look! There was the house with the red door which had caused such a commotion among the neighbours when it was painted. Only brown doors, preferably "grained" by the painter were acceptable, but the wife of the teacher who lived in this house was English and had foolish notions. She might live here for a hundred years but would never be accepted by the local people.

Mrs. Atkinson, who lived near the teacher, we could see had been doing her washing and there it was. Her clothesline was rigged like a man-o'-war, a ship of the line in full sail, the white sheets flapping madly in the wind. It was all charming, all delightful and familiar. Nowhere in the world could be more wonderful and welcoming to us.

We drew to a rattling, shuddering halt as the bus rounded a bend in the road, with a great screech of brakes and were shot to the door like pebbles from a catapult. There stood Uncle Richard and Aunt Esther who had come to meet us. Our suitcases were handed down by the driver and set on the side of the road. Uncle Richard, after hugging and kissing us, lifted them into the little farm cart which was only used for light loads and easy transport into Ballyronan on farm business. The large cart was used for the main work of the farm. Both, like all Ulster farm carts, were painted brilliant orange with a proud royal blue trim.

He drove off to the house with the cases, and we walked the short distance, over the little stone bridge and along the winding road which led to the Mill House. As we walked, one on each side of Aunt Esther, her arms round our shoulders and ours twined round her waist, we passed the house where Peter and Martin Hadden lived. These two old brothers, who lived together and slept in the same bed at nights, had not spoken to each other for twenty years. They had fallen out over the treatment of a sick cow – and while they argued about what should be done the cow died. Each blamed the other and then the Great Silence descended. Peter came to the door and waved to us as we passed. Martin, who was trimming his hedge grumpily told us that it was a brave day but there would be rain by evening.

Clinging to Aunt Esther with love, we talked excitedly of all the things here which meant so much to us. How were the dogs, I asked. The Uncles always had water-spaniels with their black or brown close-curled coats and amber eyes. Like all gun dogs they were gentle with children and now, as we approached the house one of them, Brownie, came lolloping out to meet us, barking softly in welcome and licking our hands as we knelt to stroke him.

Brownie, rushing round in circles, preceded us down the sloping yard to the front door of the house, which stood open, for it was only closed at night when darkness fell. At other times it was left open, welcoming all who entered. It led into a narrow hallway which ran, not from front to back, but from side to side of the house. In the jamb wall, built to keep draughts from the door out of the kitchen, just in front of the door there was a tiny triangular aperture and a few feet to the right of this was the kitchen door, leading to the hub of the house. The jamb wall kept the kitchen warm and snug in spite of the ever-open door and the small window-like hole allowed anyone who was in the kitchen to see who was coming in.

As we entered the house a tiny figure in a black dress with a foamy white lace collar fastened with a cameo brooch appeared at the door of the kitchen, with arms outstretched. This was Aunt Esther's mother, our great-aunt, whom we called "Granny McMaster". She was Grandma Martha's sister Sarah. To Mama she was "Aunt McMaster" and because of her close relationship to the redoubtable Martha she was endowed with a certain mystique.

Granny McMaster had "married well", better than her sister. Her husband, dead now for many years, had owned two farms of land which he had welded successfully into a large, prosperous unit. He had also owned a large tract of land on the shores of Lough Neagh. Money had never been a problem in this family and they could hold their heads up anywhere. When something was bought it was of the best quality and no one quibbled over the price. Uncle Richard, Uncle Robert and Aunt Esther lived tranquilly here with their mother, for their other sister was married and lived abroad.

Granny McMaster hugged and kissed us fondly. We were Anna Martha's children, the grandchildren of Granny McMaster's elder sister Martha (married to William Davison) who had died before we were born, and to her we seemed precious, fit subjects for cosseting and spoiling. Nothing could have suited me better. I was ripe for spoiling.

Once through the door our hats and coats were whisked away and we were ushered into the kitchen where tea awaited us. Tea, that is, consisting again mostly of milk, so that we might be "built up" by the fresh creamy milk produced by the Salterstown cows. Aunt Esther had baked a cake specially for us, frosted with pink icing and decorated with jelly dewdrops. There was also her famous wheaten bread, which no one could match, baked from the wheaten meal milled by Uncle Robert on the premises, slim scones baked on the griddle with currants in them, and a large pat of bright yellow butter made by Aunt Esther and decorated on top with a print of acorns and oak leaves. Homemade jam completed this mid-afternoon snack and I sat in the warm kitchen contentedly swinging my legs on a dear, familiar, rail-backed, rush-seated chair, looking out through the window with its white net curtains looped back at either side, at the garden beyond, feeling loved, wanted and safe.

The Mill House was set low in a hollow beside the road. The mill dam, which lay spread out before it on the level of the road, was deep and exciting and was the one place where we were forbidden to go alone. Uncle Robert was the miller, and when the mill was working and the great water wheel was turning it was the most wonderful and exciting place in the world. I could never quite work out how it all functioned, but when the wheel turned I watched in fascination, staring at the cascading water as it spilled from the little compartments. We rushed in through the mill door every now and then to stand just inside upon the shaking floor. The machinery was working, the huge mill stones grinding the wheat and corn, and there stood Uncle Robert in the midst of it all, in a light brown cotton coat, instructing his helpers, George and Alfie. His hair and eyebrows were covered in the white dust from the grain, which made him look strange. Assured and confident, he was like the captain on the bridge of his ship. Here he was master, in full command of everything, and not at all like the shy, kind man we knew in the house.

We were not allowed to step across a line painted on the floor a yard or so inside the mill door, and this rule was strictly observed. We might be hurt somehow or other, or fall against the machinery, Uncle Robert said, so only when the mill stopped were we allowed to proceed further – and of course then we did not want to, because all the excitement of the shuddery, juddery place had gone.

Across the yard from the mill lay the kiln. When the fire to dry the grain was burning, it was a warm, cosy place, the heat rising to the store above, where the sacks of corn and wheat were kept before being ground into meal. This store had a large sliding door at one side which could be pulled back on rollers, allowing the sacks of grain to be unloaded from carts, and sacks of meal to be removed when ready. Each year Uncle Robert sent a sack of wheaten meal to Mama who felt that no other wheaten meal in the whole world could possibly be its equal.

The store was a wonderful place to play, and we spent hours clambering up and down the piles of sacks and jumping from one pile to the next, feeling through the jute sacking the shifting grains of corn under our bare legs. We never tired of it. Round and round the store we wove, never touching the floor, and then, if the sliding door was open, we jumped through it, the three-foot drop to the road giving us a mild thrill. Back down through the yard we ran, into the kiln, up the little staircase in the corner and back to the store, like puppies chasing our own tails.

The house was peculiar in that its front door opened out into the yard, which was surrounded by stable, byre, dairy, the mill, the kiln and the mill dam. Round a corner was the pig-sty, positioned here because of the smell, though like all else here, the pigs were kept in near-clinical conditions. The house was set low down from the road and was cosily sheltered from storms and gales. The back door led out from the "back kitchen" – really a bright airy scullery where the dishes were washed in a large porcelain sink and thereafter neatly stacked in cupboards with glass doors – to a flower garden.

Someone, long years before, had planted this garden with care and love, and it was still delightfully old-fashioned. It was square, and one side adjoined the house, from which it was overlooked by the kitchen window and the window of the spare bedroom on the ground floor. We slept in this bedroom and Mama had warned us always to keep the window shut, for long ago a member of the family who lived here had been sleeping peacefully in this very room when a drunk man lost his way home and stepped right through the open window into this room. He lay down on top of the bed, the tale went and went to sleep, whilst its occupant slept on, oblivious. When she did awaken and found this stranger stretched out over the coverlet, Mama said she "went mad" and had to be taken to the County Asylum, although Mama added a rider to the effect that of course "he hadn't touched her". Presumably he had been too drunk.

At one of the far corners of the garden was a small group of cedars. These sheltered a summer-seat cut out of the centre of a small-leaved holly bush. The scrubbed pinewood seat was really just a small plank, and when I sat in this tiny arbour I had to beware of the prickly leaves of the holly. It was a splendid place for dolls' tea parties.

The four sides of the square had beds of old-fashioned roses, lupins, golden rod and tall flowers of all kinds, but the rest of the space was taken up by a tracery of small sandy brown paths which surrounded tiny flower-beds, each one bordered by a foot-high, neatly clipped box hedge. The little beds were crammed with small flowers like pansies and French marigolds, and some contained clumps of herbs like thyme, rosemary, mint and basil. Only the mint was used in cooking, for mint sauce to be eaten with roast lamb. The other herbs were grown simply for the pleasant scent they cast on the air after a shower of rain on a warm evening. Ulster cooking was plain and wholesome, and it would never have occurred to anyone to flavour it with the herbs which grew so easily.

I examined each flower-bed with care, the smallness of it all catching my imagination afresh. Then I ran back indoors, through the kitchen and into the long, bright, north-facing pantry, which was scrubbed out each morning. Bread, freshly made daily, was kept here, and the cupboards were full of good things, homemade jams and jellies; tins containing cakes, cherry, sultana and walnut, made by Aunt Esther so that the household would not be taken unaware and unprepared if a visitor should call. Pretty canisters of exotic teas, Lapsang Souchong and other scented teas from China, sent by the daughter abroad, lined the top shelf, but they were never used, as everyone preferred a good strong Indian brew. Once, long ago, when the strange teas first arrived, they were tried out, but the reaction of the menfolks, and truth to tell, the women themselves, was such that the canisters were consigned to the top shelf and never opened again.

Down the centre of the pantry, overhanging the floor space and fastened to the ceiling, were three cages containing song birds. These were Uncle Robert's and, though they were dull and brown in colour, their trilling sweet songs filled the house. They were called "mules" and I think were crosses between thrushes and canaries. They sang divinely, especially when the sun shone outside and fell upon their cages. They longed to escape, I felt, and to feel the fresh warm air of summer on their wings.

When I had finished enjoying the garden and had seen the familiar pantry with the plaintive birdsong, I went through the kitchen again and out into the long hallway. On the right was the spare bedroom, and at the other end of the hallway was the dining room. On the wall hung a huge stuffed fish in a glass case – caught by one of the uncles in the dim past. How fierce it looked, with its mouth open and its eyes protruding balefully. Shivering slightly I went into the dining room with its heavy mahogany furniture and its red damask wall covering, the large fireplace flanked by two small leather-covered seats. Beneath their lids were box-like spaces filled with children's books. Satisfied that these books were still here for my delectation, I went upstairs, passing on the way another glass case containing an array of stuffed birds which made me quake with fear. The largest of these was an owl and its eyes seemed to follow me greedily, as though ready to take a peck at me if I turned my back.

Upstairs I peeped into the Uncles' rooms, stiff and neat, with no soft chairs and only pictures like "The Soldier Boy's Farewell" and "Goodbye Old Friend" which showed a battlefield and a soldier shooting his dying horse. These made me sad and I was glad I did not have to sleep here. Aunt Esther and Granny shared a bedroom on the same landing and this was bright, with flowery curtains. Embroidered pincushions hung from each side of the glass on the dressing table and one made of red satin in the shape of a heart sat plumply on the mantelpiece. These were never used for pins, and their purpose was purely ornamental; they were bought from time to time at Sales of Work at the church and came home to roost here.

The flower in the buttonhole of the house was the bathroom, bright and airy, with tiled walls and floor – unheard of luxury in a remote farmhouse and rare enough even in a country town. Granny and the Uncles, together with Aunt Esther, had made a special journey to Belfast, staying overnight with Mama, to choose the bath and wash-hand basin and lavatory, which were the largest, the best and the most expensive they could find. A shower attachment was a glamorous extra, and a glass cubicle at one end of the huge bath sheltered the showerer and protected the floor, with its thick mats of jade green. All the equipment was there, in lavish array. The only drawback was that the water had to be pumped by hand. This was the duty of one of the servant-men, Pat, who greeted our arrival with mixed feelings, because it meant that the bath was used every night, and pumping water was back-breaking and not his favourite task. The water was rusty-red in colour and I think this was due to the peaty soil though which it flowed. The gleaming taps and glass and the luxurious bath towels – jade green to match the bath mats – were delightful, but I was fairly reluctant to get into this strangely coloured liquid. I was afraid that I might turn the same colour, like the whin-dyed eggs at Easter, but Mama had brought me up to be agreeable and not to complain, so that even if the stuff which came out of the taps had been pitch, I would have stepped into it without too much demur.

The upstairs drawing room was a wonderful place. A small bedroom led off it, furnished with camphor wood furniture which had been sent by Granny's daughter from the Far East. Apart from having a permanent smell of mothballs due to the camphor wood, it was a pretty little room with its pale green sprigged curtains, watered silk counterpane and white walls. The drawing room itself was carpeted with a thick silk embossed carpet from Tientsin sent by the daughter in Hong Kong. Glass-fronted cabinets lined with cream raw silk covered two walls and were filled with ivory figurines and carved curios. We were not allowed to remove these from their cases, but could gaze on them to our hearts' content, and I spent many happy hours contemplating them as they stared back at me with Oriental passivity.

The Mill House was a delight and so were the yard and farm buildings around it. The yard was always clean, swept and tidy, as was everything else. The dairy fairly sparkled and so, to a lesser degree, did the byre and stables. Cattle were Uncle Richard's passion and he bred pedigree shorthorns. He brought these to the Balmoral Show in Belfast each year and to his great delight one year won the Supreme Championship with his bull "Salterstown Butterfly".

It was the custom to ring bulls so that they could be more easily led and controlled, and once when I was at Salterstown I saw a bull being ringed. I was idling an afternoon away dreamily with the dolls in the garden with the little box hedges, when I heard sounds coming from the yard at the front of the house. Loud shouts and low muffled roars of anger and pain filled the air. Anxious not to miss anything interesting, I shot through the house and out into the yard to the scene of action.

There stood a bull with two men leaning heavily on either side of it, each armed with a short stick and hanging on to a rope around its neck. Uncle Richard stood in front of the bull's head with what looked like a pair of tongs in his hands, gripping the unfortunate animal's nostrils. Each of the round bits at the end of the shafts of the tongs had a round hole in it. A few yards away another man was bending over a small brazier, and as I watched he drew out of the red-hot coal fire, with a pair of pincers, a red-hot metal bolt. He pushed the bolt through the holes in the tongs held by Uncle Richard and of course through the end of the bull's nose. The poor beast roared with pain, but before it realised what had happened, or could gear itself to retaliate, a ring was pushed through the hole in its nose which the red-hot bolt had made. The bull began to kick, the four men at its sides held on and were tossed up and down like flies. After a time it calmed down as Uncle Richard talked to it crooningly and stroked its head and neck, and eventually it was led back to its pasture.

My eyes were standing out like organ stops when Granny came bustling out to see what the commotion was about and she scolded the men for letting me see such a sight. "You might have frightened the life and soul out of the child – sure you know she's from the city and you should have had more sense!" she berated her unfortunate son.

"Och, Mama, how was I to know she was there? Weans should be kept in the house anyway . . . ," he replied feebly.

"Kept in the house?" she answered tartly. "I suppose you would like me to keep her in one of the cabinets with the ivories! I tell you she's here to get the fresh air and I'm bound and determined she'll get it. These men and their beasts . . . " she concluded, muttering to herself as she shepherded me back into the kitchen and took down the sweetie tin with a picture of Edward VII on it, from which she took two black balls, one for me and one for herself. "These things have to be done to animals," she said to me, "and they don't feel it at all – at least I hope they don't," she finished as she shooed me back to the garden and the game I had left so abruptly.

During the day the household was increased by two servant men, Pat and Jamesy, and Lizzie. Lizzie was a widow who lived down the road in a whitewashed cottage with her two sons, George and Sammy. She was a large woman, both in body and spirit. She had jet black hair piled high in a bun on top of her head, swarthy skin and curiously hoarse voice. Lizzie did all the housework, cleaning, polishing and washing everything in sight, singing loudly all the time such songs as "The Dacent Irish Boy", "Let Him Go, Let Him Tarry", "Magherafelt May Fair" and "The Meeting of the Waters". She sang "Danny Boy" if she felt melancholy, the plaintive air echoing through the house, but this was not often, for usually she was cheerful and laughed and chatted and sang as she worked, her hands busy and her dark eyes sparkling. She went home each day at three o'clock, her work completed, so that her sons would come home from school to find a fine fire burning on the hearth and their tea on the table.

I loved to visit Lizzie's little house, where there was always company. There was a jamb wall here, too, sheltering the fire from the draughts from the open door. The tiny window in the wall was diamond-shaped, and as at the Mill House, one could sit by the fire and look out to see who was approaching if footsteps were heard. Windows were small in this cottage and sometimes could not be opened if Lizzie had painted the frames and they had stuck, but the door was always left open, as in all other houses around there, except at night. Visitors never knocked but just walked in, sure of a welcome, and sat down by the fire to join in the chat after the usual greetings had been exchanged. Lizzie continued meantime with her work, among the assembled company, going back and forth with her farls of bread between the bakeboard on the table and the griddle which hung from the crane over the turf fire on the hearth or folding her clean, dry washing into a huge wicker basket. Smoothing was not done in the presence of strangers, as she felt that intimate garments could not be displayed and someone might catch a glimpse of clean underwear, either her own or the boys', with resultant embarrassment to everyone. This Puritan attitude was rife, and was carried to great lengths. If a woman wore a V-necked dress she had to add a "modesty vest", a small piece of lace pinned inside the V to cover bare flesh. Legs were called "limbs" and women's dresses rarely had anything other than wrist-length sleeves.

I asked Mama to put a pack of playing-cards in my case when I went on holiday, for I might need to while away a wet afternoon with a game of Patience. Lizzie's visitors were pleased to see me arrive with these cards, which were in their view slightly sinful, but exciting, for they were never allowed in their own homes. They enjoyed playing games with me and we had pleasant sessions of "Old Maid", "Sevens" and "Rummy" together. I must have been able to impart enough knowledge of these games for them to participate and my standards cannot have been too high, for we all had a good time and excitement and laughter mounted as the Queen of Spades, the "Old Maid" card, was plucked from one hand to another as we sat round Lizzie's kitchen table.

There was an upstairs bedroom over the kitchen, approached by a ladder in the corner. The boys slept here, and Lizzie slept in the small bedroom off the kitchen. There were just three rooms, no water – that had to be carried from a pump some distance away – and no conveniences of any kind. There was an outside lavatory at the back, whitewashed inside and out regularly, and its wooden seat scrubbed daily with carbolic soap by Lizzie. There was no lavatory paper, but there was, hanging from a hook on the wall, a bunch of squares of newspaper, cut neatly to size and threaded together on string. This was not uncommon, for it cost nothing and served its purpose. In some, outside lavatories the newspaper was not cut up, but was placed in its entirety beside the seat, so that anyone using the convenience might catch up with the local news before tearing off a piece for a more practical use.

The cottage had an air of comfort and welcome, with its bright delft on the dresser, the walls decorated with printed texts and rosy calendars from the grocer in Ballyronan, one with a little booklet of dates stuck on, for it was the current year's, the others bereft of the dates for they were of former years, but remained to adorn the white walls. One or two had paper "pockets" where Lizzie kept any letters she might receive. The chairs, rush seated, were scrubbed every Saturday and set outside to dry, for Lizzie was fanatical about cleanliness. Her own chair, where she sat by the fire but always hospitably yielded up to a visitor, had a soft cushion embroidered with sprays of forget-me-nots worked by Lizzie herself.

The table by the window was used for everything. Meals were eaten at it, clothes were smoothed on it, bread was baked on it and dishes were washed in an enamel basin set at one end of it.

Lizzie scrubbed it daily and it was snow white. In its drawer she kept a writing pad, some envelopes and a wooden pen holder with a steel nib, together with a small bottle, corked tightly, of Stephens' Blue-Black Ink. These were rarely used, for Lizzie was not much of a correspondent, but she liked to have them ready in case she wished to write to her brother Andy in Boston.

Lizzie's bedroom was small, but the bed had white pillow shams and a brightly coloured patchwork quilt. This was "pieced" by her in the dark winter evenings by the light of the paraffin lamp which was only lit then. There was a text on the wall, stitched in wool on canvas in a black wooden frame which said:

> "God is the Head of This House
> The Unseen Guest at Every Meal,
> The Silent Listener to Every Conversation."

This frightening thought did not deter Gracie, a young girl who lived a mile or so away and who was forbidden by her strict father to have a boyfriend, from bringing her sweetheart David to Lizzie's house on occasional Sunday afternoons. Then after a short chat with whoever might be sitting by the fire, she would withdraw with him into Lizzie's bedroom and remain there for the entire afternoon. The pair emerged flushed and tousled, but totally unembarrassed, in time to join the rest of the company for tea. As I sat with the other visitors in the warm kitchen listening to the talk and laughter going on all round me, I thought to myself how tired these two must be, after their cycle ride from home, to remain in bed for such a long time, and how soundly they must sleep not to be disturbed by the noise in the kitchen. This happened two or three times when I was there and innocently I spoke of it to Aunt Esther, telling her how tired Gracie and David must have been. Her eyebrows shot up to her hairline and her face turned a dull red.

"Don't mention this to Granny," she warned, and then changed the subject quickly, asking me whether I wished to have sultana or cherry cake for tea.

Somehow I never went back to Lizzie's on Sunday afternoons after that. Aunt Esther always had something else for me to do, perhaps going for a walk along the lough shore, or visiting a family in Ballyronan related to us by marriage. I continued to visit the cottage during the week and in the evenings when I could escape, but never again on Sundays.

On Sunday mornings we drove to church in the trap, dressed in our best. Church was very different here. It was the Church of Ireland and in the eyes of all my Presbyterian relatives, just one step from Rome. Granny had been born a Presbyterian, naturally, but had converted upon marriage to please her husband, and like most converts was extra zealous for the Faith. This was considered by her relatives to be a strange foible on Granny's part, for they were all good solid Presbyterians with their feet, but certainly not their knees, on the ground.

I found the service interesting, exciting and with tremendous audience participation.

The rector's white robes gave it a party atmosphere and his approach to worship made his God seem altogether different – a much more debonair Being than the God of Wrath who ruled the Meetings in Coagh and Castledawson. It was as though John Knox had been suddenly supplanted by Charles II. I could never find my place in the prayer book but this did not matter, as everyone around me was muttering, responding with great alacrity to anything the rector said. I wondered what God – the real God who was naturally a Presbyterian True Blue – would think if He could see me here in this strange church listening to psalms from the Bible instead of singing the good old psalms in metre.

It was strange and fascinating and I enjoyed it all. The rector certainly had a busy time compared with our black-robed ministers with their Geneva tabs, who remained in the pulpit from beginning to end of the service. Here was a man who was continually on the move, from altar to reading-desk to pretty little pulpit, singing, reading, praying, preaching, never still for a minute. No wonder his head was in such a whirl that he had to read his prayers out of a book instead of making them up as he went along.

When at Salterstown we were always invited to take tea one afternoon with Miss Porte. Miss Porte lived with her brother Alex in a lovely old whitewashed house set in an old-fashioned garden with masses of peonies forming great banks of colour on either side of the pebbly driveway leading to the front door and scarlet fuchsias hanging over the white garden wall. There was a small lawn and a large and beautiful peacock called Herbert who lived there, strutting about showing off his blue breast feathers and shaking his head with its tiara if we approached, though I always kept at a respectful distance. Sometimes he spread his wonderful jewelled tail and we looked in awe at the "eyes" revealed in it. He was so exotic, so out-of-place in this environment that it was like catching a glimpse of the Arabian Nights.

This house had climbing pink old-fashioned cabbage roses on the walls and was nestled in a grove of tall trees sheltering it from the outside world. Here the brother and sister lived quietly together, for all the world like Matthew and Marilla in Green Gables. Alex had lost an arm in an accident so that he could no longer farm, but his land was let to a neighbour and he tended his vegetable garden very competently, producing all kinds of strange things like Jerusalem artichokes and kohlrabi. His orchard was carefully pruned and cared for and the crops from his plum and damson trees were the talk of the country.

We had tea in the drawing room, cool and green-shaded by the trees outside, but quietly elegant with white paint and delicate mahogany framed chairs.

Miss Porte had been engaged to be married long ago, but her sweetheart had been drowned in a boating accident on the lough. Her hair had turned white overnight and she had never looked at another man. She was kind and had a quiet dignity, but her dark eyes still held the memory of pain, especially when she looked at a child. She and Alex had grown old together and were content, but the house had an air of unfulfilled expectancy.

Further along the road and nearer the lough lived another family, distinguished for me by the fact that the mother had recently suffered a severe attack of scarlet fever. She had been quickly removed from her husband and children lest they too develop the disease, and was taken to the local fever hospital, where she remained for six weeks. Her long dark straight hair was shaved off completely, for this was the custom then, if one had scarlet fever, which was a dangerous illness.

When she returned to the bosom of her family she wore a small knitted cap to cover her scalp, but, wonder of wonders, as her hair grew again it grew curly! There she was for all to see, with a mass of tight springy curls all over her head. How I envied her! How I wished that I, too, might have scarlet fever and have my straight fair hair shaved off so that I could end up with a riot of curls! I had long abandoned the idea of obtaining instant curls by eating vegetables and had realised that Father was not telling the truth when he forecast this result. I never achieved the longed-for curls, nor scarlet fever with its accompanying excitement of being whipped off to hospital and being viewed through glass by anxious relatives, which had happened to several of my school friends.

he McMasters: back row – Uncles Richard & Robert;
front row - their mother, Hilary's great-aunt Sarah
(Granny McMaster) and their sister Esther

Salter's Castle, cottage and farm, c. 1930

Chapter 12

The Place of Dreams

The Uncles' second farm, known as the Castle Farm, joined with the Mill Farm and the house belonging to it was less than a mile down the road. Each day we walked down to the long low white building which lay quietly in the shadow of the ruined walls of an old fortress castle built by the Salters Company at the time of the Plantation of Ulster.

It was hard for me to imagine that the two walls which remained standing had once been part of where real people had lived. Now they were overgrown with creepers and pink plumes of valerian issued like smoke from crevices high up. The cottage, however, was clean and homely and a man who worked on the Castle Farm lived there.

There was always a fire in the hearth and an ever-open door, and the smell of the burning turf greeted us in the soft air as we approached. Crickets chirped the day long, and everyone believed that if they left, the house would fall into decay.

Freshly-baked bread was sent down every day from the Mill House and all provisions were despatched by farm cart twice weekly so that the men working here might enjoy good meals. Nearby was an orchard, but only one of the trees, a huge pear, covered with white blossom in springtime, bore worthwhile fruit. A flock of geese dwelt here. These were fattened to provide Christmas dinners for everyone on the farm and one was always sent to us in Belfast. I liked to climb the bars of the orchard gate and watch them waddling busily around like small white boats, under the creamy saucers of the elder trees in flower hanging over the stone wall. The gander quacked and hissed crossly at all his wives, who seemed nervous and afraid to quack back. They gathered in a small group and looked as though they were discussing his bad behaviour.

A strange thing about the Castle Farm was that when the

time changed in the spring for British Summer Time and everyone put their clocks forward, the clock in the kitchen of the low white house remained as it was. I do not know why this strange custom obtained, or who decided to be different, and I never knew another place which adhered to "old time" during the summer months when all other households went by "new time".

Outside, in the July heat, were enormous clouds of midges apparently motionless. These insects, indigenous to Lough Neagh, did not bite but clung irritatingly to hair and clothes and it was impossible to avoid them as they hung in huge misty balls in the still air. As we walked along the lough shore at the Castle Farm, we took off our shoes to feel the warm pale sand on our toes and, brushing past the grassy hedgerows with their confetti of wild flowers, the brilliant scarlet fuchsia hedges hanging over us, we searched for pieces of petrified wood and intoned the old rhyme:

"Lough Neagh hones, Lough Neagh hones,
You put them in sticks and you take them out stones."

Bathing in this part of the lough was strictly forbidden. It was dangerous and in spite of the innocent-seeming sandy shore there were deep holes not far out in the lough. If a grownup were with us we could paddle in the ripples at the very edge where the water was clear and cold, but that was all. Tales were told of children drowned here and we were cautioned never to venture into the water unsupervised, even to paddle.

Sometimes we brought a picnic and I whiled away the time by "popping" the red fuchsia buds in the hedges, bringing the bright flowers to premature birth with my inquisitive fingers before we began on the good things packed by Aunt Esther in the basket.

Each Thursday Uncle Richard went to the market in Magherafelt to conduct the business of the farm and when evening came we watched eagerly for his return. After he had exchanged news with Granny he would put his hand in his greatcoat pocket and bring out a paper bag containing a pound of boiled sweets. There was a mixture of clove rock, aniseed balls, black balls, pineapple rock, bulls' eyes, lemon drops and cough drops. A whole pound of sweets! We kissed him and opened the bag instantly, handing them round to anyone who was present, and then choosing our own favourites. Then Granny came to the table, took the bag, smoothed and folded the top of it, removed Edward VII from his perch above the stove, put the bag into the tin, closed it with a snap and replaced it out of our reach. Uncle Richard would say, "Now, Mama, let them have the sweets when they want them," and she always replied, "Yes, yes, sure you know I will." We knew, however, that we must only ask for them after meals, and then she never denied us.

There was a tiny shop just across the back lane which ran along one side of the garden, and we were allowed to go there alone. We went through the iron gate which squeaked on its hinges and was kept un-oiled so that an approaching caller could be heard. Over to the Taylors' farm we went, where Mary Anne, known to us children as "Miss Taylor" lived with her brothers in the farmhouse and ran the shop as a sideline. Here she sold bootlaces, spools of thread, bars of soap, boot-polish, matches, candles and various other odds and ends. She also stocked sweets, and I remember especially the liquorice pipes with pink sugared ends, and peppermint rock. Mary Anne's rock was just like seaside rock, white with a pink outside coat, but without a name running through it. It was slightly different, too, in that the sticks were small and thin and cost a halfpenny each. I loved these very much because Mary Anne did not have a quick turnover of her stock and by the time she sold the rock it was at that chewy degree of softness which meant it could be bitten and did not, unlike fresh rock in larger sticks, have to be hammered on a table with a heavy knife-handle to reduce it to eatable proportions.

Mary Anne loved children and I think this was partly why she kept the shop. She had a regular flow of callers that way, children being sent to buy bootlaces or leather "whangs" for their fathers' working boots, or candles if their mothers had run short, or a bar of Lux toilet soap if someone in the family was going into hospital. To each child she would give, by way of a bonus, a few dolly mixtures or perhaps a toffee or a scented conversation lozenge with a message: "When shall I see you?", "You are Beautiful" or "You are the Person I love Best" – was written in tiny red letters on its pale pink, lilac, yellow or green sugary surfaces.

I was staying at Salterstown recuperating from a bad attack of whooping cough one summer, when Ambrose, Mary Anne's younger brother, a man of about fifty, found a peewit or lapwing, with a broken wing. Tenderly gathering it up in his big hands, he brought it to the square garden, asking for me at the back door. Thinking that the sick child and the sick bird would help each other to recover, he had brought it to me, knowing it could live unmolested in the garden where the summer-seat was, and as we sat there he told me how I should feed it and care for it. Then he set it down gently on the path and came back to the house with me to tell Aunt Esther about the bird. She was used to such things and took it all in her stride. Together she and I went several times a day to see the peewit and feed it, and Ambrose came each evening to check on the healing wing. After a few weeks it was able to flutter, and very soon Ambrose was able to take it back to the field where he had found it, and set it free.

Uncle Richard and Uncle Robert were aficionados of cockfighting, an illegal sport which only took place at weekends or evenings at some out-of-the-way rendezvous. The cruelty of the practice never seemed to strike them, kind men that they were in all other ways; in fact they bred the small fighting cocks. The subject was not mentioned in the house as Granny disapproved of this form of entertainment and her sons were still to some degree under her thumb, but I would hear talk of it at Lizzie's as I played Patience at her kitchen table, or perched on someone's knee close to the fire if the evening were cold.

Opinions were exchanged about chances of the battling birds and arrangements were made to meet and attend the fights. Lizzie would sometimes intervene in the conversation with a warning, "Now, now, mind the wean!" – meaning that I might overhear and tell Granny, but I had learnt my lesson when I told Aunt Esther about the lovers in Lizzie's bed on Sunday afternoons, and had determined not to repeat any more gossip.

The remoteness of Lough Neagh meant it was virtually impossible for the police or authorities to hear of or find these clandestine meetings – indeed it was said that some of the police themselves were keen attenders at and gamblers on this sport. Father went once or twice with the Uncles when he was staying on one of his rare visits to the farm, but he did not have the stomach for the cruelty of it.

In my earliest days when Aggie was with me as well as

Joyce, Mama and Father, at Salterstown, there was a large party one Sunday. After church and a large Sunday dinner, everyone set off to visit a bird sanctuary on one of the islands in Lough Neagh. We drove to a small quay and embarked in two large rowing boats. As we drew near the island the water grew shallow and we had to transfer from the larger boats into small dinghies. Aggie and I were the last to be landed and as the boatman, Isaac Bates, lifted me from the dinghy and set me down on dry land I looked down at the ground. I was small and my eyes were not more than two and a half feet above it, and I can still remember the absolute horror of the moment. There was not a square foot of ground that was not covered with birds' nests. Some still contained unhatched eggs, some young birds all with their beaks wide open and chirping noisily. In others birds still sat on their eggs, frightened by these humans, and all around us were birds flying here and there. I have never been so terrified and the memory comes back even eighty years on to haunt me.

I screamed at the top of my voice, alarming the birds still further and also alarming the rest of the party. I climbed up Isaac Bates as though he were a pine tree, and I a squirrel, burying my head in his shoulder and howling with fright. I would not even look at Aggie as she tried to hold my hand. Isaac, I reasoned, was six feet tall and Aggie only five feet. I felt safer six feet from the ground, as far as possible from those dreadful beaks and feathers and small spindly legs. I still do not know why the party elected to visit this place. I suppose they did not realise what a bird sanctuary really was and they thought it would be an unusual place to go, something different in the way of entertainment. Isaac carried me for the duration of our stay on the island and I kept my eyes tightly shut until I was safely back in the boat. Since then I have never willingly approached a bird, any kind of bird, living or dead except Jack, the parrot at home, and Ambrose's peewit.

I was never sent to bed early at Salterstown, and if I were not at Lizzie's cottage or there were no visitors at the farm, I often went for a walk with Aunt Esther in the evening, through the soft calm air from the lough, when the midges had disappeared. Sometimes we called at a neighbour's house, especially at the Misses Collins.

Hannah and Agnes Collins were twins, alike in every

respect, small and plump like two little performing seals, with smooth grey hair drawn to the back of their heads in a bun. So much at one were they in everything that they called each other "sister" all the time. They lived together in their neat little stone house which was tightly corseted about with a close-clipped golden privet hedge, and having sold the family farm after their parents' death they were able to live in some comfort and did not need to worry about money.

They were expert needle-women and had embarked upon a major project for the church, executing, in exquisitely delicate needlepoint, covers for all the kneelers. To a Presbyterian child like me, who had been taught never to bow the knee to anyone, not even to God, this seemed a fanciful extravagance, but I could see how their House of God – and such a glamorous and soigné God, too – would be beautified by their work. Each time we called with the twins they brought out their needlework, wrapped in a white linen cloth, to show us and we always made them happy by exclaiming sincerely over the lovely designs, the soft colours and the tiny stitches.

One evening as Aunt Esther and I were strolling down the road past the Collins' house, I stopped to pick a bunch of cloudy grass from the side of the road to add to the bowl of sweet pea which had been brought in from the garden that day.

Suddenly Miss Hannah rushed out in great agitation. "Esther, dear, come in, come in," she squeaked, her voice sounding jerky and odd. "Sister wants to speak to you."

Aunt Esther was so amazed by her urgency that she immediately stopped in her tracks and turned to follow Miss Hannah who had disappeared, like the White Rabbit, back into the tiny hall. Forgetting all about me they both went into the kitchen and I followed, unnoticed, still clutching the bunch of grasses. As I went through the hall I saw a strange thing. A man's hat hung from a hook on the hall stand which was usually empty except for the two hymnbooks and prayer books which the sisters kept there for use at church on Sundays.

In the kitchen by the fire sat Miss Agnes with a clean white apron thrown over her face. Moans issued from beneath it and Aunt Esther went over and turned down a corner, exposing Miss Agnes' face which was red and swollen with tears. "What under goodness has happened, Agnes? You would think all belonging to you were dead!" exclaimed Aunt Esther.

"Och, och, och, indeed I wish they were!" gasped Miss Agnes tearfully, between sobs. Miss Hannah's face drooped pitifully at this and her sister quickly grasped her hand, saying, "Not you, sister dear, but all else! All else!" she repeated. She broke into near hysteria. "Tell her, sister, tell her the worst!" she commanded, her voice rising to a crescendo. I was fascinated. It was like a play going on in front of my eyes.

"Well, Esther," said Miss Hannah, who was infinitely calmer than her twin, though still upset. "You wouldn't remember our brother, Henry John. It all happened before you were born. Well, he was only a young lump of a boy, but he had a hot temper, a very hot temper. So indeed had my father, and Henry John took after him. One day in the field – and it was harvest time – Henry John and my father had words, and Henry John ran away from home that very night. We never saw him again, nor heard from him, and my father wouldn't even let us mention his name, for he said he was dead as far as he was concerned, and good riddance to him. He was a hard man, my father, and he never forgave Henry John. We always thought that he had maybe died away somewhere in a foreign land long years ago. But today," and she rolled her eyes up to Heaven, "a man came to the door and said he was Henry John! He said he wasn't dead at all and that he'd come home and wanted to end his days with Sister and me! And we've been so happy here, just the two of us," she concluded, and broke into fresh floods of tears.

"He's a stranger to us, Esther," broke in Miss Hannah. "I think he's our brother right enough, but he's a total stranger. Sixty years ago it all happened. And he went and left my father with a field of corn half cut!" she ended, a note of extreme irritation entering her voice.

"We don't know where he's been all these years and he won't tell us. Just says he's come home and we must take him in. He talks about streetcars and sidewalks like all those that come home out of America, so maybe he's been there. Oh, Esther, what in the name of all that's good are we to do?" Miss Agnes and Miss Hannah spoke this last sentence in unison, their small worried red faces looking imploringly at her as she sat down on a chair to digest the news.

"Well, I don't know. I don't know. This beats all," she murmured to herself as she thought over the problem. "I'll tell you what," she said finally, and then anxiously asked, "Where is he now?"

"Out for a walk, taking a stroll over the fields, he said," replied Miss Hannah, her voice rising shrilly.

"Well, then," said Aunt Esther, her voice growing more assured now that she knew Henry John was not actually on the premises. "I'll go home and talk to Richard and Robert and get them to come down here tomorrow, all unexpectedly by the way, and have a talk with him. Yes, that's the best thing to do." She stood up, fastening her light summer coat which she had unbuttoned in the heat of the moment.

"Tomorrow! Tomorrow!" gasped the sisters. "What use is that to us? How under goodness can we be expected to sleep through the night with a strange man in the house, even if he is our own brother? He's a total stranger to us. A total stranger!" and their tears flowed afresh. Then, gathering herself together, Miss Hannah said firmly, "No, Esther. Richard and Robert must come down here tonight and hoke out of him the whole root of the matter. We'll come up and stay with you and your mother while they're about it," and they removed their aprons, smoothed their slightly ruffled hair and put on their coats.

Aunt Esther was slightly taken aback at this swift development in the drama; she would rather have gone home alone to break the news to her mother and brothers before deciding finally on a plan of action. The sisters, however, gave her no choice. Out into the road we all trooped, leaving the door open. Each of the twins took one of my hands absentmindedly; in their tremendous agitation they hadn't greeted me or acknowledged my presence. I had to walk quickly to keep up with them as they trotted along, talking all the time about Henry John and his misdemeanours, and I remembered with disappointment that I had left my bunch of grasses on the kitchen table.

Down the slope into the house we marched, Aunt Esther leading the fray, through the front door and into the kitchen, where Granny stood with her hand on the kettle, ready to make the umpteenth pot of tea that day.

"Mamma," said Aunt Esther, "Hannah and Agnes have something to say to you." "Sit down, sit down," said Granny hospitably indicating the cushioned seat by the fire.

Miss Hannah and Miss Agnes, still clutching me between them like a buffer, sat down heavily and began to cry again. "Daughters dear, stop crying and tell me your trouble," said Granny anxiously. "Has the house burned down, or has the cow died?"

Trying to save time, Aunt Esther related the story of the day's happenings in the Collins' house. Granny gasped disbelievingly and went tck-tck-tck with her false teeth.

Pleased at her reaction, and growing calmer now, the twins stopped crying and said in unison, "And now, Mrs. McMaster, we want Richard and Robert to go down and talk to Henry John and find out all the ins and outs of what he's been doing and where he's been these past sixty years! We'll not rest till they do."

"I remember the day he ran away," mused Granny, as she measured the tea into the pot and poured on the boiling water. "Your father was a hard man and drove the boy beyond his strength. Your mother never had a day's health afterwards, fretting for him. So now he's back! Wonders will never cease. I suppose in the end everyone wants to come back to their own people, to die among them."

"That's just what he said," put in Miss Hannah. "He said the very words, 'I want to end my days with you girls', he said. He still thinks we're young girls like we were when he was at home. But we're not. We're not getting any younger, and besides that, Henry John's an old man now. We were all right the way we were if he would only leave us be. What under the shining sun are we going to do, Mrs. McMaster, dear?"

"First of all," said Granny, "we'll drink a cup of tea, and then when Richard and Robert come home I'll send them down to have a talk with Henry John. They're away at Moses Johnston's wake – he dropped dead in his field this morning, and left his poor wife with six children and the hay not in – but they'll be home soon. Tomorrow we'll have to send for the Rector. It's too late tonight and he'll be getting ready for bed and likely on his knees saying his prayers, but tomorrow will do."

"Bed," wept Agnes once more, "it's well for the Rector, for

263

he has his own good warm bed and a big house forbye and a housekeeper to see to his needs, but where under goodness will Henry John sleep? The bed in our spare room hasn't been used for years, and if he did sleep in it he'd get his death. We don't want him here at all, but we don't want the neighbours saying that our brother came home after sixty years and caught his death in a damp bed!"

This left the next move up to Granny, who said, reluctantly, "I suppose that just for one night he could sleep here, in the wee room off the drawing room."

Much gratified at this solution to their immediate problem, the sisters drew up chairs to the table that they might more easily enjoy their tea and sponge cake which Aunt Esther brought from a tin in the pantry. "This is the first food that has passed our lips since this morning, when Henry John came to the door," they confided as they dried their tears and began to eat.

After a short time the Uncles came home and were instantly told of the situation down the road. When they had digested the news and got over their initial astonishment at the return of the Prodigal, whose name had passed into local legend since his disappearance, they reluctantly agreed to talk to him. Putting on their hats again they trudged off down the road, leaving the women clucking like a flock of hens that have seen a fox.

They came back after an hour or so, interrupting the by now peaceful chat about cake recipes and domestic matters. They hung up their hats on the pegs inside the hall door and Uncle Richard announced, "It's all settled. Henry John seems a quiet and peaceable man, but he's bound and determined that here he is and here he'll stay. He says he was born here and he'll die here and be buried with all his family, even though he never liked his father and doesn't want to be buried in the grave next to him. He says when the time comes the girls are to make sure he's buried beside his mother."

"I don't know why he's so fussy," added Uncle Robert, "after the way he treated her, never letting on where he was all these years. I don't know how he'll have the nerve to rise and face her when the Last Trump sounds." The sisters gave uneasy mews of dissatisfaction.

"However," said Uncle Richard, "he has agreed to sleep the

night here so that his own bed can be aired." He sat down and waited for another pot of tea to be made as he had missed the earlier round.

After a minute or two Granny handed him his own large cup and saucer and poured another for Uncle Robert, asking eagerly, "Did you find out where he had been all these long years?"

"Not at all, woman dear, I did not," replied her son. "We only talked about the weather and the state of the crops, but he does have a Yankee twang in his voice, so I think he must have been in America. Leave all that to the Rector to find out when he comes tomorrow," he advised, and with that the women had to be content.

Soon Miss Hannah and Miss Agnes put on their coats again and went home, but I was in bed and asleep when Henry John arrived to stay the night, and was not up when he left early the next morning. I heard afterwards that the Rector had come later that day and had closeted himself in the parlour with Henry John for some hours, but when they came out he was none the wiser. Henry John went to his grave five years later still carrying his secret. In the meantime he made himself useful around the house and garden and kept the golden hedge neatly trimmed. His sisters grew to tolerate him, but when he died they had their small revenge. He was buried as he had wished, in the family plot beside his mother, but Miss Hannah and Miss Agnes refused to have his name inscribed on the tombstone, so his place in the graveyard is unmarked, as was his place in his family for the long years of his absence.

Every evening we sat, before bedtime, around the kitchen table, the adults drinking their last tea of the day, and I with a warm milky cup of Ovaltine. Soon the candles were lighted and handed to each member of the household as they departed to bed. Uncle Richard put out the lamp and extinguished the soft light which bloomed under its pink glass shade in the corner. Goodnight kisses were exchanged and everyone wished me pleasant dreams.

Every dream was pleasant at Salterstown. The whole place was like a dream, a beautiful dream which vanished almost overnight. Granny, who was the lynch-pin of the McMaster family, died. Her passing heralded changes within the family, and its members parted to live their own lives. I instinctively knew that for me the enchantment had gone. It was the end of an era, and uncertainty became my watchword. The old secure life that I had always known was slipping away, and my small world became a colder place. Only the happy memories remain, of that earlier period, as bright and clear now as the reality was then.

— ooOoo —